Excommunication and Outlawry in the Legal World of Medieval Iceland

# The Northern World

NORTH EUROPE AND THE BALTIC C.400–1700 AD
PEOPLES, ECONOMIES AND CULTURES

*Editors*



VOLUME 92

The titles published in this series are listed at *brill.com/nw*

# Excommunication and Outlawry in the Legal World of Medieval Iceland

*By*

Elizabeth Walgenbach

BRILL

LEIDEN | BOSTON

Cover illustration: Folio 12 recto from AM 347 fol. (Belgdalsbók). With kind permission of the Árni Magnússon Institute for Icelandic Studies/Stofnun Árna Magnússonar í íslenskum fræðum. ©Photograph by Jóhanna Ólafsdóttir.

Library of Congress Cataloging-in-Publication Data

Names: Walgenbach, Elizabeth, author.
Title: Excommunication and outlawry in the legal world of medieval Iceland / by Elizabeth Walgenbach.
Description: Leiden ; Boston : Brill, [2021] | Series: The Northern world, 1569-1462 ; volume 92 | Based on author's thesis (doctoral - Yale University, 2016) issued under title: Outlawry as secular excommunication in medieval Iceland, 1150-1350. | Includes bibliographical references and index.
Identifiers: LCCN 2021007397 (print) | LCCN 2021007398 (ebook) | ISBN 9789004460911 (hardback) | ISBN 9789004461468 (ebook)
Subjects: LCSH: Outlawry–Iceland–History–To 1500. | Excommunication (Canon law)–History–To 1500.
Classification: LCC KKG20.5.O87 W35 2021 (print) | LCC KKG20.5.O87 (ebook) | DDC 262.9094912/0902–dc23
LC record available at https://lccn.loc.gov/2021007397
LC ebook record available at https://lccn.loc.gov/2021007398

Typeface for the Latin, Greek, and Cyrillic scripts: "Brill". See and download: brill.com/brill-typeface.

ISSN 1569-1462
ISBN 978-90-04-46091-1 (hardback)
ISBN 978-90-04-46146-8 (e-book)

# Contents

**Acknowledgements** IX
**Spelling and Other Conventions** X
**Abbreviations** XII

**Introduction** 1
1 Outlawry, Excommunication, and Icelandic Legal History 1
2 Methodology and Approaches 3

1 **Excommunication** 5
1 Excommunication 6
2 Secular Sanctions and Excommunication 8
3 Rituals of Excommunication in the Period before Canonical Reforms 10
4 Excommunication and Damnation 12
5 Consecrated Burial 13
6 Later Legal Views on Excommunication and Damnation 15
7 Developments in Canon Law 17
7.1 *Major and Minor Excommunication* 17
8 The Canon *Si quis suadente* and *latae sententiae* Excommunication 18
9 Excommunication for Disobedience to Church Authority 19
10 Excommunication in the Church Courts 20
11 Excommunication in Political Conflicts 21
11.1 *Excommunication as a Political Weapon* 22
12 Excommunication in Icelandic Sources 23
12.1 *Early Sources* 23
12.2 *Early Law Texts: Grágás* 26
13 Sources after 1275 28
13.1 *Later Bishops Sagas* 32
13.2 Árna saga 32
13.3 *Bells, Candles, and Ritual* 33
13.4 *Lárentíus saga* 34
14 Conclusions 36

2 **Outlawry** 38
1 Origins of Outlawry? 38
2 Outlawry in Icelandic Sources before 1275 43

2.1 *Full Outlawry in Grágás* 44
2.2 *Consequences of Full Outlawry* 45
2.3 *Escaping or Annulling Outlawry* 46
2.4 *Helping or Associating with an Outlaw* 47
3 The Problem of Lesser Outlawry (*fjǫrbaugsgarðr/fjǫrbaugsmaðr*) 49
3.1 *Fjǫrbaugr as a Fine* 50
3.2 *Fjǫrbaugsgarðr as Banishment with Limited Protections in Iceland* 50
3.3 *Offenses Leading to the Sanction of Fjǫrbaugsgarðr* 51
3.4 *Interpreting Fjǫrbaugsgarðr in Grágás* 52
4 Outlawry in the Sagas 54
5 Outlawry in the Contemporary Sagas 56
6 Relationship to State Power and Statelessness 57
7 Norwegian Influence and later Icelandic Law Sources 60
8 Outlawry's Afterlife: From Saga to Folklore 63
9 Conclusions 63

3 **Outlawry as Secular Excommunication** 65
1 Previous Scholarship 66
2 The Legal Sources, Reading *Grágás* 68
3 Similarities between Excommunication and Outlawry 72
3.1 *Legal Formulations* 75
3.2 Lesser Outlawry in *Grágás* and Minor Excommunication 75
3.3 *Burial in Consecrated Ground* 76
3.4 *Outlawry and the Soul* 83
3.5 *Outlaws at the Church Door* 85
4 Cooperation between Legal Systems 87
5 How Independent Were Secular and Church Law? 91
6 Outlawry for Offenses against Christian Law 93
7 Conclusions 95

4 **Excommunication and Outlawry in Sturla Þórðarson's *Íslendinga saga*** 99
1 *Íslendinga saga* and Sturla Þórðarson 100
2 Narration of the Conflict 102
2.1 *First Steps in the Conflict (1203–1207)* 102
2.2 Phase Two of the Conflict, Escalation (*1208*) 105
2.3 *Phase Three of the Conflict, the Bishop Driven from His See* 107
2.4 *Phase Four of the Conflict: Consequences* 109
2.5 *Part Five, Miracles and Endings* 112

3 Sturla's Use of Vernacular and Canon Law 115
3.1 *Engagement with Vernacular Law* 115
3.2 *Engagement with Canon Law* 115
4 Thomas Becket 120
5 Conclusions 124

**5 Stories of Aron Hjǫrleifsson, Outlaw and Pilgrim** 127
1 Aron's Life in Brief 130
2 Aron and His Enemies 130
3 Guðmundr Arason and Aron 136
4 How to Redeem an Outlaw 139
5 Outlawry as Hell 139
6 Outlawry as a Political Consequence 140
7 Aron the Pilgrim 142
8 Outlaws and the Kings of Norway 147
9 Kings and Icelanders 150
10 Conclusions 152

**Conclusion** 154

**Bibliography** 157
**Index** 174

# Acknowledgements

This book is based on my Yale University doctoral thesis. The research and writing were made possible by generous support from the Birgit Baldwin Fellowship, the Haugen Memorial Scholarship (both administered by the Society for the Advancement of Scandinavian Study), the Leifur Eiríksson Foundation, the American Scandinavian Foundation, the MacMillan Center, and the Yale Graduate School of Arts and Sciences.

My Ph.D. supervisor Anders Winroth has been consistently helpful through the years of my studies and early research career, offering excellent advice and key suggestions throughout the writing and research process and reading many drafts. My committee members Paul Freedman and Carolyne Larrington have been generous with advice, suggestions, and invaluable critiques. Sverrir Jakobsson, as the external reader of the thesis, offered many helpful comments and corrections. All errors that remain here are, of course, my own.

The bulk of the research for this book was carried out at the Stofnun Árna Magnússonar í íslenskum fræðum, where I had the opportunity to be a guest researcher during my Ph.D. studies. The final revisions were undertaken as an Árni Magnússon Research Fellow at the same institute, and my thanks to researchers and colleagues there are many. I thank especially the director of the institute Guðrún Nordal, Guðvarður Már Gunnlaugsson, and all of my colleagues in the manuscript division.

For help and advice on diverse aspects of the research and writing that went into this book, including opportunities to present early results, my thanks to Torfi Tulinius, Úlfar Bragason, Haraldur Bernharðsson, Allegra di Bonaventura, Lára Magnúsardóttir, and Lena Rohrbach.

For advice, many illuminating chats over coffee, help with accessing tricky materials both before and during a global pandemic, and moral support through the long research and writing process I especially thank Agnieszka Rec, Erika Sigurdson, Annalena Müller, Giselle Gos, Lara Hogg, John Burden, Marita von Weissenberg, Kristen Mills, Agnieszka Backman, Emily Lethbridge, Beeke Stegmann, Jóhanna Katrín Friðriksdóttir, Ana del Campo, Nicole Marafioti, Silvia Hufnagel, Anita Sauckel, Viðar Pálsson, Katelin Parsons, Margaret Cormack, Ryder Patzuk-Russell, Tiffany White, Þórdís Edda Jóhannesdóttir, and Oren Falk. Warm thanks to my family and tengdafjölskylda for their support— especially my parents — and to Freyja.

To Gunnar, my thanks, more than I can express. This book is for you.

# Spelling and Other Conventions

Throughout this book I use the Old Norse-Icelandic forms of names and place names so: Guðmundr rather than Guðmundur and Skálaholt rather than Skálholt, except in cases where modern place names are widely known in English. I use Trondheim to refer to the district in the region of Norway that is now modern Trondheim and Niðaróss to refer to the episcopal see and town there. I refer to King Óláfr Haraldsson/St. Óláfr/St. Olav as St. Olaf although I have kept variant spellings in direct quotations that refer to him.

The dating of many events discussed in this book can be established from various more or less reliable sources. For the dating of events that are narrated from the contemporary sagas (*samtíðarsögur*), I have taken the expedient of using the dates supplied by the 1946 editors of these texts: Jón Jóhannesson, Magnús Finnbogason, and Kristján Eldjárn (eds.), *Sturlunga saga,* 2 vols. (Reykjavík: Sturlunguútgáfan, 1946).

When making references to Gratian's *Decretum* I distinguish between the first and second recension as argued for by Anders Winroth.[1] When available, I refer to the newest edition of Gratian's text edited by Winroth and available at Gratian.org.[2] For portions of the *Decretum* not yet available there as well as the *Liber extra*, I refer to Friedberg's editions.[3]

References to the different manuscripts of *Grágás* refer to Vilhjálmur Finsen's editions: *Grágás efter det Arnamagnæanske Haandskrift Nr. 354 fol., Staðarhólsbók* (Copenhagen: Kommissionen for det Arnamagnæanske Legat; Gyldendal, 1879); *Grágás: Islændernes Lovbog i Fristatens Tid, udgivet efter det kongelige Bibliotheks Haandskrift* (Copenhagen: Fornritafjelag Norðurlanda í Kaupmannahöfn, 1852), and *Grágás: Stykker, som findes I det Arnamagnæanske Haandskrift Nr. 351 fol. Skálholtsbók og en Række andre Haandskrifter* (Copenhagen: Kommissionen for det Arnamagnæanske Legat; Gyldendal, 1883), with the manuscript in question given with each reference. I also give the volume and page numbers in the two-volume English translation: Andrew Denis, Peter Foote, and Richard Perkins (trans.), *Laws of Early Iceland: Grágás, the Codex Regius of Grágás, with Material from other Manuscripts*, 2 vols. (Winnipeg: University of Manitoba Press, 1980–2000).

1 *The Making of Gratian's Decretum* (Cambridge: Cambridge University Press), 5, 197–227.

2 Accessible at Gratian.org, edition last updated on the 5th of October 2019.

3 Emil Friedberg (ed.), *Corpus iuris canonici*, 2 vols. (Leipzig: Ex Officina Bernhardi Tauchnitz, 1879–1882).

References to the Kristinréttr Árna Þorlákssonar, Bishop Árni Þorláksson's Christian laws for Iceland, are generally given to Magnús Lyngdal Magnússon's edition, with the orthography slightly simplified: "Kristinréttur Árna frá 1275: Athugun á efni og varðveizlu í miðaldahandritum," (Master's thesis, Háskóli Íslands, 2002). This edition has the same chapter numbering as the edition in the fifth volume of *Norges gamle love* edited by Gustav Storm: *Norges gamle love indtil 1387* (Christiania: Grøndahl, 1890), 5.16–56. This numbering differs from that in the edition published by Sögufélagið in 2005: *Járnsíða og Kristinréttur Árna Þorlákssonar*, ed. by Haraldur Bernharðsson, Magnús Lyngdal Magnússon, and Már Jónsson (Reykjavík: Sögufélag, 2005), which begins the Kristinréttr at chapter 8 of the two previously mentioned editions.

References to Anglo-Saxon laws are to Felix Liebermann's edition, *Die Gesetze der Angelsachsen*, 3 vols. (Halle: Max Niemeyer, 1903–1916), using Liebermann's editorial titles and numbering.

I have silently expanded abbreviations in quotations from early modern editions of canon law texts and in these cases rendered "æ" as "ae" and standardized the use of "v" and "u." In references to Icelandic sagas, I give both the chapter and page number when these are both available. Throughout this book, I cite published English translations when these are available. Other translations are my own.

# Abbreviations

*Diplomatarium Islandicum* — *Diplomatarium Islandicum: Íslenzkt fornbréfasafn*. Copenhagen and Reykjavík: Hið íslenzka bókmenntafélag, 1857–1972.

KLNM — *Kulturhistoriskt lexicon för nordisk medeltid från vikingatid till reformationstid*. Malmö: Allhem, 1956–1978.

*Norges gamle love* — *Norges gamle love indtil 1387*. Ed. by Rudolph Keyser, P.A. Munch, Gustav Storm, and Ebbe Hertzberg. 5 vols. Christiania: Chr. Gröndahl, 1846–1895.

# Introduction

Much has been written on the topic of outlawry in Iceland, including studies focused on outlawry as a literary motif, its role in bloodfeud, and its relationship to Iceland's unique landscape. Less attention has been devoted to a sanction that, in many ways, functioned in the same way as outlawry—excommunication, the chief sanction imposed by the laws of the medieval Church. In its most severe form, this sanction forbid others from interacting with offenders, deprived them of Christian burial, and perhaps even condemned them to hell. This book argues that outlawry can be much better understood if we place it within a context in which it has been little examined—the legal system of the medieval Church.

This book argues that outlawry in medieval Icelandic sources is heavily influenced by canon law concepts of excommunication. Excommunication and outlawry resemble one another, often closely, in a range of Icelandic texts, including lawcodes and narrative sources such as the contemporary sagas. Although outlawry and excommunication likely spring from different origins, in Iceland in the thirteenth and fourteenth centuries, they were sanctions that shadowed one another closely, suggesting a legal culture that was not sharply divided between secular and sacred. Canon law influenced not only the lives of bishops and monks but also helped to shape the outlines of secular justice.

An understanding of canon law is essential for understanding the legal world of medieval Iceland. This book considers a specific aspect of canon law to highlight this point. It addresses the ways that excommunication and its interpretation by the educated elite in Iceland helps to explain both legal and narrative texts produced in and about this period. Excommunication in canon law explains some of the key ways that outlawry was discussed and used, even as we can see that excommunication too, was adapted into the Icelandic cultural and legal landscape.

## 1 Outlawry, Excommunication, and Icelandic Legal History

Although outlawry was not a uniquely Icelandic legal sanction, existing as it did in medieval England, the Carolingian Empire, Norway and Sweden among other places, Iceland is often discussed as a special case because it functioned without an executive authority until it submitted to the Norwegian crown

 | DOI:10.1163/9789004461468_002

in the 1260s.[1] In the absence of such an authority to carry out punishments such as execution, outlawry was the most severe sanction available in the pre-submission legal system.

Outlawry has been extensively studied within this system, mostly as represented by the manuscripts of *Grágás*, the earliest surviving legal code for Iceland, often bolstered with material from the so-called outlaw sagas and other sagas of Icelanders.[2] Outlawry did not disappear once the Norwegian king began to wield executive power and *Jónsbók* was adopted (in 1281) although its vocabulary and range of use shifted. Ideas of outlawry lived on (in altered form) well into the early modern period with its *útilegumenn*, fugitives surviving on the margins of society.[3]

Alongside Iceland's complicated legal system for regulating conflict, with its panels of appointed judges and formal procedural rules coexisted another legal

1 For discussions of these legal and political structures, often referred to as an "acephalous" type of government see, for instance, William Ian Miller, *Bloodtaking and Peacemaking* (Chicago: University of Chicago Press, 1990); Jesse L Byock, *Feud in the Icelandic Saga* (Berkeley and Los Angeles: University of California Press, 1982); and Jón Viðar Sigurðsson, *Chieftains and Power in the Icelandic Commonwealth*, trans. by Jean Lundskær-Nielsen (Odense: Odense University Press, 1999).

2 Andreas Heusler, *Das Strafrecht der Isländersagas* (Leipzig: Duncker & Humblot, 1911); Andreas Heusler, *Zum Isländischen Fehdewesen in der Sturlungenzeit* (Berlin: Verlag der Königl. Akademie der Wissenschaften, 1912), 74–101; Miller, *Bloodtaking and Peacemaking*; Byock, *Feud in the Icelandic Saga*; Lúðvík Ingvarsson, *Refsingar á Íslandi á Þjóðveldistímanum* (Reykjavík: Bókaútgáfa Menningarsjóðs, 1970), 96–173. There has also been extensive study of outlawry from the perspectives of literary studies. See recently, Joonas Ahola, "Outlawry in the Icelandic Family Sagas," (Ph.D. Dissertation, University of Helsinki, 2014); Sarah Harlan-Haughey, *The Ecology of the English Outlaw in Medieval Literature: From Fen to Greenwood* (London and New York: Routledge, 2016); Timothy S. Jones, *Outlawry in Medieval Literature* (New York: Palgrave Macmillan, 2010); Rebecca Merkelbach, "'He Has Long Forfeited All Kinship Ties': Monstrosity, Familial Disruption, and the Cultural Relevance of the Outlaw Sagas," *Gripla* 28 (2017): 103–137; and Jeremy DeAngelo, *Outlawry, Liminality, and Sanctity in the Literature of the Early Medieval North Atlantic* (Amsterdam: Amsterdam University Press, 2019). On outlawry as a social phenomenon in Iceland see, Frederic Amory, "The Medieval Icelandic Outlaw: Lifestyle, Saga, and Legend," *From Sagas to Society: Comparative Approaches to Early Iceland*, ed. by Gísli Pálsson (Middlesex U.K.: Hisarlik Press, 1992), 189–203.

3 In the early modern period, *útilegumenn* ("outlaws" or people who placed themselves outside the law by leaving settled areas) were often convicted thieves who fled settled areas to escape punishment and often survived by further theft. The most famous example is probably Fjalla-Eyvindur (Jónsson), an *útilegumaður* who lived in the eighteenth century and is attested in both documentary sources and in folklore. Although often called "outlaws," útilegumenn were not sentenced to outlawry per se. On the *útilegumenn* of early modern Iceland see especially Ólafur Briem, *Útilegumenn og auðar tóttir*, 2nd ed. (Reykjavík: Bókaútgáfa Menningarsjóðs, 1983). On Fjalla-Eyvindur as an historical person see, Þorsteinn Bjarnarson, "Fjalla-Eyvindur og niðjar hans," *Blanda* 7 (1940–1943): 91–96.

system — that of the Church. Christian laws played a role in Icelandic legal culture from the earliest periods of written legal texts. The two earliest complete *Grágás* manuscripts each contain a section on Christian laws (Kristinna laga þáttr), and many early documents, including some of the oldest preserved charters from Iceland, are inventories of church property that the Christian laws of *Grágás* dictated ought to be written.[4] Christianity brought with it an emphasis on written law and written sources but also the influences of a Church that increasingly saw itself as an independent authority and source of justice throughout all of Christendom.

This book offers a fresh contribution to the growing field of studies addressing the local usage of wider legal traditions (*ius particulare*) in medieval Europe.[5] It focuses on how medieval Icelanders adapted to and within wider European legal traditions, in this case the legal traditions of the *Corpus juris canonici*, canon law. It is a work of legal history that also employs historical methods, literary sources—particularly Icelandic saga texts—and manuscript studies.

## 2 Methodology and Approaches

In this book I draw on a range of disparate sources to evaluate the legal world of Medieval Iceland, principally working with legal texts and saga narratives within the genre of the Contemporary sagas (*samtíðarsögur*). I also consider

4 The Kristinna laga þáttr of the earliest *Grágás* manuscripts calls for written inventories to be made of all of a church's possessions. *Grágás Konungsbók*, Kristinna laga þáttr 4, ed. Finsen, 1a.15, trans. Denis et al. 1.32–33. Many of these inventories, called *máldagar*, survive, a few in originals, many in later copies. See Margaret Cormack, *The Saints in Iceland: Their Veneration from the Conversion to 1400* (Brussels: Société des Bollandistes, 1994), 25–29.

5 Anthony Perron, "Local Knowledge of Canon Law, ca. 1150–1250," *Cambridge History of Medieval Canon Law*, ed. by John C. Wei and Anders Winroth (Cambridge: Cambridge University Press, Forthcoming); Lára Magnúsardóttir, *Bannfæring og kirkjuvald á Íslandi, 1275–1550* (Reykjavík: Háskólaútgáfan, 2007); Anders Winroth, "The Canon Law of Emergency Baptism and of Marriage in Iceland and Europe," *Gripla* 29 (2018): 203–229; Anders Winroth, "Goffredus och Västgötalagen," *Kyrkohistorisk årsskrift* 1:119 (2019): 183–188; Bertil Nilsson, *De Sepulturis: Gravrätten I Corpus iuris canonici och i medeltida nordisk lagstiftning* (Stockholm, Almqvist and Wiksell, 1989); Kristoffer Vadum, "Bruk av kanonistisk litteratur i Nidarosprovinsen ca. 1250–1340," (Ph.D. Dissertation. University of Oslo, 2015); and Joel Anderson, "Bishop Guðmundr's Roman Redemption: Imagining and Suspending Papal Government in Medieval Iceland," *Speculum* 95 (2020): 657–688. For an early medieval perspective see, Nicole Marafioti, "Secular and Ecclesiastical Justice in Late Anglo-Saxon England," *Speculum* 94 (2019): 774–805.

the manuscript transmission of these texts, focusing as much on the time when manuscripts were written as on the time when we think any one text may have been originally composed in some form. This is particularly important when working with legal materials, which in the case of Iceland survive mostly in manuscripts written in the mid-thirteenth century and later.

Chapters 1 and 2 outline the history of excommunication (chapter 1) and outlawry (chapter 2) and their treatment in medieval Icelandic sources. In chapter 3 I make a detailed argument that outlawry as it appears in surviving Icelandic sources is derived from canon law ideas about excommunication, using the material evidence of surviving manuscripts, detailed comparison of legal texts, and a general reevaluation of the evidence.

Chapters 4 and 5 are case studies. In chapter 4 I discuss outlawry and excommunication in stories documenting the conflict between Bishop Guðmundr Arason and the chieftain Kolbeinn Tumason, a conflict that took place in the early thirteenth century in north Iceland that continued to be written about into the fourteenth century when there was a formal attempt to canonize Bishop Guðmundr. Chapter 5 concentrates on the outlaw Aron Hjǫrleifsson (ca. 1200–1255) and the stories told about him. It addresses the porous boundary between being outlawed and being excommunicated displayed by writers and readers in the fourteenth century. Throughout this book I seek to demonstrate how outlawry and excommunication functioned within the same legal world in Iceland in the thirteenth and fourteenth centuries. They were sanctions that reflected, amplified and sometimes blurred into each other.

CHAPTER 1

# Excommunication

This chapter provides a brief history of excommunication in medieval Europe, focusing on the ways the sanction changed from the early to the high and late Middle Ages and tracing how it was disseminated in Iceland. I emphasize several arguments about excommunication within this account: different ideas circulated about how closely excommunication was linked to damnation—earlier medieval sources are more likely to associate excommunication with damnation. Legal sources, especially from the twelfth century onward, developed complex concepts and terminology to further define and often limit the impact of excommunication; these texts are more likely to argue that excommunication did not automatically damn a person and to entertain the possibility that excommunication could be unjust. It can be difficult to say how widely these ideas spread outside of learned circles, and older ideas about excommunication also persisted.[1] In Iceland as elsewhere in Europe in the thirteenth century we can see a shift, mostly in legal but also in narrative sources, towards the use of excommunication as a technical and bureaucratic weapon although this shift was neither instantaneous nor total.

Excommunication in narrative sources is likely to focus on specific conflicts. In high-profile cases involving disputes between lay magnates and church officials, excommunication often appears in disputes over jurisdiction. In these cases, excommunication is most likely to be invoked as a sanction for disobedience or contumacy, for refusing to bend to or acknowledge the Church's, often novel, claims.

Many Icelandic sources produced in or discussing the period before the late-thirteenth century present excommunication not as a complex legal sanction but as a forceful sentence used in political conflicts. In these sources, excommunication is often tied to unconsecrated burial, sometimes to curses, and I argue it is likely, to damnation. Excommunication is not generally discussed at great length in these narratives—it is simply deployed with little comment before the narrative continues. This means that the precise meaning of any one excommunication can be difficult to interpret.

1 On the persistence of older ideas about excommunication see, Genevieve Steele Edwards, "Ritual Excommunication in medieval France and England, 900–1200," (Ph.D. Dissertation, Stanford University, 1997).

 | DOI:10.1163/9789004461468_003

Part of this picture is due to the nature of the surviving sources about excommunication in Iceland, which are often narratives either about bishops or conflicts involving bishops and are almost always in the vernacular, including most legal and documentary sources. Another factor is probably the persistence of older attitudes toward excommunication, which did not necessarily change immediately after churchmen began advocating for new legal ideas or decrees. As Lára Magnúsardóttir has argued, there is a shift in Icelandic sources in the late thirteenth century when there begins to appear more focus on precise canon law concepts and terminology,[2] but these developments took time.

## 1 Excommunication

Excommunication was the most severe and often the only available sanction used by the medieval Church.[3] It is a concept with a long history it existed in one form or another from the earliest Christian churches, survived the Reformation, including in many Protestant sects, and continues in use in some churches today. It can be difficult to separate the definition of excommunication from the history of its development in legal sources because the concept itself changed even when the words (and sometimes the texts being cited) remained the same.

---

2 Lára Magnúsardóttir, *Bannfæring og kirkjuvald*, 297–440.

3 F. Donald Logan, *Excommunication and the Secular Arm in Medieval England: A Study in Legal Procedure from the Thirteenth to the Sixteenth Century* (Toronto: Pontifical Institute of Medieval Studies, 1968); F. Donald Logan, "Excommunication," *Dictionary of the Middle Ages*, ed. Joseph R. Strayer (New York: Charles Scribner's Sons, 1984), 4.536–538; Elisabeth Vodola, *Excommunication in the Middle Ages* (Berkeley: University of California Press, 1986); Paul Hinschius, *System des katholischen Kirchenrechts*, 6 vols. (Berlin: Guttentag, 1869–1897), 4.698–705, 799–806; Alexander Murray, *Excommunication and Conscience in the Middle Ages: The John Coffin Memorial Lecture, 13 February 1991* (London: The University of London, 1991); Richard H. Helmholz, "Excommunication as a Legal Sanction: The Attitudes of the Medieval Canonists," *Zeitschrift Der Savigny-Stiftung fur Rechtsgeschichte, Kan. Abt.* 68 (1982): 202–218; Richard H. Helmholz, "Excommunication in Twelfth Century England," *Journal of Law and Religion* 11 (1995): 235–253; Richard H. Helmholz, *The Spirit of Classical Canon Law* (Athens, Ga.: University of Georgia Press, 1996), 366–393; Rosalind Hill, "The Theory and Practice of Excommunication in Medieval England," *History* 42 (1957): 1–11; Rosalind Hill, "Public Penance: Some Problems of a Thirteenth-Century Bishop," *History* 36 (1951): 213–226; Lára Magnúsardóttir, *Bannfæring og kirkjuvald*; Torstein Jørgensen, "Excommunication – an act of expulsion from heaven and earth," *The Creation of Medieval Northern Europe: Christianisation, Social Transformations, and Historiography, Essays in Honour of Sverre Bagge*, ed. Leidulf Melve and Sigbjørn Sønnesyn (Oslo: Dreyer Forlag, 2012), 58–69; and Edwards, "Ritual excommunication in medieval France and England."

Excommunication had roots in the earliest Christian churches.[4] The early sanctions almost always involved a ban on participation in the ritual of communion, from which the term derives. In the earliest sources, excommunication can be difficult to separate from penance, which was often public and usually demanded fasting and other outward signs of repentance in addition to a forbidding a person's access to the sacraments. This sanction was meant to be medicinal and corrective, eventually welcoming the person back into the Christian fold.[5]

By the seventh and eighth centuries, public penance had faded out of favor. Penance became increasingly a private matter between confessor and sinner, and excommunication became more distinct, focusing on public sins and offenses against the Church, which were crimes under Church law.[6] These offenses were conceptualized as acts that hurt the community or indeed other people's hope of salvation. Heresy, for example, was seen as a threat to the salvation of others and was the focus of much writing on excommunication in the Middle Ages.[7]

Bishops, as heirs of the Apostle Peter, had the authority to excommunicate.[8] It was usually required that offenders be given a warning to cease their offending behavior or end a forbidden relationship (such as a marriage between closely related people) before they were given the full sentence of excommunication.[9] This type of excommunication would later be referred to as excommunication *ferendae sententiae*, pronounced verbally (or by letter) by a bishop to a an individual as a consequence of a specific action.

---

4 On Bible passages often used to explain excommunication see, Jørgensen, "Excommunication – an act of expulsion," 59.

5 Vodola, *Excommunication*, 7–12; Logan, "Excommunication," 537–538.

6 Vodola, *Excommunication*, 12; Norman Tanner and Sethina Watson, "The least of the laity: the minimum requirements for a medieval Christian," *Journal of Medieval History* 32 (2006): 405–408; Logan, "Excommunication," 536. Public penance did not necessarily disappear completely or immediately, see, Mary C. Mansfield, *The Humiliation of Sinners: Public Penance in Thirteenth-Century France* (Ithaca: Cornell University Press, 1995).

7 Vodola, *Excommunication*, 30–34. The discussion goes at least as far back as Augustine writing against the Donatists in the early fifth century.

8 An early eleventh-century articulation of this can be found in Burchard, Bishop of Worms, *Decretorum libri XX, ex consiliis et orthodoxorum patrum decretis, tum etiam diversarum nationum synodis seu loci communes congesti*. ed. by Gérard Fransen and Theo Kölzer (1548 Cologne edition; repr: Aalen, 1992), 11.1 folio 144v.

9 Vodola, *Excommunication*, 5–7; 31. X 2. 28. 26, *Liber extra*, ed. Friedberg, 2.418–419. The Biblical basis for these warnings, with an increasing degree of public exposure, and for excommunication itself comes from Mt. 18:15–18.

Consequences of the sentence, once incurred, varied. The most intrinsic consequence was being banned from the sacraments, especially receiving communion (and with the exception of extreme unction). Other protections and privileges of the Church that were also denied to excommunicants under many medieval laws were the right to seek sanctuary in churches and burial in consecrated ground.[10] Excommunication also affected how others were supposed to interact with an excommunicated person. Continuing to associate and conduct business with an excommunicated person was itself grounds for excommunication.[11] This provision was modified by Pope Gregory VII in 1078 in a canon known as *Quoniam multos*, to emphasize that it was those who were actively participating in wrongdoing with an excommunicant who were excommunicated. Others were simply supposed to go to confession. Sin was not hereditary, and immediate family members were not forbidden to interact with excommunicated members, particularly if the excommunicated person was a head of household. In 1078 Pope Gregory VII further suggested that people ought not to fulfill oaths and other obligations toward an excommunicated person.[12]

## 2 Secular Sanctions and Excommunication

In the early Middle Ages, severe secular sanctions often followed excommunication, particularly if an offender remained defiant. Under the Carolingians (in

10 The denial of consecrated burial, and indeed the concept of consecrated burial, are ideas that developed unevenly over time. They were not always a part of Christian law or custom. On the development of the idea of consecrated burial see, Nilsson, *De Sepulturis*, 37–165; Donald Bullough, "Burial, Community and Belief in the Early Medieval West," *Ideal and Reality in Frankish and Anglo-Saxon Society: Studies Presented to J.M. Wallace-Hadrill*, ed. by Patrick Wormald (Oxford: Blackwell, 1983), 177–201; and Bonnie Effros, "Beyond cemetery walls: early medieval funerary topography and Christian salvation," *Early Medieval Europe* 6 (1997): 1–23. One of the early sources to attest to the idea of excommunicants being forbidden consecrated burial is found in a letter of Pope Leo I in the 5th century. Gratian, *Decretum*, C. 24 q. 2 c. 1 (first recension). The logic of the ban on excommunicated person's seeking sanctuary was that those who had already offended against the Church should not enjoy its special protections.

11 Vodola, *Excommunication*, 8, 16–18, 24–25. Pope Gregory VII was the first pope to comment explicitly on the contagion of excommunication. But the idea itself has existed long before he issued *Quoniam multos*. Jørgensen, "Excommunication – an act of expulsion," 61. For the canon see, Gregory VII, *Das Register Gregors VII*, ed. by E. Caspar, 2nd ed., Monumenta Germaniae Historia, Epistolae selectae (Berlin: Weidmann, 1967), 2.372–373.

12 Vodola, *Excommunication*, 22–23. On early articulations of the bans and limits on interaction with excommunicants see, Vodola, *Excommunication*, 8–10, 17.

the eighth and ninth centuries) excommunication was, according to Elisabeth Vodola: "transformed into a fully public criminal sanction" enforced by both secular lords and the bishops, many of who were themselves also territorial lords.[13] Excommunication under this system could entail not just exclusion from Church services and the sacraments but also punishment at the hands of worldly authorities, including imprisonment and execution. The laws often coordinated with each other, with those remaining in excommunication given secular sanctions if they refused to amend their offending behavior, often within a specified period.[14]

A characteristic early medieval voice on excommunication is the Carolingian Archbishop Hincmar of Rheims (d. 882), writing about how incest separates people from the church and from society: "Because they do not wish to obey divine and human laws, such that they separate themselves by this incest, according to the sacred canons they are cast out from the sacred community of the body and blood of Christ and from the society of all Christians [...] we brothers and the sons, who you have not taught letters, know what is called in our language anathema, that is, alienation. Such that these people are alienated from Christ, in whose [name] they are called Christians, and from and from the society of Christians and from communion, until they separate themselves from this illicit connection."[15] Incest, according to Hincmar, broke

13 Vodola, *Excommunication*, 12. The same can also be argued for Anglo-Saxon England, where most of the early preserved laws about excommunication are royal codes issued by kings often in consultation with bishops. Elaine M. Treharne, "A unique Old English formula for excommunication from Cambridge, Corpus Christi College 303," *Anglo-Saxon England* 24 (1995): 190–191; and Nicole Marafioti, "Unconsecrated Burial and Excommunication in Anglo-Saxon England: A Reassessment," *Traditio* 74 (2019): 58. Marafioti cautions, however, that this does not necessarily prove that there was no distinction made in the period between secular and ecclesiastical jurisdiction, ibid.

14 A clear example of this can be found in a capitulary associated with the Frankish King Childebert. *Pactis legis Salicae*, Capitulare 6, ed. Eckhardt, 267. trans. Katherine Fischer Drew, *The Laws of the Salian Franks* (Philadelphia: University of Pennsylvania Press, 1991), 157: "Qui uero episcopo suo noluerit audire, excommunicatus fuerit, perenne conditione apud Deum susteneat et de palatio nostro sit omnino extraneus, et omnes res suas parentibus legitime admittat. qui noluerit sacerdotis sui medicamenta sustinere." [He who does not wish to listen to the bishop will be excommunicated; he shall sustain this condition perpetually before God and be a stranger in all things from our palace. And he who does not wish to accept relief (*medicamenta*) from his priest shall lose all his property to his legitimate relatives.]

15 Hincmar of Reims, "Hincmari episcopi Remensis Epistolae Synodales," *Acta conciliorum et epistolae, decretales ac constitutiones Summorum Pontificum*, ed. by Jean Hardouin alias Jo. Harduinus et al. (Paris 1714), 6 (part one).349: "quia obedire divinis et humanis legibus noluerunt, ut se ab ipso incestu disjungerent, secundum sacros canones a sacra communione corporis et sanguinis Christi et ab omnium Christianorum societate abjecti sunt [...]

both human and divine law and should have resulted in total separation from Christian society. The alienation Hincmar posited was conceived of as temporary, however. It was essentially the offenders themselves who had removed themselves from community by violating its standards. If this behavior ceased, the separation from community could be reversed.

In one extreme example from a canon of the Council of Tribur in 895, it was decreed that unrepentant excommunicants could be killed with impunity.[16] Such provisions suggest that the sanction of excommunication was viewed as severe. They do not, however, provide much evidence about how and how often a consequence like execution was enforced. Indeed, Elisabeth Vodola has argued that the very severity of some of the secular punishments decreed for unrepentant excommunicants suggests just how difficult it could be to enforce excommunication.[17]

## 3 Rituals of Excommunication in the Period before Canonical Reforms

Early medieval sources about excommunication are not particularly plentiful.[18] Moreover, most of these sources are not what we might label typical sources of canon law: they are not from church councils or papal letters, but are often rather texts that document the ritual of excommunication, probably for pastoral use, or are secular laws that themselves punish excommunicants.[19]

vos fratres ac filii, qui litteras non didicitis, scitote quid sonat in nostra lingua anathema, id est alienatio. Ut a Christo, in quo nominantur Christiani, et ab Christianorum societate atque communione sint tales alieni, donec ab illa inlicita conjunctione se separent." Anathema was sometimes defined as a distinct and more severe sentence than excommunication but, as Vodola has demonstrated, this is not convincingly or consistently justified by the sources, *Excommunication*, 14–16. Cf. Jørgensen, "Excommunication – an act of expulsion," 60, 64.

16 Alfredus Boretius and Victor Krause (eds.), *Capitularia Regum Francorum* 2, Monumenta Germaniae Historica (Hannover: Hahn, 1897), 214–215: "Si interficiantur, iaceant absque compositione." [If they are killed, they fall without right to compensation.] On this council see Vodola, *Excommunication*, 18–19.

17 Vodola, *Excommunication*, 18–19.

18 Edwards, "Ritual Excommunication," 10–11; Treharne, "Formula for excommunication," 189.

19 See Treharne, "Formula for excommunication," 190–191: "In the Anglo-Saxon period, the secular law codes of the kings provide much of the evidence for excommunication, […] There is evidence to suggest that the penalty of excommunication may have been more frequently implemented than previously recognized and yet, regardless of its utter damnation of the offender, it was not effective when used by the church alone;" and Edwards, "Ritual Excommunication," 3: "at present excommunication is not well understood by historians, especially for the period before the thirteenth century, when canon law treatises

One early source about excommunication in medieval Europe is formulas for excommunication. These survive in a variety of manuscripts and were, for example, translated into vernacular languages including Old English.[20] Many of these formulas can be traced back to the work of Bishop Burchard of Worms (ca. 950/965–1025) who wrote a widely-disseminated handbook on pastoral care, designed to help priests carry out their duties.[21]

Burchard discusses a wide range of pastoral and disciplinary concerns. Book eleven (there are twenty books in his *Decretum*) focuses on excommunication, discussing why people might be excommunicated, how to conduct an excommunication, people who die excommunicated, and how excommunicants can be reconciled with the Church.[22] He includes a detailed description of an excommunication, clearly to be conducted in person by a bishop, including both words to say and actions to perform. The first element is the pronouncement of the excommunication, which in these formulas is clearly an oral sentence. This is done in no uncertain terms; it is to be pronounced that: "we separate you from the society of all Christians and exclude you beyond the boundaries of Holy Mother Church in heaven and on earth. We say that you are anathemized and judge you damned with the devil and his angels and all reprobates in eternal fire [...]"[23] Next it calls for twelve priests to throw twelve

on the subject began to be written. Too often the sanction is considered solely from a legal standpoint, usually papal, and a post-Tridentine understanding of excommunication is read back into events occurring centuries earlier."

20 On translations into Old English see, Treharne, "Formula for excommunication," 201–211.

21 For more about this text as both a work useful to ordinary priests and as a work of canon law see, Greta Austin, "Jurisprudence in the Service of Pastoral Care: The 'Decretum' of Burchard of Worms," *Speculum* 79 (2004): 929–959. See also John Burden, "Reading Burchard's *Corrector*: canon law and penance in the High Middle Ages," *Journal of Medieval History* 46:1 (2020): 77–97. DOI: 10.1080/03044181.2019.1671892 Burchard drew on other sources, particularly on Regino of Prüm's early-tenth-century *De ecclesiasticis disciplinis et religione Christiana*. Austin, "Jurisprudence in Service," 935. See also, James A. Brundage, *Medieval Canon Law* (London and New York: Routledge, 1995), 31–32.

22 Burchard, *Decretorum libri XX*, folio 143v–153v.

23 Burchard, *Decretorum libri XX*, 11.3. folio 145: "a societate omnium Christianorum separamus, et a liminibus sanctae matris Ecclesiae in caelo et in terra excludimus, et excommunicatum, et anathematizatum esse decernimus, et damnatum cum diabolo et angelis ejus, et omnibus reprobis, in igne aeterno judicamus: nisi forte a diaboli laqueis resipiscat et ad emendationem et paenitentiam redeat et Ecclesiae Dei quam laesit satisfaciat. Et respondeant omnes tertio amen, aut, fiat fiat, aut, anathema sit. Debent enim XII. sacerdotes episcopum circunstare [sic], et lucernas ardentes in manibus tenere, quas in conclusione anathematis vel excommunicationis projicere debent in terram, et conclucare pedibus. Post haec episcopus plebi ipsam excommunicationem communibus verbis debet explanare, ut omnes intelligant quam terribiliter damnatus sit, et ut noverint quod ab illa hora in reliquum non pro Christiano sed pro pagano habendus sit."

lighted candles to the ground and trample on them.[24] Then the pronouncement is to be repeated in the "common tongue" so that the person being sentenced (as well as any observers) understands the severity of the sentence.[25] We do not know if or how often this ritual was carried out, but it provides a vivid image of excommunication and suggests that excommunicants were faced with damnation in no uncertain terms.[26]

## 4 Excommunication and Damnation

A recurring concern in the historical interpretation of excommunication brought out in these texts is the relationship between excommunication and damnation. Did people believe that the excommunicated were destined for hell? The basic source material is open to multiple interpretations, with earlier sources more likely to see excommunication leading more or less directly to damnation,[27] whereas later sources tend to see excommunication as a tool for correction and enforcement of policy, not as a direct route to hell.

---

The same or similar formulas appears in a variety of contexts (and languages) throughout the Middle Ages. See for example, Clyde Pharr, "A Thirteenth Century Formula of Anathema," *The American Journal of Philology* 66 (1945): 135–150. Genevieve Edwards presents a list previously published examples as well as additional unpublished formulae with translations: "Ritual Excommunication," 133–336. On liturgical curses more generally see, Lester K. Little, *Benedictine Maledictions: Liturgical Cursing in Romanesque France* (Ithaca and London: Cornell University Press, 1993).

24 This is to be done by twelve priests. Burchard, *Decretorum libri XX*, 11.3. folio 145: "Debent enim XII. sacerdotes episcopum circunstare [sic], et lucernas ardentes in manibus tenere, quas in conclusione anathematis vel excommunicationis proijcere debent in terram, et conclucare pedibus." [Then twelve priests are to stand around the bishop, holding flaming candles in their hands, which at the end of the anathema or excommunication they are to throw to the ground and trample with their feet.] This passage appears in Gratian, *Decretum*, C. 11 q. 3 c. 106 (second recension), ed. Friedberg, 1.674. In terms of the persistence of ideas of excommunication and damnation, it is important to emphasize that this is a canon added in the second recension of the *Decretum*.

25 Burchard, *Decretorum libri XX*, 11.3, fol. 145: "communibus verbis."

26 Logan, "Excommunication," 537: "A study of over 15,000 persons excommunicated in English ecclesiastical courts did not reveal even one performance of the solemn rite." For further caution about interpreting such texts see, Philippe Buc, *The Dangers of Ritual: Between Early Medieval Texts and Social Scientific Theory* (Princeton: Princeton University Press, 2009). Against these considerations, the sheer *number* of surviving formulae must be weighed.

27 As is strongly suggested, for example, in Burchard, *Decretorum libri XX*, 11.3. fol. 145: "in igne aeterno judicamus." See also, Lára Magnúsardóttir, *Bannfæring og kirkjuvald*, 16; Murray, *Excommunication and Conscience*, 17–22. Treharne suggests that the body was

Excommunication formulas suggest a strong association with damnation. These survive from a variety of contexts and can often be traced to common sources, particularly the passage from Burchard's *Decretum* cited above. An Anglo-Saxon formula, for example, minces no words: "We excommunicate, damn, and anathemize [you] and sequester [you] at the threshold of God's holy church."[28] It is not possible to be certain if these texts were used frequently or their imagery believed, but they do leave an impression of excommunication as a fearful threat.

The secondary literature on the topic can be divided on unclear on this particular issue, with some voices more than others convinced that excommunication was, effectively, a sentence of damnation.[29] This confusion is largely a reflection of the sources, their diversity, and the difficulty of interpreting how they related to practices or beliefs.[30] It is not always possible to be certain how a particular writer understood the relationship between excommunication and damnation although the earlier and further from Rome the sources, the greater the likelihood that excommunication was strongly associated with damnation.[31]

## 5 Consecrated Burial

The issue of damnation is linked to a common consequence or threat that often went hand in hand with excommunication: denial of consecrated burial.

An early canon often cited to support the ban on consecrated burial for excommunicants was written by Pope Leo I (440–461) in a letter to the Bishop of Narbonne. He insisted that "those whom we have not communicated with

being damned in excommunication rituals, but not the soul, a claim that she cites no sources for, "Formula for Excommunication," 208 note 102.

28 This text is from the manuscript Cambridge, Corpus Christi College 303 edited by Elaine M. Treharne in the appendix to her article, "Formula for Excommunication," 210: "excommunicamus, dampnamus, anathematizamus, atque a liminibus sancte Dei ecclesie sequestramus." A similar text is also in the vernacular in the same manuscript. It is possible that the formula is itself derived from Burchard's text although the two are not identical, Treharne, "Formula for Excommunication," 203.

29 Murray, *Excommunication and Conscience*, 17–22; Lára Magnúsardóttir, *Bannfæring og kirkjuvald*, 16; Treharne, "Formula for excommunication," 190–191; and Edwards, "Ritual Excommunication," 111–132.

30 Vodola, *Excommunication*, 2.

31 Edwards, "Ritual Excommunication," 111–132.

while they were living, we cannot communicate with when they are dead."[32] The usual interpretation of this during the Middle Ages was that non-Christians and certain other groups, usually including heretics, excommunicants, and sometimes other types of criminals, should not be buried alongside members of the Christian community in consecrated graveyards (or inside churches).[33] Denial of consecrated burial for excommunicants seems to have been a common practice by the eleventh century if not earlier.[34] Through the high Middle Ages we can see consecrated burial being withdrawn or withheld, sometimes pending a posthumous absolution.[35] Consecrated burial was also forbidden during interdicts and constituted part of their coercive power.[36] Although consecrated burial did not guarantee salvation, it was a mark of belonging to the Christian community as well as, many believed, a help to the souls of those buried, not least because it often meant that graves were in the near vicinity of regular masses and prayers.[37]

Although it was not synonymous with excommunication, unconsecrated burial was strongly associated with severe crimes and, from the eleventh century at least, with excommunication and damnation in a variety of northern lawcodes—particularly in Anglo-Saxon, Norwegian, and Icelandic codes. In these cases, whether it is a king or the Alþingi, it is often secular authorities that dictate that certain individuals should not be granted a consecrated burial.[38] This secular and ecclesiastical blending of punishments will be explored

---

32 Gratian, *Decretum*, C. 24 q. 2 c. 1 (first recension): "quibus viventibus non communicavimus mortuis communicare non possumus." The full letter can be found in the *Patrologia Latina*, 54.1205B–1206A.

33 A group that, notably, also included infants who died before they were baptized.

34 Consecrated burial was not common among of the first Christian communities in Europe, who tended to retain ancestral burial practices. Bullough, "Burial, Community and Belief," 179, 192; Bonnie Effros, "Beyond cemetery walls," 1–23; Nilsson, *De sepulturis*, 37–41. Nicole Marafioti has argued that in England before the eleventh century, unconsecrated burial was actually primarily a secular punishment, "Unconsecrated Burial and Excommunication," 55–123.

35 For discussion of the development of a "topography of salvation" in Christian burial practices see Effros, "Beyond cemetery walls," 1–23. On posthumous absolution See also X 5. 39. 28, *Liber extra*, ed. Friedberg, 2.899–900.

36 Peter D. Clarke, "A Question of Collective Guilt: Popes, Canonists and the Interdict c. 1140–c. 1250," *Zeitschrift der Savigny-Stiftung für Rechtsgeschichte, Kanonistische Abteilung* 116 (1999): 104–146.

37 Effros, "Beyond cemetery walls," 3–4.

38 According to Donald Bullough, there is no evidence for the formal consecration of cemeteries before the Carolingian period (ca. 780–900), "Burial, Community and Belief," 189, 199. For further discussion of those forbidden consecrated burial in Nordic lawcodes see, Nilsson, *De sepulturis*, 242–290.

further in chapter 3. Although the details varied, it is clear that during the high Middle Ages unconsecrated burial was a serious consequence that both individuals and their surviving family members were at pains to avoid or, in some cases, posthumously correct via reinternment.[39]

Not all writers subscribed to this view. Indeed, it seems reasonably clear that for the canonist Gratian, for example, excommunication was first and foremost a sanction and treatment for the living, not something that could or should be imposed on the dead.[40] Nevertheless, a wealth of medieval sources suggest that other views were also common, views that associated unconsecrated burial with earthly disgrace, disinheritance, and damnation.

## 6 Later Legal Views on Excommunication and Damnation

Legal thinking by the thirteenth century was moving away from any absolute connection between excommunication and damnation. At the First Council of Lyon in 1245, for example, Pope Innocent IV declared that excommunication in and of itself did not affect one's salvation. This idea was taken up by some thinkers, notably the theologian Thomas Aquinas, but there is little evidence that it was widely understood or discussed in broad circles in the thirteenth century.[41]

Gratian's *Decretum* (from the mid-twelfth century), more than earlier sources, considers the possibility of unjust excommunication, an idea that also argues against an automatic connection between excommunication and

39 This could involve money payments or, at least one Anglo-Saxon law suggests, proving a dead relative's innocence through an ordeal. See, Marafioti, "Unconsecrated Burial and Excommunication," 86–99. On debt payments to allow reburial in consecrated ground see Vodola, *Excommunication*, 38–39.

40 Nilsson, *De sepulturis*, 256–257.

41 Vodola, *Excommunication*, 42–43. See also Edwards, "Ritual Excommunication," 16: "A council at Meaux and Paris in 845–6, presided over by the famous reformer Hincmar, Archbishop of Reims, repeats the old Early Church strictures against depriving anyone of communion 'sine certa et manifest peccati causa' […] cautioning that […] 'anathema is damnation to eternal death.' This last is a claim that careful theologians and canonists in the High and Late Middle Ages would have been at pains to refute, but it is implicit in both word and gesture of excommunication rituals from this time on and well into the Reformation era." The potential for unjust excommunication and the punishment of the innocent more generally was also a major point of discussion with regard to interdicts, Margaret Murphy, "Ecclesiastical Censures: An Aspect of Their Use in Thirteenth Century Dublin," *Archivium Hibernicum* 44 (1989): 92–93; and Clarke, "A Question of Collective Guilt," 104–146.

damnation. Gratian cites Bishop Atto of Vercelli (885–961) who wrote that: *Non in perpetuum dampnamur, cum iniuste iudicamur* "we are not damned in perpetuity when we have been unjustly judged."[42] Gratian discusses this as a real possibility that should be guarded against and fought,[43] but nevertheless the authority of one passing the sentence was to be respected.[44] These warnings about excommunication were codified and reiterated at the Fourth Lateran Council, which required a clear warning, reasonable cause, and the presence of witnesses before an excommunication and provided pathways for someone fighting an unjust excommunication to seek remedies.[45]

This shifting attitude toward damnation and excommunication (and the initially limited reach of that shift) is a small indication of larger shifts in canon law surrounding excommunication. F. Donald Logan has characterized this as a shift from seeing excommunication primarily as a judicial sentence, to its use "as a means of imposing ecclesiastical discipline [...] Excommunication, the severest penalty of the Christian church, became the coercive edge to even routine decrees."[46] In other words, rather than a sentence that was pronounced after a specific breach or action, excommunication was increasingly held up as

42 Gratian, *Decretum*, C. 24 q. 3 c. 5 (first recension). The attribution of this passage in the *Decretum* to Rabanus is inaccurate.

43 Gratian, *Decretum*, C. 11 q. 3 c. 8 (first recension): "De episcopis, qui innocentes aut minimis causis culpabiles excommunicant. Item ex Concilio Agatensi. [c. 3]. Episcopi, si sacerdotali moderatione postposita innocentes aut minimis causis culpabiles excommunicare presumpserint, aut ad gratiam baptismi festinantes fortasse recipere noluerint, a uicinis episcopis eiusdem prouinciæ litteris moneantur, et si parere noluerint, communio illis usque ad tempus sinodi a reliquis episcopis denegetur, ne forte per excommunicationis peccatum excommunicati longo tempore morte preueniantur." [Concerning bishops, who excommunicate innocent people or those guilty of the most trivial violations. Likewise, from the Council of Agde [c. 3]. Bishops, if, putting aside priestly moderation, presume to excommunicate innocent people or those guilty of the most trivial violations, or perhaps do not wish to accept those hurrying to the grace of baptism, are to be warned by bishops of a neighbouring province with letters, and if they do not wish to yield, let communion with them be denied by the remaining bishops up to the time of a synod, lest perhaps through the sin of excommunication, those excommunicated for a long time are speeded on to death.]

44 Gratian, *Decretum*, C. 24 q. 3 c. 1 (first recension): "Sententia pastoris, siue iusta siue iniusta fuerit, timenda est." [The sentence of the shepherd, whether it be just or unjust, is to be feared.]

45 Lateran IV (1215), canon 47, available digitally at: http://www.internetsv.info/Archive/CLateranense4.pdf. The best edition is, Antonio García y García, et al eds., *The General Councils of Latin Christendom: From Constantinople IV to Pavia-Siena (869–1424)*. Corpus Christianorum, Conciliorum Oecumenicorum Generaliumque Decreta vol. 2.1 (Turnhout: Brepols, 2013).

46 Logan, "Excommunication," 536.

a possibility for those not obeying new decrees, a threat before any action was committed.

## 7 Developments in Canon Law

The laws of the Church and the legal systems and bureaucracy surrounding them developed throughout the Middle Ages. This came as a part of the expansion of academic canon law and the increasing literacy and professionalization of the clergy.[47] These developments changed, some argue radically, the face and uses of excommunication in medieval canon law.[48]

### 7.1 *Major and Minor Excommunication*

With the development of more formal systems of canon law in the twelfth century, excommunication was more closely defined and was also often separated into two different types. Major excommunication is the penalty that the casual observer likely associates with excommunication, it was an exclusion from the Christian community, forbidding one to enter churches, receive sacraments, or enjoy legal status under canon law. Minor excommunication, by contrast, became a more medicinal, less punitive form of the sanction, those under it were forbidden the Eucharist and other sacraments but were allowed, indeed expected, to continue to attend mass.[49] According to Logan, minor excommunication "simply referred to the consequences of mortal sin."[50] Minor excommunication was also the sentence, according to many canonists, imposed on those who associated with excommunicants.[51]

One of the earliest canonists to offer a formal distinction between major and minor excommunication was Goffredus of Trano (ca. 1200–1245), who wrote in the mid-thirteenth century. He carefully distinguished between major and minor excommunication by name (he also saw anathema as equivalent to major excommunication, seeing it as a foreign word that translated into Latin

47 Brundage, *Medieval Canon Law*, 44–69.

48 Vodola, *Excommunication*, 192–193.

49 Vodola, *Excommunication*, 41–42: "The full contagion of excommunication now affected only those whose contact with the excommunicate was criminal—they conspired or participated in the crime—or those who associated with someone excommunicated 'with all his communicatores' because of the gravity of his crime."

50 Logan, "Excommunication," 536.

51 Previously there was no formal distinction between different types of excommunication although there is evidence that excommunication could vary considerably in severity. Edwards, "Ritual Excommunication," 14–15.

as major excommunication). For him major excommunication entailed a public separation from the Christian community, a ban not only on the sacraments but also on entry into churches and "the community of the faithful" whereas minor excommunication forbade a person the sacraments.[52] In other words, according to Goffredus, those under minor excommunication were forbidden from taking communion, for example, but not from entering a church building or attending mass, a visible punishment but not a complete separation from the community.

## 8 The Canon *Si quis suadente* and *latae sententiae* Excommunication

By the high Middle Ages excommunication pronounced by a bishop, excommunication *ferendae sente*ntiae, was joined by the controversial but frequently invoked excommunication *latae sententiae*, or by an already pronounced sentence. This type of excommunication, particularly associated with the canon *Si quis suadente* (first promulgated in 1139 at the Second Lateran Council), needed neither a specific warning nor the pronouncement of a bishop to come into effect. Performing a forbidden action was enough to bring the sentence upon oneself without the need for a bishop or any formal process.[53] It was sometimes referred to as excommunication *a jure* "by law" or ipso facto as opposed to excommunication *ab homine*, i.e. pronounced by a person.

The canon original focused on protecting clerics from all physical violence. It decreed that physically assaulting a cleric with *violentas manus* "violent hands" was an action that led to excommunication (the word used within the

52 Gottofredo da Trani (Goffredus Tranensis), *Summa super titulis Decretalium* (Lyon, 1519. Reprint Aalen: Scientia, 1968), 483. Available at: http://works.bepress.com/david_freidenreich/17. "Una est que dicitur anathema que excludit ab ingressu ecclesie a communione fidelium et sacramentis. hec dicitur maior excommunicatio. alia que separat a sacramentis et hec dicitur minor excommuicatio ut superius dictum est." [One is that which is called anathema, which excludes from the entrance into church, from the communion of the faithful, and the sacraments. This we call major excommunication. The other, which separates from the sacraments, is called minor excommunication as is said above].

53 The canon is associated with increasing papal claims to power and the so-called papal monarchy. See, Richard Helmholz, " 'Si quis suadente' (C.17 q.4 c.29): Theory and practice," *Proceedings of the Seventh International Congress of Medieval Canon Law, Cambridge, 23–27 July 1984*, edited by Peter Linehan (Vatican City: Biblioteca Apostolica Vaticana, 1988), 425; Vodola, *Excommunication*, 28–29. For Iceland specifically see, Elizabeth Walgenbach, "The Canon *Si quis suadente* and Excommunication in Medieval Iceland," *Gripla* 30 (2019): 155–185; and Lára Magnúsardóttir, *Bannfæring og kirkjuvald*, 78–104, 153–154.

canon is *anathema*) without a formal procedure.[54] Moreover, such an excommunication could not be absolved without referral to the pope "except in cases of imminent danger of death."[55] This sentence was automatic; it required no formal warning, or technically even a witness, before it went into effect.

The number of offenses that could lead to such a sentence grew throughout the Middle Ages, with some manuscripts containing long lists of offenses. What was most distinctive about this concept was that, at least technically, it required no bishop, judge, or other official procedures in order to come into effect. The canon itself—as well as the perceived seriousness of the offenses that fell under *latae sententiae*—served as an official warning against would be offenders, who were then said to bring the sanction on themselves by their actions. The threat (or perceived threat) of heresy justified the use and expansion of preemptive sentences of excommunication. This was especially true on the continent between the twelfth and thirteenth centuries.[56] Indeed, in some legal texts, including the *Decretum* of Gratian, much of the discussion of excommunication comes in the context of the legal issues surrounding heresy.[57]

## 9 Excommunication for Disobedience to Church Authority

Further developments shifted the focus in major excommunication away from excommunication as a formalization of sin's consequences and towards an attitude holding that excommunication, for contumacy, could be the result of simple disobedience to specific church precepts or demands.[58] It was now possible and indeed likely for a person to be excommunicated not for grievous sins or heresy but rather a failure to obey new rules promulgated by the Church. As framed by Logan: "contumacy now meant the refusal to obey a mandate of the church and did not necessarily imply a general rejection of church authority."[59]

---

54 Gratian, *Decretum*, C. 17 q. 4 c. 29 (second recension), ed. Friedberg, 1.822.

55 Gratian, *Decretum*, C. 17 q. 4 c. 29 (second recension), ed. Friedberg, 1.822: "nisi mortis urgente periculo."

56 Vodola, *Excommunication*, 69.

57 My discussion of heresy is very limited in this book. Heresy was not a concern in Iceland during the period from 1150–1350.

58 Logan, "Excommunication," 536.

59 Logan, "Excommunication" 536. Vodola takes an extreme view on this, suggesting that almost all if not all connection with sin was lost and excommunication became mostly a tool of the church courts, *Excommunication*, 36. Others have questioned this view see, Lára Magnúsardóttir, *Bannfæring og kirkjuvald*, 82: "[…] er ég ósammála Vodola um að bann af sjálfu verkinu hafi fyrst og fremst verið notað sem vopn í réttarhöldum um önnur

Some papal letters ended with the threat of an automatic excommunication for those not obeying the new dictate.[60]

## 10 Excommunication in the Church Courts

Excommunication also created legal handicaps; those under the sentence could not bring cases into court, an effect which made excommunication a popular tool in developed ecclesiastical court systems because failure to appear in court could itself lead to excommunication. (i.e., a person could be excommunicated for contumacy when failing to appear). Excommunication could also be appealed in these same courts, which was sometimes used as a delay tactic in itself.[61] There was also the risk of being excommunicated due to a lawsuit that misrepresented the facts of a case, an acknowledged problem that was never fully solved by the papal courts.[62]

These uses of excommunication in legal battles as well as the proliferation of actions that could lead to automatic excommunication led to the sentence being proclaimed more and more often. As the number of sentences increased, calls for restricting the use of excommunication became increasingly prominent. The potential for the abuse of excommunication was one of the issues discussed during the Reformation when it became a point that reformers were keen to attack. This was also true for the counter Reformation when, for example, in 1563 it was concluded at the Council of Trent that

mál á síðmiðöldum. Þvert á móti benda heimildir til þess að flest þau verk sem vörðuðu bannfæringu samkvæmt íslenska kristinréttinum frá 1275 hafi fallið án þess að dómari hafi komið þar nálægt." [I disagree with Vodola that excommunication *latae sententiae* was first and foremost a tool of the courts used in the course of other cases in the late Middle Ages. On the contrary, sources suggest that most excommunications according to Icelandic Christian law from 1275 fell automatically, without a judge coming near them.]

60 Or for, for example, not paying a new tithe. Pope Nicholas III, for example, approved of the lifting of an excommunication on the Greenlanders, which had fallen because they failed to pay a crusading tithe in a timely fashion, a reasonable decision given that it was rather unlikely that the Greenlanders had even learned that the tithe had been imposed. *Diplomatarium Islandicum*, 2.160.

61 Logan, "Excommunication," 537.

62 Many papal judgements were given with the caveat, implicit or explicit, that the facts presented were an accurate representation of the case, otherwise the decision could be invalid. On this issue see Stanley Chodorow, "Dishonest Litigation in the Church Courts, 1140–98," *Law, Church, and Society: Essays in Honor of Stephan Kuttner*, ed. by Kenneth Pennington and Robert Somerville (Philadelphia: University of Pennsylvania Press, 1977), 187–206.

"when [excommunication] is imposed rashly and in slight matters, then the penalty will be more despised than feared and will produce more harm than good."[63] Excommunication was a double-edged sword for the Church—not least because of the increasing service it was expected to perform in helping to enforce new legislation.

In many cases, it is difficult to determine how widely these ideas about excommunication were disseminated or how deeply they were applicable outside a narrow world of lawsuits brought before Church courts. Excommunication outside of the most technical of legal sources often looked rather different.

## 11 Excommunication in Political Conflicts

Court cases were not the only place that excommunication was a frequent feature. Particularly in the high Middle Ages, excommunication was also a tool of political conflict. It was a step that could bring a conflict to a crisis. The most compelling stories of excommunication from the Middle Ages were not courtroom battles or careful theological arguments about access to salvation and the Eucharist, nor were they about heresy, which was often used as a test case in, for example, Gratian's *Decretum*.[64] They were political excommunications, attempts by Church leaders to wield the full power of the sanction against the secular magnates on whose physical protection they were often dependent.

One widely disseminated example is the story of the conflict between Thomas Becket and the English king Henry II. This story of a stubborn archbishop intent on asserting the Church's rights as he saw them and the equally stubborn king who opposed him was written and rewritten across Europe. It both fueled and was fueled by the popularity of Canterbury, the site of the archbishop's martyrdom, as a pilgrimage site. The story came to Iceland soon after the events took place and was translated and adapted into at least two Old Norse-Icelandic versions.[65] Unlike in the Carolingian world, where

63 25th session of the Council of Trent (December 1563), *Canones et Decreta sacrosancti oecumenici Concilii Tridentini* (Lipsiae: Ex officina Bernhardi Tauchnitz, 1863), *Decretum de reformatione*, chap. 3, 189: "si temere aut levibus ex rebus incutiatur magis contemni quam formidari et perniciem potius parere quam salute;" trans. Logan, "Excommunication," 538.

64 Most of the discussion about excommunication in Causa 24 of Gratian's *Decretum*, for example, is focused on excommunication in the context of heresy.

65 KLNM 18.244–245, s.v. "Thomas Becket," by Hans Bekker-Nielsen; KLNM 18.249, s.v. "Thomas Becket (Norge)," by Lilli Gjerløw; KLNM 18.249–251, s.v. "Thómas saga erkibiskups," by Hans Bekker-Nielsen; and Eiríkr Magnússon, introduction to *Thómas saga*

excommunication was often more or less enforced by secular authorities, in these stories, excommunication was turned against these same secular powers.

Alongside the high-profile excommunications of individual leaders, the related and controversial sanction of interdict was sometimes used.[66] This sanction fell not on an individual person but rather on a particular area. It put a stop to the performance all of the sacraments except baptism and extreme unction and was designed to enlist a community to persuade one of its members to correction. Interdict was especially potent, although not necessarily more effective, because it had consequences not just for the person or persons being punished but for the whole community. There is no evidence that an interdict was ever imposed on Iceland although church buildings were on occasion closed because they had been defiled by bloodshed.[67]

### 11.1 *Excommunication as a Political Weapon*

In many conflicts in which bishops deploy excommunication against powerful secular leaders, what is being fought over is not sin per se so much as power. Excommunicated leaders were usually not excommunicated for obvious moral offenses such as murder, but rather for refusing to obey or accept churchmen's ideas about legal jurisdiction – ideas that were often novel. The popes and bishops who used excommunication could not, however, physically enforce the sentence. Excommunication, for all its dire overtones, could also mark a failure in conflict resolution. It was an empty punishment if it could not be enforced or was not recognized. In some narratives and political conflicts excommunication marks an impasse, and one that was not necessarily resolved or resulted in concessions that were only temporary.[68]

---

*Erikbyskups, A Life of Archbishop Thomas Becket, In Icelandic with English Translation,* Notes and Glossary vol. 2 (London: Longmans, 1883), vi–clxxv.

66 For a detailed discussion of interdict see, Peter D. Clark, *The Interdict in the Thirteenth Century: A Question of Collective Guilt* (Oxford: Oxford University Press, 2007).

67 On when and how churches could require re-consecrating after bloodshed see Árni Þorláksson, "Kristinréttr Árna," chap. 12, ed. Magnús Lyngdal Magnússon, 158. For a saga example of this see, Sturla Þórðarson, *Íslendinga saga, Sturlunga saga efter membranen Króksfjarðarbók udfyldt efter Reykjarfjarðarbók*, ed. by Kristian Kålund, 2 vols. (Copenhagen and Kristiania: Kongelige nordiske oldskrift-selskab, 1906, 1911), 1.289, trans. by Julia McGrew, *Sturlunga saga* vol. 1 (New York: Twayne Publishers and the American Scandinavian Foundation, 1970), 25: 145.

68 Or it could result in the exile of the bishop or archbishop who pronounced the sentence, as was the case for Archbishop of Niðaróss Jón rauði, who died in exile in Skara (Sweden) amid conflicts with powerful laymen in Norway. See, Eldbjørg Haug, "Concordants, Statute and Conflict in *Árna saga biskups*," *Collegium Medievale* 28 (2015): 87–89.

Excommunication was not always an effective tool. It was both very powerful and useless depending on the willingness of others to recognize it (and recognize it as just). Some particularly powerful rulers seem to have had little trouble continuing to rule without hindrance despite papal excommunication, including Emperor Frederick II (1194–1250) who seemed untroubled by his two excommunications in 1227 and 1239, or Emperor Louis IV (1282–1347) who continued to rule as he pleased despite being excommunicated.[69]

We have reason to suspect that the stories that do survive are exceptional. Narratives of excommunication had the potential for drama and pathos. They were also a useful way of narrating and framing conflicts between churchmen and the secular leaders who resisted their increasing claims on property and power. Excommunication was powerful in these stories because of its imagery, its associations with damnation, and also because of the rituals that could release a person from the sentence. These features appear in Icelandic sources that concern excommunication, which will be under discussion in the rest of this chapter.

## 12 Excommunication in Icelandic Sources

### 12.1 *Early Sources*

Few scholars have investigated excommunication in an Icelandic context.[70] The major exception to this is Lára Magnúsardóttir, who focuses on the period after 1275. Before this time, the evidence about excommunication in Iceland is limited.[71] Moreover, most of the sources that document the period before 1275 are preserved in later manuscripts that may be influenced by later ideas and terms.[72] Some of the arguably earliest sources attesting to

69 Logan, "Excommunication," 537. Another example is King John, See, C.R. Cheney, "King John's Reaction to the Interdict on England," *Transactions of the Royal Historical Society* 31 (1949): 129–150.

70 For a detailed discussion of the (limited) historiography of excommunication in Iceland and some of the biases that have hampered study see, Lára Magnúsardóttir, *Bannfæring og kirkjuvald*, 139–215.

71 Some of the sources that do survive about the history of the Church in Iceland in this period are little studied. There is for example, a penitential associated with Bishop Þorlákr (in later manuscripts) that is almost never discussed. See, Sveinbjörn Rafnsson, "Skriftaboð Þorláks Biskups," *Gripla* 5 (1982): 77–114.

72 This may well be the case, for instance, in the various sagas about Bishop Guðmundr Arason, who lived in the first half of the thirteenth century but was written about extensively in the early fourteenth. KLNM 5.542–543, s.v. "Guðmundar saga biskups Arasonar," by Björn Sigfússon. Stefán Karlsson suggests that "It is unlikely that any *Guðmundar saga* covering the bishop's whole life was written before the exhumation [in 1315]."

excommunication in Iceland are a group of letters preserved in a fifteenth-century manuscript AM 186 4to (Hvanneyrarbók). One of these letters was sent from Rome to the Archbishop of Niðaróss; the others were sent to Iceland from the archbishop.[73]

The first of these letters was sent to the Icelandic bishops and other men in Iceland, probably in 1173. The letter reminds the bishops and priests to set a good example and exhorts them to remember "those deeds which drag [one] to eternal death." The archbishop also reminds the bishops that "anyone who misuses a cleric with hostile hand is under God's ban and the pope's and may not be absolved of the killing or maiming of a cleric or a monk. except in the presence of the pope."[74] This letter clearly addresses contemporary concerns in canon law, particularly the increasing attempts to define the clergy as a separate, protected group.[75] It also shows excommunication being used as a threat; the threat being suggested is eternal punishment in hell, rather than a later, more circumscribed understanding of excommunication.

Another letter is a brief missive in Latin, firmly reminding the archbishop that clerics were not to bear arms; Pope Clement III does not discuss excommunication directly but admonishes all clerics that it is "a danger" to "involve ourselves in physical conflicts" and that "we prohibit this with our universal apostolic authority."[76] This letter has been dated to 1189, about 50 years after *Si quis suadente* was first promulgated. Similar warnings are preserved in a letter attributed to Archbishop Eiríkr, writing (in Old Norse-Icelandic) to the Icelandic Bishops Þorlákr and Brandr, suggesting that the archbishop was dutiful in transmitting papal directives on to Iceland.[77]

---

Stefán Karlsson, "Guðmundar sögur biskups," *Medieval Scandinavia: An Encyclopedia*, ed. by Phillip Pulsiano et al. (New York and London: Garland, 1993), 245–246. The conflict between Bishop Guðmundr and the northern chieftains is the subject of chapter 4 of this book.

73 *Diplomatarium Islandicum*, 1.218–223; 1.258–264; 1.284–289.

74 *Diplomatarium Islandicum*, 1.222: "hverr er sa j gudz banne og papans er misþyrmer kenne manni med heiptugri hendi. og ma hvergi lavsn taka vm drap. eda afhögg kenne manz eda mungs. nema þar sem papinn er."

75 This passage can be tied to specific developments in canon law, particularly the canon *Si quis suadente*. See, Lára Magnúsardóttir, *Bannfæring og kirkjuvald*, 121–122 and Walgenbach, "The Canon *Si quis suadente*."

76 *Diplomatarium Islandicum*, 1.284: "periculosum est uobis et professioni uestre penitus inimicum bellis uos carnalibus immiscere [...] Inde est quod uniuersitate uestre auctoritate apostolica prohibemus."

77 This letter is also dated to 1189 in the *Diplomatarium Islandicum*, 1.285.

This same letter to Þorlákr and Brandr addresses excommunication directly. Clerics who persist in bearing weapons and involving themselves in secular conflicts are first warned and then excommunicated.[78] Excommunication also appears as a sanction for marriage within the prohibited degrees of kinship and for remarriage while the first spouse is still living, both of which the archbishop forbids. The first remedy the archbishop suggests is for the parties to cease their illicit union, but if they persist, they are excommunicated.[79]

The terminology used for excommunication in these sources is generally: *forboð*, *bann*, or *bannsetja* and their lexical variants. The verb *banna* did not mean exclusively "to excommunicate" but could also simply mean "to forbid." A *farbann*, for example was a ban on travel.[80] In some cases, *forboð* seems to mean more simply a warning, rather than a technical sentence of excommunication although it can be difficult to be certain.[81] There is also some uncertainty about whether *forboð* and *bann* were used consistently to differentiate between major and minor excommunication.[82] There is little consensus on this issue, and my own readings suggest that there is no consistent use of *forboð* as "minor excommunication." It sometimes appears to be used as a warning or caution before a sentence of excommunication, which is not how minor excommunication was generally used. This imprecise vocabulary is perhaps not all that different from the situation in Latin sources, however, in which there are some

78 *Diplomatarium Islandicum*, 1.288–289. "Kenne menn bere eigi vopn. og skulv vera fridsamer vit olærda menn. þviat olærder menn sæta miclvm stormælvm ef þeir vinna aa kenne monnum [...] En ef kenne madr verdur hirtur af odrum hvorum yckrum og vill eigi at lata. epter þvi sem ec hefe tied yckur. fyr j rite minv. þa se fyst aa honum forbod en sidan bansettning." The editors suggest that this letter was originally written in Latin and was later translated into the vernacular, *Diplomatarium Islandicum*, 1.285.

79 *Diplomatarium Islandicum*, 1.286: "Nv ef madr firi lættur konv sina. og tekur adra konv. þa skal hann vit skiliazt þa konu er hann tok sidar. En taca hina fyre. eda se j forbodum. En ef madr tecr vitande frændkonv sina. eda sifkonu at fimta manni. eda gudsifiv sina. þa kemur þar forbod firi. ef eigi lætur af." In *Grágás*, knowingly marrying within the prohibited degrees of kinship is sanctioned with lesser outlawry, *Grágás Konungsbók*, Festa-þáttr 144, ed. Finsen, 1b.31, trans. Denis et al., 2.55. For further discussion of marriage within the prohibited degrees and incest in medieval Iceland see, Már Jónsson, *Blóðskömm á Íslandi 1270–1870* (Reykjavík: Háskólaútgáfan, 1993), 27–66.

80 On Old Norse-Icelandic words used for excommunication see, Lára Magnúsardóttir, *Bannfæring og kirkjuvald*, 44–48, 82. See also the definitions s.v. *bann*, *banna*, *bannsetja*, and *forboð* in Ebbe Herzberg's glossary to *Norges gamle love*, 5.88–89, 200.

81 As for instance in the letter of 1189 previously cited, *Diplomatarium Islandicum*, 1.288–289: "þa se fyst aa honum forbod en sidan bansettning."

82 Johan Fritzner, *Ordbog over det gamle norske Sprog* (Kristiania: Norske forlagsforening, 1886), 1.111–112; KLNM 4.79 s.v., "Excommunicatio og interdikt," by Andr. Seierstand; and glossary to *Norges gamle Love*, s.v. *forboð*, 5.200.

attempts to see *anathema* and *excommunicatio* as separate concepts but also many cases in which they are used as synonyms.[83]

The earliest surviving manuscript to discuss excommunication in Icelandic is arguably the Icelandic Homily Book, which survives in a manuscript dated to around 1200 and contains a number of homilies in Old Norse-Icelandic, most of which are based on earlier Latin sermons.[84] In a passage discussing the holding of the Lord's day, the custom of taking communion is discussed, a practice that is said to be less common in Iceland than in other places. It is suggested that all those who are not *fra skiliþr* i.e. "separated" from the church should go to confession and take communion at least once a year. Lára Magnúsardóttir has suggested that this is probably a reference to excommunication and, particularly given that it comes in a discussion of taking communion, her reading is probably correct.[85] The passage further goes on to say that a person who separates *themselves* from communion for small causes rather than because of *gløpsko* "wrongdoing" will not be separated from eternal celebrations on judgement day.[86] The focus of this passage is on encouraging listeners to go to confession and trust in God's mercy and not on excommunication itself, but it does seem to imply that those excommunicated from the Church would have needed to seek other remedies beyond simple confession in order to have such bright prospects on judgement day.

### 12.2 *Early Law Texts: Grágás*

The manuscripts of the lawcode generally referred to as *Grágás*, the earliest surviving law texts from Iceland, display limited interest in excommunication

83 As in the example from England cited above, Treharne, "Formula for Excommunication," 210: "excommunicamus, dampnamus, anathematizamus, atque a liminibus sancte Dei ecclesie sequestramus." See also, Vodola, *Excommunication*, 14–16.

84 David McDougall, review of Andrea de Leeuw van Weenen, editor. *The Icelandic Homily Book, Perg. 15 4° in the Royal Library, Stockholm* and Sigurbjörn Einarsson et al., editors. *Íslensk hómilíubók: Fornar stólræður. alvíssmál* 5 (1995): 107–111; *The Icelandic Homily Book, Perg. 15 4° in the Royal Library, Stockholm*, ed. by Andrea de Leeuw van Weenen (Reykjavík: Stofnun Árna Magnússonar á Íslandi, 1993), 17–18.

85 See also Lára Magnúsardóttir, *Bannfæring og kirkjuvald*, 45. I am less convinced by her suggestion that *rekningar* "outcasts" in this same homily book is also a term for excommunicants as it seems to be as often a reference to groups that were never really considered a part of the Christian community such as Jews.

86 *The Icelandic Homily Book*, ed. de Leeuw van Weenen, 43r (orthography simplified from the diplomatic edition); *Íslensk hómilíubók: Fornar stólræður*, ed. by Sigurbjörn Einarsson, Guðrún Kvaran and Gunnlaugur Ingólfsson (Reykjavík: Hið íslenska bókmenntafélag, 1993), 139. de Leeuw van Weenen identifies a homily by Caesarius of Arles as the source for this particular homily, *The Icelandic Homily Book*, 11.

directly. In these codes most breaches of church law are punished with *fjǫrbaugsgarðr* "lesser outlawry."[87] This limited range of sanctions is similar to the situation in early Norwegian Christian laws, in which outlawry or banishment are the sanctions for some breaches of church law, including sacrificing to heathen gods and exposing infants.[88]

Although there is a distinct possibility that at least some of the terms being used, such as *gerer til utlægðar i kristnum rette* "made outlawed in Christian law" are in fact referring to excommunication.[89] Another possible explanation, in tune with Carolingian and some Anglo-Saxon secular sanctions on excommunicants,[90] is that these sanctions can be interpreted as secular reinforcement of the Christian sanction of excommunication.[91] The degree to which these sources are prescribing excommunication itself, which only bishops had the authority to impose, is open to debate, but given that the offenses that they name are specifically breaches of Christian law and custom it seems likely that they are connected, at least indirectly, with ideas about excommunication. As will be discussed in more detail in chapter 3, from the earliest surviving Icelandic legal sources, including *Grágás*, consecrated burial was an important concern for legislators whether secular or ecclesiastical, and issues over rights to consecrated burial were connected both to people's position within the Christian community (and legal rights to pass on their property) as well as their status in the afterlife.[92]

87 *Grágás* is itself not one text but a several manuscript versions of a similar law code. The two most complete copies are Konungsbók and Staðarhólsbók. It is generally held that these manuscripts were always "private" texts rather than official copies of valid law. KLNM 10.13–15, s.v. "Kyrkostraff," by Magnús Már Lárusson. I discuss the use of "lesser outlawry" at more length in chapters 2 and 3.

88 *Den eldre Gulatingslova*, 22, ed. Eithun et al., 45, trans. Larson, *Earliest Norwegian Laws*, 50 (exposing infants); *Ældre Frostathings Lov (III)*, 15, ed. R. Keyser and P.A. Munch, *Norges gamle love*, 1.152, trans. Larson, *Earliest Norwegian Laws*, 251 (pagan sacrifice); and *Ældre Frostathings Lov (III)*, 24, ed. R. Keyser and P.A. Munch, *Norges gamle love*, 1.155–156, trans. Larson, *Earliest Norwegian Laws*, 255 (general breach of Church law).

89 *Ældre Frostathings Lov (III)*, 24, ed. R. Keyser and P.A. Munch, *Norges gamle love*, 1.155–156, trans. Larson, *Earliest Norwegian Laws*, 255. Lára, *Bannfæring og kirkjuvald*, 46. This is not to say that excommunication and secular punishments were seen as interchangeable.

90 Treharne, "Formula for Excommunication," 190–197; Vodola, *Excommunication*, 12.

91 *Ældre Frostathings Lov (III)*, 21, ed. R. Keyser and P.A. Munch, *Norges gamle love*, 1.154, trans. Larson, *Earliest Norwegian Laws*, 254. This is the only explicit reference I have found to excommunication in the earliest Norwegian codes.

92 On burial in Scandinavian and Icelandic lawcodes see Nilsson, *De sepulturis*, 228–290.

## 13 Sources after 1275

In the late thirteenth-century more sources were produced both in Norway and in Iceland that address the topic of excommunication specifically. These include a large number of lawcodes that survive from this time as well as sagas that consider the administrative tasks and legal positions of bishops in more detail than earlier sagas. This is a time when Iceland was a part of the Archiepiscopate of Niðaróss. Icelandic bishops attended regional church councils in Norway and, largely via Norway, Iceland had access to an increasing stream of canonical texts and evolving ideas about excommunication and the uses of excommunication for both pastoral care and asserting clerical rights.[93]

Later Icelandic and Norwegian lawcodes provide evidence for shifts in the amount of knowledge about excommunication that was present in Iceland.[94] There is also increasing evidence in this period that canon law works were accessible in Iceland, particularly general manuals such as the one by Goffredus of Trano and the *Summa* of Raymond of Penyafort.[95]

93 Evidence about which texts were available to clerics in Niðaróss province is of three types, sources mentioned in inventories, wills, or sagas; preserved translations (usually of short excerpts); or fragments of Latin texts. There seems to be one surviving manuscript of an entire canonical commentary that was known to be in Niðaróss province in the Middle Ages, a copy of Goffredus of Trano's *Summa*. This manuscript was probably owned by the Bishop of Bergen but is now preserved in Uppsala as Cod. Upsal. C 564. For more detailed discussion of these sources see, Sveinbjörn Rafnsson, "Skriftaboð Þorláks biskups," 97; and Sigurður Líndal, "Um þekkingu Íslendinga á rómverskum og kanónískum rétti frá 12. öld til miðrar 16. aldar," *Úlfljótur Afmælisrit 50*, ed. Þórólfur Jónsson (1997), 241–273. A number of Latin fragments connected with canon law survive in the Norwegian national archives. Kristoffer Vadum lists them in, "Canon Law and Politics in Grímr Hólmsteinsson's Jóns Saga Baptista II," trans. by Alan Crozier, *Intellectual Culture in Medieval Scandinavia, c. 1100–1350*, ed. by Stefka Georgieva Eriksen (Turnhout: Brepols, 2016), 178 note 10.

94 Magnús Lyngdal Magnússon, "Kátt er þeim af kristinrétti, kærur vilja margar læra: Af kristinrétti Árna, setning hans og valdsviði," *Gripla* 15 (2004): 43–90; Lára Magnúsardóttir, *Bannfæring og kirkjuvald*, 297–440.

95 Fol. 19v of AM 544 4to (Hauksbók) contains a fragment of a translation into Old Norse-Icelandic of Goffredus's *Summa decratalium*, discussing interactions with excommunicants, i.e. minor excommunication. Finnur Jónsson ed., *Hauksbók: udgiven efter den arnamagnæanske Håndskrifter no. 371, 544 og 675 4to samt forskellige Papiershåndskrifter* (Copenhagen: Kongelige nordiske oldskrift-selskab, 1892), 1.187. This same fragment is also in AM 351 fol. (Skálholtsbók eldri), which in addition has a passage from Raymond of Penyafort's *Summa*, another canonical commentary. Christian Westergård-Nielsen, introduction to, *Skálholtsbók Eldri, Jónsbók etc. AM 351 fol.* (Copenhagen: Rosenkilde and Bagger, 1971), 20. Several vernacular translations of portions of canonical commentaries are persevered in a range of Icelandic legal manuscripts. The most common texts are passages from Goffredus of Trano and Raymond of Penyafort. Both of these canonical commentaries were widely disseminated throughout medieval Europe.

It is also from the period after 1275 that sources that might best be thought of as direct adaptations of canon law texts begin to survive. These include texts that can be traced to both the *Decretum* of Gratian and the *Liber extra* as well as canonical commentaries elaborating and explaining these texts. A useful example from Norway in 1280, for example, restates the canon *Si quis suadente* in Old Norse. Article five of this statute from a local church council states that if someone assaults a cleric or a monk, "then that one falls by his own deed into the papal ban."[96] This is closely followed by a passage (probably translated from the *Liber extra*) that puts those who had the power to stop a violent act against clerics but did not under excommunication.[97]

Kristinréttr Árna, or Árni's Christian laws for Iceland (from 1275) offers a more thorough presentation of excommunication, reflecting (and indirectly confirming) Bishop Árni's education in canon law—Árni himself came to Iceland with a copy of either the *Decretum* or the *Liber extra* when he was ordained as Bishop of Skálaholt in 1269.[98] The lawcode associated with Árni, which was produced in cooperation with the Norwegian Archbishop Jón rauði, draws on the *Liber extra* and arguably also the *Decretum* of Gratian as well as Christian laws produced for Gulathing and Frostathing law provinces in Norway.[99]

Excommunication appears in Kristinréttr Árna as a sanction for a number of offenses, especially violence against clerics. In chapter 14 of this code the punishment for a person who misuses a cleric or monk with a hostile hand is in excommunication by his own deed (i.e. *latae sententiae* or by already passed sentence). Offenses against church property are to be punished by *forboð*, probably minor excommunication, and money payment. Recalcitrant offenders are

96 Statutes of Archbishop Jón, 1280, ed. R. Keyser and P.A. Munch, *Norges gamle love*, 3.234: "þa feller sa af sialfs sins werki i pafans bann." The comparison with *Si quis suadente* is made by Vadum, "Bruk av kanonistisk litteratur," 398. Vadum has, moreover, identified the source of this material as the *Summa de paenitentiae* by Raymond of Penyafort, "Canon Law and Politics," 201–203.

97 Vadum makes this comparison with the *Liber extra* X 5. 39. 47, "Bruk av kanonistisk litteratur," 398.

98 There is some debate about what exactly is meant by the *Decretales cum apparatu* that Bishop Árni is reported to have brought to Iceland. *Árna saga*, ed. Guðrún Ása Grímsdóttir, 8: 13; both Gratian's *Decretum* and the *Liber extra* have been suggested, although the latter seems more likely. See, Agnes S. Arnórsdóttir, *Property and Virginity: The Christianization of Marriage in Medieval Iceland 1200–1600* (Aarhus: Aarhus University Press, 2010), 88.

99 Much more work has been done comparing Árni's Christian Law to Norwegian codes than has been done to compare it with broader canon law sources. See, Magnús Lyngdal Magnússon, "Kátt er þeim af kristinrétti," 54 et passim.

then to be referred to worldly authorities.[100] In this instance it seems likely that *forboð* is being used in the sense of "minor excommunication" given that it occurs in a context in which major excommunication is referred to as *bann*. No Icelandic source specifically explains the distinction between *forboð* and *bann*, however, and as I argued above, the terms are not used consistently.

At other times in Árni's Christian law, those who committed offenses against church law, including incest, are made *friðlauss*, i.e. are sanctioned with outlawry.[101] *Friðlauss* is not the traditional Icelandic term for an outlaw, and this usage almost certainly reflects the Norwegian sources used in the composition of Árni's code.[102] The terminology of outlawry will be discussed in more detail in the next chapter. Árni's code also specifies that *vdaða menn*—a group that includes convicted thieves, *flugu menn* "assassins," unabsolved excommunicants, murderers and those who committed suicide are not to be buried in church yards, although it might be possible for their survivors to seek

100 Árni Þorláksson, "Kristinréttr Árna," chap. 14, ed. Magnús Lyngdal Magnússon, 160–161: "huerr er heiptugri hendi misþyrmir clerc æða clavstra manni þa ær hann ibanni af sialfs sins verki þar til er hann fær lavsn eptir gvðs lagvm með forsia byscops [...] Nu þarf at greina um eigor kirkna eþa þat sem varðueitt er iheilagri kirkio þo at aðrir eigi. hver refsing aliggr ef þvi er rangliga rascat. Enn þessor refsing atuefolld at vera. forboð. oc fegialld [...] oc forðaz hann eigi þvi helldr rettliga refsing af veralldar hofðingiom."

101 Árni Þorláksson, "Kristinréttr Árna," chap. 27, ed. Magnús Lyngdal Magnússon, 177: "Enn þer convr ero er enn liggr meira við ef ver vinnvm aþeim vdaða verc oc leggiomz með þeim. Nu er ein moðir manz. Aunnor systir. þriðia dottir. iiij. stivp moðir. v. sonar kona [...] Enn ef maþr verðr at þvi kvnnr oc sannr. at hann legz með þeim conum. Þa er sa maþr friðlauss oc beþi þau þar til er þau taca skriðt þa er byscop leggr aþau. oc beði hafa þau firir gert hveriom peninngi fear sins. beði ilondom oc lausom aurom."

102 The passage itself derives from Norwegian sources, esp. Nyere Gulatings kristenrett I, *Norges gamle love*, 2.322–323, 2.334–335 and Nyere Borgartings kristenrett II, *Norges gamle love*, 4.175–176 (Note that Bjørg Dale Spørck has convincingly argued that the latter text is better identified as Nyere Gulatings kristenrett II, see afterword to, *Nyere Norske Kristenretter (ca. 1260–1273)*, Thorleif Dahls Kulturbibliotek (Oslo: Aschehoug, 2009), 166–168). *Friðlauss*, meaning "outlawed," is a term well-attested in Norwegian legal sources, including those that were used to aid in the composition of Icelandic legal texts; it does not appear in *Grágás* texts. The usage in Kristinréttr Árna is marked as unusual in the Lexicon of Medieval Nordic Law, s.v. 'friþlös.' A Lexicon of Medieval Nordic Law. http://www.dhi.ac.uk/lmnl/nordicheadword/displayPage. On *friðlauss/friedlosikeit* in a wider context see, Lundgreen, M. "Friedlosigkeit (Acht)," *Reallexikon der Germanischen Altertumskunde*, Band 9 (Berlin: Walter De Gruyter, 1995), 613–621; see also KLNM 4.592–596, s.v. "Fredløshed – Danmark," by Poul Meyer; KLNM 4.596–601, s.v. "Fredløshed – Sverige o. Finland," by Ragnar Hemmer; KLNM 4.601–3, s.v. "Fredløshed – Norge," by Arne Bøe; and KLNM 4.603–608, s.v. "Fredløshed – Island," by Magnús Már Lárusson.

absolution and reburial for them in some cases.[103] *Vdaða menn* here and in other sources is a rather difficult term to understand precisely. It clearly means "criminals" but it seems likely that there are a number of other connotations, perhaps not least with the idea that *udaða menn* would be denied entry into heaven, a suggestion I make based on the way the term is used in lawcodes and in some of its other early attestations, particularly in sagas about St. Olaf.[104]

In addition to the Norwegian and Icelandic lawcodes, there also survive a number of documents that are connected with canon law, and often associated with Bishop Árni Þorláksson and other bishops.[105] These documents have often been edited in the *Diplomatarium Islandicum*, but the editorial principles of these volumes can obscure both the context and the volume of these materials, which is large and under-catalogued. These documents include a penitential and a series of statutes (*skipanir*) on Church law as well as a wide variety of shorter passages addressing specific questions of canon law, such as impediments to ordination; the manuscripts are from as early as 1300 and as late as ca. 1500.[106] To take just one example: in a statute attributed to Árni on the subject of excommunication (in AM 135 4to, ca. 1345–1525, the passage in question is in a part of the manuscript dated to the end of the fifteenth century) a provision reads "that person who has fallen into papal excommunication [i.e. major excommunication] by his own deed [i.e. *latae sententiae*], he shall swear before he be absolved to go to the papal palace with the bishop's advice and will."[107] These legal sources were drawing on and in some cases translating directly from general works of canon law widely distributed through Europe in the Middle Ages. Recent work has shown that some of the sources translated into Old Norse-Icelandic include not only passages from the

---

103 Árni Þorláksson, "Kristinréttr Árna," chap. 18, ed. Magnús Lyngdal Magnússon, 163–65. A marginal notation in AM 49 8vo, the earliest surviving manuscript of Kristinréttr Árna, suggests that the main source of this law is "Gula þ[ings bok]." Árni Þorláksson, "Kristinréttr Árna," chap. 18, ed. Magnús Lyngdal Magnússon, 163.

104 A Lexicon of Medieval Nordic Law, defines an *ódáðaverk* as a "crime." 'ódáðaverk,' A Lexicon of Medieval Nordic Law. http://www.dhi.ac.uk/lmnl/nordicheadword/displayPage/3869(04/21/2020). I also base my suggestions about the connotations of the word on the entries listed under *ódáðamaður* in the Dictionary of Old Norse Prose, https://onp.ku.dk/onp/onp.php?o58092 (last accessed 2 March 2020).

105 Agnes S. Arnórsdóttir, *Property and Virginity*, 88; Lára Magnúsardóttir, *Bannfæring og kirkjuvald*, 303. The texts can be found in *Diplomatarium Islandicum*, 2.23–61.

106 *Diplomatarium Islandicum*, 2.23.

107 *Diplomatarium Islandicum*, 2.35: "sa er fallit hefir j pafa bann af verki sínu sialfs skal sueria adr hann se leystur at fara a pafa gard med biskups radi og uilia." The same text also has a provision about the posthumous excommunication of family members, *Diplomatarium Islandicum*, 2.35.

*Decretum* of Gratian and the *Liber extra* but also from some of the more popular canonical commentaries of the high Middle Ages. Some of these passages have long been identified (not least because the sources are named) but other passages with no named source have been recently identified and it is likely that there are many more both within lawcodes and as short texts within different manuscripts.[108]

### 13.1 *Later Bishops Sagas*

Later saga sources, especially *Árna saga biskups* and *Lárentíus saga* engage directly with newer canon law concepts about excommunication.[109] Both of these sagas were probably written in the fourteenth century. *Árna saga* is likely slightly earlier; it was once often attributed to his nephew Árni Helgason, who died in 1320.[110] *Lárentíus saga* is later still.[111] Laurentius died in 1331 and his saga was probably written by Einarr Hafliðason sometime after 1346 and before Einarr's death in 1393, although the earliest surviving manuscript, AM 180 b fol. is dated to ca. 1500.[112]

### 13.2 Árna Saga

Bishop Árni was known for being learned in canon law and his use of excommunication in his saga attests to his knowledge. *Árna saga biskups* uses Latin

108 Some passages are attributed in the manuscripts to "meistari Goffridus" i.e. Goffredus of Trano and to "Raymondus" i.e. Raymond of Penyafort. For texts attributed to Goffredus see, for example, *Diplomatarium Islandicum*, 2.218 and Raymondus, *Diplomatarium Islandicum*, 2.216. Other passages have also been identified see, Joel Anderson, "Disseminating and Dispensing Canon Law;" Vadum, "Canon Law and Politics," 201–203; and Winroth, "The Canon Law of Emergency Baptism," 203–229.

109 For discussion of bishops' sagas as historical sources, particularly with regard to the sagas written in the fourteenth century, see, Erika Sigurdson, *The Church in Fourteenth-Century Iceland: The Formation of an Elite Clerical Identity* (Leiden and Boston: Brill, 2016), 30–47.

110 Árni himself died in 1298. KLNM 1.251, s.v. "Árna saga biskups," by Magnús Már Lárusson; Sverrir Tómasson, "The Middle Ages. Old Icelandic Prose," *A History of Icelandic Literature*, ed. by Daisy Neijmann (Lincoln: University of Nebraska Press, 2006), 90: "The nineteenth-century scholar Guðbrandur Vigfússon was of the opinion that the saga was written by Bishop Árni Helgason [...] This opinion has since been refuted, but all scholars now agree that the saga was written during the bishopric of Árni Helgason and under the auspices of Skálhot."

111 For the sake of consistency, I spell the bishop's name as Laurentius but the saga *Lárentíus saga*, as is done in the most recent edition by Guðrún Ása Grímsdóttir.

112 Árni Björnsson, "Laurentius saga biskups," *Medieval Scandinavia: An Encyclopedia*, ed. by Phillip Pulsiano et al. (New York and London: Garland, 1993), 381–382; KLNM 10.354–355, s.v. "Laurentius saga," by Magnús Már Lárusson; and Sverrir Tómasson, "Old Icelandic Prose," 91–92.

terminology directly,[113] referring at one point to simony (the selling of ecclesiastical offices) in Latin.[114] The same saga also translates and uses technical concepts like the idea of excommunication *latae sententiae* in the vernacular as in this passage, said to have been spoken by Bishop Árni: "I see after your report that you have brought a papal ban on yourselves by your own action, and you are by no means absolved, and will not be before you swear the oath which the laws of the church offer and restore the priest to his rights."[115]

It is in these later bishops' sagas as well that documents and books of canon law begin to appear with any frequency. Laurentius is reported to have had a notable collection of canon law books that were only narrowly saved when he was imprisoned by enemies in Norway.[116] There is also evidence of the use of written records to enforce church claims to property. For instance, Bishop Árni refers to *máldagar* (inventories of church property) when discussing disputed benefices.[117] These types of claims do not appear routinely in earlier bishops' sagas.

### 13.3 *Bells, Candles, and Ritual*

The rituals or formulas associated with excommunication and preserved in a number of continental sources from the eleventh century on also appear in

113 This same extensive use of Latin terminology has made some literary critics dismissive of the saga, suggesting that it is often little more than a collection of Latinate words and terms. Sverrir Tómasson, "Old Icelandic Prose," 90: "the narrative is mostly dry, a simple report full of Latin loanwords." For a reevaluation of the saga see particularly, Richard Cole, "Árna saga biskups / Kafka / Bureaucracy / Desire," *Collegium medievale* 28 (2015): 37–69; and Haki Antonsson, "*Árna saga biskups* as Literature and History," *Journal of English and Germanic Philology* 116 (2017): 261–285.

114 *Árna saga*, in *Biskupa sögur III, Árna saga biskups, Lárentíus saga biskups*, ed. by Guðrún Ása Grímsdóttir, Íslenzk fornrit 17 (Reykjavík: Hið íslenzka fornritafélag, 1998), 102: 146: "Eigi lítz mér sem bróðir minn hafi *simoniam* framit í þessum skiptum." [*emphasis mine*] Also note that the Latin is used and conjugated as a noun in the accusative following Latin rules for declension.

115 *Árna saga*, 49: 70: "Sé ek eptir ykkrum flutningi at þið hafit fellt páfabann á ykkr af sjálfu verkinu, ok dugir með engu móti at þið séuð eigi leystir, ok eigi þið áðr sverja fyrir lausnina þann eið sem lög kirkjunnar bjóða en bæta prestinum rétt sinn." On the translation of *latae sententiae* into Old Norse-Icelandic see, Lára Magnúsardóttir, *Bannfæring og kirkjuvald*, 82 and Walgenbach, "The Canon *Si quis suadente*," 158–179.

116 *Lárentíus saga*, in *Biskupa sögur III, Árna saga biskups, Lárentíus saga biskups*, ed. by Guðrún Ása Grímsdóttir, Íslenzk fornrit 17 (Reykjavík: Hið íslenzka fornritafélag, 1998), 27: 303.

117 *Árna saga*, ed. Guðrún Ása Grímsdóttir, 84: 126. "Hann sagði ok at staðr í Odda ok Vatnsfjarðarkirkja ok þær kirkjur sem fornir máldagar segja byskup eiga at hafa vald yfir má engi þýða at takaz eigi fyrir konungs boðskap."

Icelandic sources starting in the late-thirteenth century.[118] In *Árna saga* it is said that Bishop Árni excommunicated a certain Klemet who had taken over a church and its property at Gnúpur: "and so [Árni] excommunicated that man [Klemet] on the same day as the previously mentioned Eiríkr with *bells ringing and extinguished candles*. This same Klemet had also driven away the priest whom the Lord Bishop had delegated to this church and held his revenues."[119] A similar incident occurs in *Lárentíus saga*, when Bishop Laurentius threatens to excommunicate a couple "with extinguished candles and bells ringing" for refusing to separate despite being too closely related.[120] This is not perfect evidence for the ritual itself ever having been enacted in Iceland, but it further underlines that continental sources and ideas were available and also being incorporated into literary texts, as here without explanation, assuming readers would have understood the reference.

### 13.4 *Lárentíus Saga*

*Lárentíus saga* is almost as determined as *Árna saga* in its uses of canon law and self-conscious knowledge of Latinate, clerical education and customs. The saga repeatedly highlights Bishop Laurentius's learning and mastery of both Latin and canon law. Indeed, it might be argued that knowledge of canon law is Laurentius's most defining feature (although an education in canon law did not stop him from fathering a son.)[121] The saga relates that Laurentius frequently spoke in Latin, and repeatedly refers to how learned he was in canon law and how much time he spent mastering books of canon law.[122]

---

118 Indeed, these sources are one of the few places where evidence for these rituals appear outside of the excommunication formulas. Of course, this instance may speak to the use of written sources in the composition of these later bishops' sagas rather than to actual use of the ritual. Cf. Lára Magnúsardóttir, *Bannfæring og kirkjuvald*, 222.

119 *Árna saga*, ed. Guðrún Ása Grímsdóttir, 114: 161. "ok því bannsetti [Árni] þenna mann [Klemet] á sama degi sem fyrrnefndan Eirík *með hringdum klukkum ok steyptum kertum*. Þessi sami Klemet hafði ok rekit í burt prest þann sem herra byskup skipaði til þessarar sömu kirkju ok helt kaupi hans." (emphasis mine).

120 *Lárentíus saga*, ed. Guðrún Ása Grímsdóttir, 44: 385. "meðr styptum kertum ok hringdum klokkum."

121 *Lárentíus saga*, ed. Guðrún Ása Grímsdóttir, 25: 300.

122 *Lárentíus saga*, ed. Guðrún Ása Grímsdóttir, 9: 235. "Kallaði herra byskup Laurentium síðan í sitt studium ok setti fram fyrir hann lektara ok þar á kirkjulögbækr; bað hann þar skemmta sér viðr."

*Lárentíus saga*, ed. Guðrún Ása Grímsdóttir, 10: 236. "Þá kallaði herra Pétr Laurentium til sín, ok bað hann dikta ok skrifa þetta bréf á latínu sem hann kunni bezt."

*Lárentíus saga*, ed. Guðrún Ása Grímsdóttir, 12: 241. "Þat er nú at segja at síra Laurentius er kominn til Jörundar erkibyskups ok gekk dagliga til studium at læra kirkjunnar lög."

In *Lárentíus saga* excommunication features frequently, often as a part of conflicts either between churchmen (in the conflict between Archbishop Jörundr and the canons of Niðaróss cathedral),[123] or between churchmen and laymen who oppose the claims that they are making.[124] Excommunication is often given as an oral sentence, as when Laurentius is asked to read the sentence of excommunication over the canons of Niðaróss cathedral.[125] Although sentences could be sent by letter and subsequently read aloud as happened in north Iceland when Laurentius was still serving as a priest.[126] In *Lárentíus saga*, for all of its emphasis on Laurentius as an expert in canon law, excommunication in this saga is still presented in much the same way it is in earlier sources. One feature that is more prominent in *Lárentíus saga* is the frequency that excommunication is used between clerics not only in the conflict with the canons of Niðaróss but also as a disciplinary measure in Iceland, for instance when Bishop Auðunn of Hólar places one of his subordinates under major excommunication, forbidding him all contact with Christian people.[127]

This evidence might not be that revolutionary in itself but in this context, it is worth emphasizing that canon law materials were available and being engaged with and used in Icelandic disputes. Iceland by the late twelfth century and certainly the thirteenth was a firmly Christian country with established churches and institutions and access to developments in wider Christian society. It was also familiar with and invested in "religious practices" that gave

123 The conflict began to escalate soon after Laurentius came to Norway, *Lárentíus saga*, ed. Guðrún Ása Grímsdóttir, 16: 245.

It culminated in Laurentius being imprisoned in Norway by the same canons whom he had once excommunicated. *Lárentíus saga*, ed. Guðrún Ása Grímsdóttir, 24–25: 292–300.

124 *Lárentíus saga*, ed. Guðrún Ása Grímsdóttir, 7: 233; 44: 385.

125 *Lárentíus saga*, ed. Guðrún Ása Grímsdóttir, 14: 248. "Um morgininn eftir svá sem í hámessu sem kórsbræðr vóru í kór ok þá varði minnst, gekk síra Laurentius upp á kór eftir boði erkibyskups ok las bréf rumor pestiferus. Var í bréfinu því sá skilningr haldandi at fyrir margar sakir ok stórar er hann á nefndi, boðaði hann bannsetta kórsbræðr, Eilíf, Auðun rauð [who later became a bishop in Iceland], Sigvat landa: skyldi ok niðr falla messuembætti ef þeir gengi eigi frá."

126 *Lárentíus saga*, ed. Guðrún Ása Grímsdóttir, 7: 233. The word used is "bannsetningarbréf."

127 Bishop Auðun excommunicates a cleric for refusing to obey him in many matters, using a severe sentence. The cleric, however, ignores this and goes to Norway. *Lárentíus saga*, ed. Guðrún Ása Grímsdóttir, 33: 341. "kom svá at síðustu at byskup setti Snjólf í it hæsta forboð, afsetjandi hann samneyti kristinna manna. Gaf Snjólfr ekki gaum at því ok fór til Nóregs." [In the end the bishop put Snjólfr under the highest ban, forbidding him to be among Christian men. Snjólfr paid no attention to this and went to Norway.] The term *it hæsta forboð* might be understood as major excommunication although this combination of words is rare.

"religious coherence through the overriding idea of eternal life."[128] People cared about their status in the Christian community, whether they died as part of the Christian community, and where they were buried.

## 14 Conclusions

Excommunication in sources before the legal reforms of the twelfth century is often a slippery concept difficult to put on firm footings. Excommunication was a diverse, heterogeneous collection of ideas, rituals, and rules, and it is not safe to assume that changing canonical definitions transferred easily or quickly in all directions. Nevertheless, they did travel and were read about and understood by educated people as far as Iceland in the late thirteenth and early fourteenth centuries.

The engagement with texts like the *Decretum* and the *Liber extra* came later in these northern countries than in more centrally located places, but even before these books were available in their entirety in Iceland, Icelanders were already familiar with the idea of excommunication, which appears in the earliest surviving Christian sources, often connected with the idea of damnation for breaking rules and taboos of the Church. These ideas associating excommunication with damnation also continued to be present in a wider European context, as demonstrated by the numerous and widely spread evidence for excommunication formulas and statements in vernacular lawcodes.

Excommunication as depicted in Icelandic sources produced before the late-thirteenth century and often after this time is closer to the excommunication of Burchard of Worms than that of Innocent IV, with a focus on bishops as agents of excommunication and strong connections between excommunication as a sentence for actions and excommunication as ritual exclusion. Excommunication in this period was often an oral sentence imposed by a bishop on an individual. Sometimes for a particular recalcitrant sinner, such as a priest continuing to live openly with a concubine, but at least as often a sanction imposed on a secular leader for exercising jurisdiction over matters that the Church was increasingly claiming control over, such as the election of bishops.

One of the stronger associations in early sources is between excommunication and damnation. One way that this association was reinforced was through

128 Arnved Nedkvitne, *Lay Belief in Norse Society, 1000–1350* (Copenhagen: Museum Tusculanum Press, 2009), 223.

the denial of consecrated burial. This seems to have been a widely held medieval idea, although not one often advocated or supported by academic canon lawyers or theologians of the late Middle Ages.

The Icelandic evidence preserved about the thirteenth century (even if it survives in fourteenth-century manuscripts) tends to adhere to what Genevieve Edwards suggests was an older, but also a persistent, view of excommunication, rooted in existing ideas and traditions rather than in canon law reforms and elaborations of the twelfth and later centuries. This was beginning to change with the spread of a more educated and professionalized clergy in Iceland and Norway from the late thirteenth century. Excommunication for the first time in lawcodes and in sagas such as *Lárentíus saga* begins to resemble more closely the legal sources preserved in places such as the *Decretum* of Gratian, although during the period of this study it is as likely to be a sentenced invoked in person by a bishop, which still remained a valid form of excommunication. Sometimes we can see a bishop not excommunicating a person directly but rather pointing out and speaking aloud that a person had already excommunicated themselves by performing a forbidden action.[129]

In Old Norse-Icelandic sources from the thirteenth and fourteenth centuries, the vocabulary of excommunication is neither standardized nor consistent. Legal sources often use secular terms to sanction breaches of church law. The appearance of excommunication *latae sententiae* is the most prominent innovation that appears in later Icelandic sources, and there is some evidence for excommunication used for internal Church discipline, especially in the later bishops' sagas.

The next chapter focuses on Icelandic and other sources about a sanction closely related to excommunication in medieval Icelandic sources, outlawry. It concentrates on the legal sources that document outlawry, when these sources were produced, and how the sentence and its consequences were articulated. The documentation of outlawry is more limited than that of excommunication, particularly before the thirteenth century, hence its history is more difficult to trace.

129 As Bishop Árni does in the passage cited above page 34. A document from the mid-fourteenth century attests that *visatores* sent to Iceland from the Norwegian archbishop recognized that people taking liberties with the rights of Grenjaðarstaðir church were already excommunicated. Þjóðskjalasafn Íslands, K 28 (Grenjaðarstaðir), edited in, *Islandske originaldiplomer indtil 1450*, ed. by Stefán Karlsson (Copenhagen: Munksgaard, 1963), 33 nr. 29.

CHAPTER 2

# Outlawry

This chapter examines the evidence documenting outlawry in medieval Iceland with a focus on the legal sources. Although it is likely that outlawry existed in Icelandic society from the time of the settlement or shortly thereafter, there is limited surviving evidence to reconstruct outlawry as an ancient, pre-Christian sanction. In this chapter I discuss the diverse and sometimes confusing legal evidence that documents outlawry, both full outlawry and the *fjǫrbaugsgarðr* "lesser outlawry" that features prominently in the manuscripts of *Grágás*. I also discuss how this relates to outlawry in the sagas of Icelanders (*Íslendingasögur*) and the contemporary sagas (*samtíðasögur*) and in later legal texts. I argue that the outlawry depicted in these sources, especially the sanction of "lesser outlawry" in *Grágás,* is influenced by the conventions of learned, Christian law.

Outlawry is often connected to Iceland's decentralized, stateless political organization, but outlawry was also a sanction in medieval polities with kings and growing royal power. In the third section of this chapter, I discuss the relationship between outlawry and state power in medieval Norway and Iceland. This is followed by a short discussion of outlawry in Icelandic sources after the submission to Norway in the 1260s.

This chapter follows a roughly chronological outline. I begin with the earliest attestations of outlawry in "Germanic" sources with a brief evaluation of early Merovingian and early English sources. These texts are diverse but all have in common that they were produced during a time when those writing them were themselves Christians. They also present a variety of interpretive problems, not least concerning the vocabulary used to denote an outlaw or outlawry. With this background in mind, I then evaluate the definitions of outlawry in the earliest Icelandic legal sources and then in narrative sources. I then discuss the relationship between outlawry and state power. The final sections address how outlawry changed in later legal and narrative sources.

## 1 Origins of Outlawry?

The origins of outlawry are impossible to trace with any certainty, not least because a wide range of sanctions and practices in different contexts might reasonably be described by the modern English word. Even given the difficulty

 | DOI:10.1163/9789004461468_004

of arriving at a satisfactory definition of outlawry in general, outlawry as a sanction based on social exclusion and loss of legal protections is not a uniquely Icelandic innovation but rather existed in European legal systems in some form from at least the Roman period.[1] It is also attested in at least some form in a variety of early Germanic cultures although here the documentation is often limited. Outlawry is also often assumed to be a very old, pre-Christian sanction in Germanic cultures.[2]

One of the earliest surviving sources cited on the topic of outlawry in a Germanic context is the Salic law, one of the so-called Barbarian codes written in Latin after various Germanic tribes established themselves in formerly Roman territories in the fifth and sixth centuries.[3] This code (or perhaps more accurately group of codes as there are divergent manuscripts from the Carolingian period) presents a type of banishment or sanction in which a person is made *wargus*, which is often translated as "outlaw."[4] In a passage that is marked as "an old law" the penalty for desecrating a grave is to be made a *wargus*, until such time as the family is willing to receive compensation for the act, when the offender can be accepted back into society.[5] During

1 This book is limited in examining medieval, western European concepts of outlawry. On outlawry in Roman criminal law see, for example, W.D. Aston, "Problems of Roman Criminal Law," *Journal of the Society of Comparative Legislation* 13.2 (1913): 213–231. Gösta Åqvist also emphasizes the difficulty of assessing precisely what early ideas of outlawry entailed, including a discussion of different terms and possible etymologies, *Frieden und Eidschwur: Studien zum mittelalterlichen germanischen Recht*. Skrifter utgivna av Institutet för rättskistorisk forskning grundat av Gustav och Carin Olin. Serien 1. Rättshistoriskt Bibliotek 14 (Stockholm: A.-B. Nordiska Bokhandeln, 1968), 229–318.

2 The idea is especially prominent in work that connects outlaws to animals such as wolves. See, for example, Mary Gerstein, "Germanic Warg: The Outlaw as Werewolf," *Myth in Indo-European Antiquity*, ed. by G.J. Larson (Berkeley: University of California Press, 1974), 131–156. Gerard Breen, " 'The Wolf is at the door' Outlaws, Assassins, and Avengers Who Cry 'Wolf!' " *Arkiv för nordisk filologi* 114 (1999): 31–43. Breen focuses mostly on characters who sometimes use animal names, such as bear or wolf (both *úlfr* and *vargr*) as a disguise, rather than the legal origins and meaning of the term; Anne Irene Riisøy, "Outlawry: From Western Norway to England," *New Approaches to Early Law in Scandinavia*, ed. by Stefan Brink and Lisa Collinson (Turnhout, Belgium, 2014), 107–109; and Joonas Ahola, "Outlawry in the Icelandic Family Sagas," 87, 309–310; Harlan-Haughey, *The Ecology of the English Outlaw*, 1–18. I am not arguing that there were never connections made between wolves and outlaws, but rather arguing against assuming that the connection is itself ancient, pre-Christian, or a primary way of understanding outlaws in all "Germanic" contexts.

3 For further discussion of the Babarian lawcodes see, Katherine Fischer Drew, introduction to, *Laws of the Salian Franks*, 3–55.

4 Drew, *Laws of the Salian Franks*, 118.

5 *Pactis Legis Salicae*, 55.4, Monumenta Germaniae Historica, Legum Sectio 1, Leges Nationum Germanicarum, Vol. 4, Part 1, ed. by Karl August Eckhardt (Hanover: Hahn,

the time that such a person is a *wargus*, he cannot be given food or help from others, including his own wife.[6] This is the only occurrence of the term *wargus* in the Salic laws.[7] Sanctions that resemble outlawry are very much the exception in this code, however: fines are stipulated for the vast majority of offenses.

This text is usually dated to the time of Clovis at the end of the fifth or beginning of the sixth century,[8] but the manuscripts are younger, mostly dating from the Carolingian period several hundred years later.[9] The Salic laws, while they are much older than surviving Icelandic sources, even if we date them based on the surviving eighth-century manuscripts, are also firmly Christian codes. A frequent prologue to many manuscripts of the 100-title version of the Salic laws begins: "In the name of the holy trinity [here] begins the prologue of the book of Salic law,"[10] the Franks are identified as a people who covered the

---

1962), 206–207, trans. Drew, *Laws of the Salian Franks*, 118. "[Et antiqua lege:] Si quis corpus iam sepultum effodierit et expoliauerit et ei fuerit adprobatum, mallobergo muther hoc est, uuargus sit usque in diem illa(m), quam ille cum parentibus ipsius defuncti conueniat, ut et ipsi pro eo rogar debeant, ut ei inter homines liceat accedere. Et qui ei, antequam cum parentibus conponat, aut panem dederit aut hospitalem dederit, seu parentes seu uxor sua proxima, DC denarios qui faciunt solidos xv culpabilis iudicetur. Tamen auctor sceleris, qui hoc admisisse probatur aut effodisse, mallobergo tornechale sunt, VIIIM denarios qui faciunt solidos CC culpabilis iudicetur." [*mallobergo muther* and *mallobergo tornechale* are part of the so-called Malberg glosses transmitted with some manuscripts of the Salic laws, see, Drew, *Laws of the Salian Franks*, 52–56.]

A different manuscript tradition of the Salic laws, preserves a similar passage without the use of the term *wargus*. *Lex Salica*, 18, Monumenta Germaniae Historica, Legum Sectio I, Leges Nationum Germanicarum, Vol. 4, Part 2, ed. Karl August Eckhardt (Hanover, 1969), 59. "Si quis corpus sepultum exfodierit et expoliauerit, soledos cc culpabilis iudicetur. Et sic parentes defuncti iudicem rogare debeant, ut inter homines non habitetur auctor sceleris; et qui ei, antequam cum parentibus sit satisfactum, hospitium dederit, soledos xv culpabilis iudicetur."

6 *Pactis Legis Salicae*, 55.4, ed. Eckhardt, 206–207, trans. Drew, *Laws of the Salian Franks*, 118.

7 In other instances that Drew discusses as outlawry, different terms are used in the text including being *extra sermonem suum*, that is outside of the king's protection (literally "speech"), *aspellis*, and *forbatuos*. For her discussion of outlawry, see introduction, *Laws of the Salian Franks*, 38. Note that *wargus* is copied as *virgo* in one of the manuscripts Eckhardt uses in his edition, *Pactis Legis Salicae*, 55.4 (A2 variant), ed. Eckhardt, 206.

8 Drew, *Laws of the Salian Franks*, 8.

9 The manuscript tradition and transmission are complex to the point that one scholar even suggested that the Salic laws are themselves a Carolingian forgery. See, Drew, *Laws of the Salian Franks*, 231–232.

10 *Lex Salica*, Prologus, ed. Eckhardt, 3: "In nomine sanctae trinitatis incipit prologus libri legis salicae."

bodies of the martyrs in jewels, and church sanctuary is mentioned.[11] In other words, *wargus* as a sanction (or status) is likely to have been influenced by Christianity and its norms.[12]

The term *wargus*, is an old Germanic word and it does appear occasionally in Old Norse-Icelandic, perhaps especially in poetry.[13] It is not, however, the standard or common term for an outlaw in Icelandic legal or narrative sources.[14] Others have argued convincingly that the etymology of *wargus* is not rooted in the word "wolf," but rather "criminal" although it later acquired the meaning and at least some of the associations of "wolf."[15]

Although Merovingian sources likely have no direct bearing on Icelandic evidence, it is useful to discuss some of the background implicit in discussions of outlawry and ask the question: are these sixth (or eighth if we rely on the dates of the manuscripts) sources likely to be direct precursors to Icelandic outlawry as seen in thirteenth and fourteenth century sources? My answer is: no. *Wargus*, though it undoubtedly is a Germanic word, in this code is an exception, not a norm. It is not necessarily permanent but could be forgiven by the family harmed, the sanction described might well be influenced by Christianity, and it existed in the context of assertive kings. There is not sufficient reason to assume Germanic continuity from the sixth century into the thirteenth.

Outlawry is better attested in Old English legal sources which, while younger than the Salic Laws, survive from much earlier than surviving Old Norse legal sources. Bryan Carella has suggested that a legal concept of outlawry occurs in Old English sources (first in Latin) from as early as the late eighth century (in at least one tenth-century manuscript Wolfenbüttel, Herzog-August Bibliothek,

11 On covering the martyrs with jewels: *Lex Salica*, Prologus, ed. Eckhardt, 8, trans. Drew, *Laws of the Salian Franks*, 171. On fleeing to a church: *Pactis legis Salicae*, Capitulare 6.2.2, ed. Eckhardt, 268, trans. Drew, *Laws of the Salian Franks*, 157.

12 Donald Bullough further suggests that early Germanic lawcodes might well be influenced by Roman law traditions on the topic of grave desecration, "Burial, Community and Belief," 187.

13 Riisøy, "Outlawry: From Western Norway," 105–111.

14 The two times that *vargr* appears in the Konungsbók manuscript of *Grágás*, it occurs as part of compounds—*vargdropi* (offspring of an outlaw who had no right to inherit) and *morð vargr* ("murderer"). *Grágás Konungsbók*, Arfa-þáttr 118, ed. Finsen, 1a.224, trans. Denis et al., 2.7, and *Grágás Konungsbók*, Vígslóði 102, ed. Finsen, 1a.178, trans. Denis et al., 1a.164.

15 Michael Jacoby, *Wargus, vargr 'Verbrecher' 'Wolf' eine sprach- und rechtsgeschichtliche Untersuchung* (Uppsala: Almqvist & Wiksell, 1974), esp. 11–45. Reviewed by John Lindow, *Speculum* 52 (1977): 382–385. *Vargr* is from a root **warg-* which had a meaning of something like "criminal."

Codex Guelf. 454 Helmstedt).[16] Outlawry appears more often in later codes associated with different Anglo-Saxon kings including the Danish Cnut, and continued to be a part of English law well after the Norman conquest.[17] In these early English sources, outlawry is often closely connected with excommunication, a topic that I will address further in chapter 3.

The case of Anglo-Saxon outlawry and its potential relationship to Icelandic sources is complex and any conclusions can only be conjectural. Anglo-Saxon sources derive from a time closer to the composition of surviving Icelandic lawcodes and there are likely to have been connections, not least through the dissemination of religious writings, between Iceland and England at this time.[18] Whether there were meaningful connections between Icelandic and English outlawry in their development is impossible to say given the surviving evidence although influence, at least indirectly via Norway, seems plausible.[19]

More than drawing out any firm conclusion about antecedents to Icelandic outlawry, what I wish to emphasize is the degree of uncertainty, the problems of the sources and the connections with Christian ideas that follow along with the earliest documented sanctions of something that might reasonably be called "outlawry" in Germanic sources. Without denying any possible pre-Christian or ancient origins for outlawry, I wish to underline that much is unknown and, as the sources stand, unknowable about the origins or pre-Christian forms of

16 Bryan Carella, "The Earliest Expression for Outlawry in Anglo-Saxon Law," *Traditio* 70 (2015): 111–143.

17 Outlawry was very much a part of the laws of Henry I and Henry II, for example. Naomi D. Hurnard, *The King's Pardon for Homicide before A.D. 1307* (Oxford: Clarendon Press, 1969), 5–30. A full evaluation of outlawry in English sources will not be attempted here. For discussions of outlawry in Old English see, Riisøy, "Outlawry: From Western Norway to England," 101–129; and Carella, "The Earliest Expression for Outlawry," 111–143. See also Elisabeth van Houts, "The Vocabulary of Exile and Outlawry in the North Sea Area around the Frist Millennium," *Exile in the Middle Ages: Selected Proceedings from the International Medieval Congress*, ed. by L. Napran and E. van Houts, International Medieval Research, 13 (Turnhout: Brepols, 2004), 13–28.

18 In this case possibly reaching Iceland via Norway, where English influence is well-documented. See, Absalon Taranger, *Den Angelsaksiske kirkes indflydelse paa den norske*. Den Norske Historiske Forening (Kristiania: Norsk Historisk Forening, 1890) and Lesley Abrams, "The Anglo-Saxons and the Christianization of Scandinavia," *Anglo-Saxon England* 24 (1995): 213–249. For the influence of Old English and other languages on the vocabulary of Christianity in Old Norse-Icelandic see, Matteo Tarsi, "On the origin of the oldest borrowed Christian terminology in Icelandic," *Orð og tunga* 18 (2016): 85–101.

19 Influence flowed in both directions, and it has been convincingly argued that the Old English word *utlah* is a loanword taken from Old Norse, probably brought by Scandinavian invaders and settlers during the Viking Age. Riisøy, "Outlawry: From Western Norway to England," 101–129; Harlan-Haughey, *Ecology of the English Outlaw*, 24 note 3.

the sanction. To point to a specific example in Old English writings, one of the frequent examples of a prototypical outcast in Old English writings is the Biblical figure of Cain.[20]

## 2 Outlawry in Icelandic Sources before 1275

Our main sources that document outlawry as a legal form in Iceland are *Grágás* and the lawcodes introduced after the submission to Norway, *Járnsíða* and *Jónsbók* (*Járnsíða* was introduced in 1271–1273 and *Jónsbók* in 1281).[21] Other law codes from Scandinavia are of similar date. The earliest complete surviving Norwegian law codes are a copy of the Gulathing law (1250–1300) and the Frostathing law (in paper copies of a manuscript of ca. 1260).[22] In this section I will be focusing on the group of Icelandic laws collectively referred to as *Grágás*.

*Grágás* survives in two main codices, Konungsbók (also known as the Codex Regius, GKS 1157 fol.) and Staðarhólsbók (AM 334 fol.).[23] In both of these codices the text is divided into sections on a variety of topics including: Christian laws, assembly procedures, inheritance, marriage, and land claims.[24] Outlawry, both full and lesser, appears in most of these different sections and in both manuscripts.

The Konungsbók manuscript declares that: "There are three kinds of legal outlawry in our country: when a man is made a full outlaw, who may not be given passage, or a lesser outlaw, or, third, when lesser outlawry has the added condition that the man has no right to return to this country."[25] What each of

20 See, for instance, Heide Estes, "Raising Cain in Genesis and Beowulf: Challenges to Generic Boundaries in Anglo-Saxon Biblical Literature," *The Heroic Age* 13 (2010). http://www.heroicage.org/issues/13/estes.php.

21 On the name *Járnsíða* and other issues having to do with the text see, Patricia Pires Boulhosa, "Narrative, Evidence and the Reception of Járnsíða," *Sturla Þórðarson: Skald, Chieftain and Lawman,* ed. by Jón Viðar Sigurðsson and Sverrir Jakobsson (Leiden and Boston: Brill, 2017), 223–232.

22 KLNM, 5.559–565, s.v. "Gulatingsloven (Gtl.)" by Trygve Knudsen; KLNM 4.656–661, s.v., "Frostatingsloven," by Trygve Knudsen.

23 The only medieval copy of *Járnsíða* is also in AM 334 fol.

24 it is difficult to say precisely how many chapters and subsections there are in these (and other) legal manuscripts, which rely a lot on visual markers such as different sizes of initials and rubrics rather than on numbered chapters as in modern editions. For a convenient table that gives an approximate view of the organization of the two main manuscripts see: Gunnar Karlsson, et al. (eds.), *Grágás: Lagasafn íslenska þjóðveldisins* (Reykjavík: Mál og menning, 1992), xix.

25 *Grágás Kongunsbók*, Þingskapa-þáttr 60, ed. Finsen, 1a.109, trans. Denis et al., 1.110.

these different types means in the context of *Grágás* is the subject of the next section of this chapter, which examines how the manuscripts of *Grágás* define and discuss different types of outlawry.

## 2.1 *Full Outlawry in Grágás*

Full outlawry appears most frequently in the section on assembly procedures (the *Þingskapa-þáttr*), on the treatment of homicide (*Vígslóði*), and quite frequently in the betrothals section (*Festa-þáttr*), which concerns marriage but also intercourse and childbearing outside of marriage. In these sections (and others) full outlawry, *skóggangr, sekt,* and their lexical variants, are named as the sanction for a variety of actions including killing, theft, and sexual offenses.[26]

An oft-cited passage about full outlawry occurs in the betrothals section of Staðarhólsbók (it is not in Konungsbók). It is a formula associated with a case of what the translators render as "intercourse" with an unmarried woman. The provision reads: "If a man wants to publish an intercourse case on an assembly slope or at Lögberg, then he shall speak in this way: 'I name witnesses to witness that I publish a case against N.N. on the grounds that he has lain with N.N. and gone so far that he could expect that they might get a child if that was destined for them. For this cause I claim that he must be under penalty as a full outlaw, not to be sustained, not to be given passage, not to be given any saving advice. I claim that all his property is under penalty, half to me and half to all the men of the Quarter to whom property under penalty is due. I claim personal compensation from his property, forty-eight ounce-units, for the principal in the case [...]' "[27] This passage, including the phrasing "not to be sustained, not to be given passage, not to be given any saving advice" is sometimes presented as a more general formula for announcing and prosecuting outlawry cases or indeed as itself a definition, but this is actually one of the few times that such a formula is presented, and it occurs in only one of the *Grágás* manuscripts.

The use of full outlawry (*skógarmaðr, skóggangr, sekr*) without comment is much more frequent in *Grágás*. Without further definition, full outlawry is

26 Discussed below in more detail. For further discussion of the vocabulary of outlawry and some of the ways that it may have shifted in response to changing social realities see, Agneta Breisch, *Frid och fredlöshet: sociala band och utanförskap på Island under äldre medeltid*. Studia Historica Upsaliensia 174 (Uppsala: Uppsala universitet, 1994), esp. 130–148.

27 *Grágás Staðarhólsbók*, Festa-þáttr 166, ed. Finsen, 2.198–199, trans. Denis et al., 2.274–275.

named as the sanction for "malicious damage," that remains uncompensated,[28] "unlawful milk usage,"[29] and a variety of non-lethal violent acts including shaking someone, knocking a person to the ground, or throttling a person.[30] Sometimes the sanction is rendered impersonally. Such a construction occurs in the following provision about false witness in the procedures section: "if a man speaks falsely or bears lying-witness at the Alþingi that becomes outlawry."[31] I have here given a rather literal translation to highlight the style of *Grágás* and the difficulties of interpreting such provisions, particularly when as here they are stated in an impersonal construction. The final phrase is "varþar þat scógang" which equates the action or deed of bearing false witness with outlawry, rather than the person committing it. The provision also gives no indication of how the sanction should or could have been enforced in this circumstance. It seems as much a moral judgement about lying as effective legislation. *Grágás* does not present a consistent picture of outlawry as an impersonal sanction designed to protect a community at large or define that community's values, nor of outlawry as a personal sanction that could be brought by a single wronged person against another individual. Nor does *Grágás* offer a single definition, instead using a collection of different words (mostly *sekr*, *skógarmaðr* and their variants) to sanction a diverse collection of offenses.

## 2.2 *Consequences of Full Outlawry*

Much as *Grágás* does not present a single, general definition of full outlawry, the consequences associated with outlawry vary within it, depending on the offense and any number of other factors such as when and where a particular law or formulation might originate from or whether someone was made an outlaw at the Alþingi or in another type of settlement. The most severe form of full outlawry is the formulation cited above, in which the outlawed

28 *Grágás Konungsbók*, Þingskapa-þáttr 51., ed. Finsen, 1a.88, trans. Denis et al., 1.92. "Nv verðr hann secr vm spell virki oc gialdaz eigi scaða bötr at ferans domi. þa verðr hann oc scogar maðr o øll."

29 *Grágás Konungsbók*, Um fiárleigur 224, ed. Finsen, 1b.153–154, trans. Denis et al., 2.167. Unconcealed taking and theft both led to outlawry. *Grágás Konungsbók*, Rannsókna-þáttr 227, ed. Finsen, 1.162, trans. Denis et al., 2.177.

30 Or thrusting something out of another's hand. These examples are all listed at the beginning of the section on homicide. *Grágás Konungsbók*, Vígslóði 86, ed. Finsen, 1a.144–145, trans. Denis et al., 1.139.

31 *Grágás Konungsbók*, Þingskapa-þáttr 25, ed. Finsen, 1a.47. "Ef maþr telr rangt. eþa ber liuguitni a alþingi. oc varþar þat scógang." Cf. with the published English translation, trans. Denis et al., 1.60. "If a man enumerates wrong or bears false witness at the General Assembly, the penalty is outlawry."

person cannot be given passage, cannot be helped, and has all of their property confiscated. Such an outlaw could be killed with impunity,[32] although in the Staðarhólsbók version, this has in at least one place the caveat that the killing must be announced and cannot have occurred in a forbidden place.[33]

The property of full outlaws was confiscated. A confiscation court (*Féransdómr*), was supposed to follow an outlawry sentence (whether full or lesser outlawry).[34] This court was to take place at the home farm of the person being outlawed. The outlaw's property was confiscated to pay debts (whether restitution for stolen goods or compensation) and also surely to ensure the defenselessness of the person sentenced.[35] In Konungsbók, the failure to hold such a court carried a penalty of lesser outlawry.[36] Less often cited are the scattered but more numerous provisions that suggest some of the ways that full outlawry could be mitigated in practice.

## 2.3 *Escaping or Annulling Outlawry*

Full outlaws could be forbidden help (as in the oft-cited provision above), but in other circumstances it was possible for them to be allowed passage out of Iceland. For instance, in the assembly procedures section some full outlaws (*scógar menn*) are allowed passage out of the country and one safe house.[37] In a similar passage a little later on, a full outlaw who is permitted passage out of Iceland, a *scogar manne ferianda*, is allowed three safe homes just like a lesser outlaw.[38] This passage further suggests that the law council the *lǫgrétta*

32 *Grágás Konungsbók*, Þingskapa-þáttr 55, ed. Finsen, 1a.96, trans. Denis et al., 1.98. "Ef þeir menn er her ero görvir scogar menn o ølir oc oferiande. þa ero þeir iafnt dræpir oc o hælgir erlendis sem her fyrir orvm löndom."

33 *Grágás Staðarhólsbók*, Vígslóði 380, ed. Finsen, 2.397–398, trans. Denis et al., 1.236.

34 *Grágás Konungsbók*, Þingskapa-þáttr 48–52, 62, 66, 69, 77; ed. Finsen, 1a.83–88, 112–116, 118, 120, 125, trans. Denis et al., 1.88–93, 112–116, 117, 118–119, 123. The last of these passages, somewhat inexplicably, specifies that a confiscation court after a spring assembly should be held on a Wednesday. *Staðarhólsbók* places less emphasis on the holding of a court but does discuss property confiscation. *Grágás Staðarhólsbók*, Vígslóði 332, ed. Finsen, 359.

35 Kirsten Hastrup, *Culture and History in Medieval Iceland: An Anthropological Analysis of Structure and Change* (Oxford: Oxford University Press, 1985), 140–142.

36 *Grágás Konungsbók*, Þingskapa-þáttr 62, ed. Finsen, 1a.115, trans. Denis et al., 1.115.

37 *Grágás Konungsbók*, Þingskapa-þáttr 55, ed. Finsen, 1a.95, trans. Denis et al., 1.98. "Þeir scogar menn er farning er mælt enda verðr eigi áttr ferans domr eptir þa scal kiósa þeim heimile eítt oc segia bvvm .v. þeim er næstir búa heimilino. enda verðr hann þar heilagr alengr at þvi heimile sem þa at kørit væri. at ferans domi. oc sva scal a goto til scips þaðan fra þvi heimili. enda scal hann lata bera þav vætte fram er honom er fars beiðt sem i ferans domin scyldi ef áttr væri nema honom væri hælgi meire mælt en fiorbavgs mane. oc þarf eigi þa at kiósa honom heimilit."

38 *Grágás Konungsbók*, Þingskapa-þáttr 52, ed. Finsen, 1a.89, trans. Denis et al., 1.93.

had the authority to mitigate some outlawry terms, at least under certain conditions, so that, although a person was not allowed to return to Iceland, they were not under perpetual penalty beyond it. This type of outlawry also seems to have been a feature of outlawry judgements that were reached as part of settlements undertaken outside of the Alþingi.[39]

There are other places in *Grágás* that hint that outlawry was not so absolute. A provision only found in Staðarhólsbók suggests, indirectly, that some outlaws could regain their lost legal standing: "Those men who have been outlawed and are afterwards led into the law must maintain their dependents, and reprieve must be allowed them on other terms."[40] This provision does not, however, specify how this particular mitigation could be arranged. A different provision (in Konungsbók) offers the idea that an outlaw could be reintegrated into society by killing another outlaw (or even having someone else kill an outlaw in his name).[41] In an appendix to the Skarðsárbók version of *Landnámabók*, a post-Reformation text, it is suggested that, in the late tenth century, it was added to the law at the advice of Eyjólfr Valgerðarson that an outlawed man could earn his freedom by killing three outlaws.[42] I would suggest that these provisions are not evidence for a society filled with roaming outlaws to be killed at almost any cost. They suggest rather an approach to legal writing that sought to capture a range of ideas, perhaps only heard or filtered through a story and attempted to fix them in the frame of a law code. These diverse provisions also urge caution in trying to frame any one definition of outlawry. *Grágás* certainly does not offer one.

## 2.4 *Helping or Associating with an Outlaw*

Helping an outlaw in *Grágás* is an act that could lead to the sanction of outlawry for those offering aid.[43] It was not, however, a requirement to kill an

39 *Grágás Konungsbók*, Þingskapa-þáttr 55, ed. Finsen, 1a.94–96, trans. Denis et al., 1.97–98.

40 *Grágás Staðarhólsbók*, Ómaga-bálkr 112, ed. Finsen, 2.143, trans. Denis et al., 2.261. "Þeir menn eigo fram at føra omaga sina er sekir hafa verit oc se lög leiddir siþan. en eigi a at lofa þeim syknona elligar."

41 *Grágás Konungsbók*, Vígslóði 110, ed. Finsen, 1a.187, trans. Denis et al., 1.170–171.

42 *Skarðsárbók. Landnámabók Björns Jónssonar á Skarðsá*, ed. by Jakob Benediktsson (Reykjavík: Háskóli Íslands, 1958), 189.

43 *Grágás Konungsbók*, Þingskapa-þáttr 55, ed. Finsen, 1a.94–95, trans. Denis et al., 1.97; *Grágás Staðarhólsbók*, Vígslóði 382, ed. Finsen, 2.402, trans. Denis et al., 1.238. In Staðarhólsbók the penalty for allowing an outlaw one had personally condemned go free is outlawry. *Grágás Staðarhólsbók*, 380, ed. Finsen, 2.397–398, trans. Denis et al., 1.236.

According to another provision in Konungsbók, there is no penalty for people who unwittingly bring an outlaw to land until three days have passed, *Grágás Konungsbók*, Þingskapa-þáttr 77, ed. Finsen, 1a.127, trans. Denis et al., 1.124. Staðarhólsbók extends this to Greenland, saying that anyone helping a person outlawed in Greenland should be outlaw.[44] In one provision (in the assembly procedures section) assisting an outlaw before the outlawry sentence had been proclaimed at an assembly, led to the sanction of lesser outlawry. After the sentence was recognized,[45] the penalty for assisting a full outlaw became full outlawry.[46] Men who brought an outlaw back to Iceland in ignorance were not necessarily sanctioned, but once they found out, they were supposed to either kill him or bring him to the man who had outlawed him.[47]

Being in the presence of outlaws without explicitly helping them could also be punished.[48] Konungsbók posits a situation in which "men share a household and one of them takes in an outlaw and the other is unwilling," in this event, "the one who is unwilling is to name witnesses to witness that he is unwilling and that it is with his disagreement and report it to five neighbors. Then he is liable to no legal penalty for sharing living quarters with an outlaw as long as he gives him assistance in no other way."[49] I would like to emphasize how similar the thinking in this passage is to the ways that canonists were considering how household members of an excommunicated person ought to be regarded, especially given that excommunication could be contagious.[50] This passage in Konungsbók imagines a situation in which an outlaw is present in a

---

prosecuted as if the case had been prosecuted at a spring assembly and not yet published at the Althingi (i.e. the sanction was lesser outlawry). *Grágás Staðarhólsbók*, Vígslóði 374, ed. Finsen, 2.389–390, trans. Denis et al., 1.235.

44 *Grágás Konungsbók*, Vígslóði 110, ed. Finsen, 1a.189. trans. Denis et al. 1.171. "Eigi er manne scyllt at drepa scogar man þott hann hitte hann at mále ef hann tecr hann eigi oc rædr honom eigi biarg ráð." See also, *Grágás Staðarhólsbók*, Vígslóði 383, ed. Finsen, 2.402, trans. Denis et al., 1.238.

45 There is some uncertainty in the manuscript reading whether this is meant to be a confiscation court or a quarter court, *Grágás Konungsbók*, trans. Denis et al., 1.97 note 119.

46 *Grágás Konungsbók*, Þingskapa-þáttr 55, ed. Finsen, 1a.94–95, trans. Denis et al., 1.97–98. Some provisions suggest that helping someone before a legal action but after an act had been committed could also lead to a sentence for the person offering aid. *Grágás Konungsbók*, Vígslóði 86, ed. Finsen, 1a.148, trans. Denis et al., 1.141; *Grágás Staðarhólsbók*, Vígslóði 343, ed. Finsen, 2.369, trans. Perkins et al., 1.226.

47 *Grágás Konungsbók*, Þingskapa-þáttr 70, ed. Finsen, 1a.121, trans. Denis et al., 1.119.

48 *Grágás Konungsbók*, Þingskapa-þáttr 77, ed. Finsen, 1a.126, trans. Denis et al., 1.124.

49 *Grágás Konungsbók*, Þingskapa-þáttr 77, ed. Finsen, 1a.126, trans. Denis et al., 1.124. "Ef menn bua saman oc tecr anar þeirra við scogar manne. en anar vill eigi. þa scal sa er eigi vill nefna vatta at þvi at hann vill eigi. oc þat er at osátt hans oc segia til .v. buom sinom siþan þa varðar honom eigi við lög samvista við scog gangs man. ef hann veitir honom i engo aðro biorg."

The same code specifies that unknowingly sharing space with an outlaw for three days or fewer (cumulative or consecutive) carried no penalty. *Grágás Konungsbók*, Þingskapa-þáttr 77, ed. Finsen, 1a.126–127.

50 See chapter 1, page 8.

household and suggests a way to limit the culpability for being in an outlaw's presence, which in this instance is acceptable as long as no other help is given, much as the contagion of associating with an excommunicated person was limited more and more to those who aided his or her crimes.

Helping an outlaw in ignorance was not necessarily punished, particularly if he was ill or injured.[51] The Konungsbók version of *Grágás* even specifies that there is no penalty if one unknowingly "gives [an outlaw] assistance because he does it for his soul's good, he is not put under penalty for such boarding in ignorance even though lengthy. He is not to give him passage from the country."[52] This passage, with its concern for one's soul, is not often cited, perhaps because it offers such a different perspective on outlawry than some of the more uncompromising pronouncements in *Grágás*. The outlaw here is presented as sick, wounded, or otherwise in need of aid. The code here presents, in other words, a picture of an outlaw as a potential object of charity to be helped or rehabilitated, much like an excommunicant being led back into the fold.

There is no single formula for full outlawry nor are the consequences always so clear cut as the one- or two-sentence summations of outlawry often given in passing suggest. Outlawry as presented in the manuscripts of *Grágás* is not one consistent sanction. Rather *Grágás* presents many ideas about outlawry, how permanent it was, how it was to be enacted as a sentence as well as how it might be mitigated.

## 3 The Problem of Lesser Outlawry (*fjǫrbaugsgarðr*/*fjǫrbaugsmaðr*)

If full outlawry in *Grágás* presents thorny problems for anyone trying to understand the sanction, *fjǫrbaugsgarðr* usually translated as "lesser outlawry," presents still more. The existence of lesser outlawry is a feature that is more often observed than explained in the discussion of Icelandic medieval law. A literal translation of *fjǫrbaugsgarðr* might be "life-money fence" or "life-ring fence."[53] What it meant in terms of legal writing and legal practice in medieval Iceland is more debatable.

---

51 *Grágás Konungsbók*, Þingskapa-þáttr 77, ed. Finsen, 1a.127, trans. Denis et al. 1.124–125.

52 *Grágás Konungsbók*, Þingskapa-þáttr 77, ed. Finsen, 1a.127, trans. Denis et al. 1.124–125. "Ef maðr veit eigi secþ manz oc bergr hann honom af þvi at hinn er siucr eða sár eða vanheill fyrir elle eða veiti hann honom af þvi at hann gørir þat til sale bótar ser oc secz hann eigi af þvi elðe þott langt se. Eigi scal af lande feria hann."

53 KLNM 4.603–608, s.v. "Fredløshed – Island," by Magnús Már Lárusson.

While various words for outlawry are attested in a wide variety of sagas and in most, if not all, of the medieval Germanic languages, *fjǫrbaugsgarðr* appears almost exclusively in Old Icelandic texts.[54] Even within these sources, the term is relatively rare although it appears in abundance in the manuscripts of *Grágás*. The term appears to be used in two distinct ways in *Grágás*. Sometimes it is a fine, and sometimes it is a rather complicated sanction involving temporary exile for three years and limited protection within defined boundaries until departure from Iceland. Gwyn Jones argues that the sanction in *Grágás* is a garbled legal confection and that the original meaning and usage of the term can be understood as follows in the context of feuding: *Fjǫrbaugr* was a sum of money, usually paid by a person judged a *fjǫrbaugsmaðr* for actions committed as part of conflict. This *fjǫrbaugsmaðr* was giving limited sanctuary rights, called *fjǫrbaugsgarðr,* until he managed to leave Iceland, a situation designed to deescalate conflict. Jones also emphasizes that this sanctuary was also (if not primarily) protection for the person who imposed it, not the person who was under it, as it limited an enemy's movements and range for revenge.[55]

### 3.1 *Fjǫrbaugr as a Fine*

*Fjǫrbaugr* could be a type of fine. For example, in section 51 of the assembly procedures section, which discusses how to conduct a confiscation court for a lesser outlaw, it reads: "A mark in legal tender is to be paid at the confiscation court to the chieftain who nominated the confiscation court. That is called a 'life ring' (*fiorbavgr*) and one ounce-unit of that money is called a 'sustenance pledge.' If that money is not paid, then he becomes a full outlaw who may not be sustained [...]"[56] The assertion that a "life ring" was a sum of money is clear. And Jones's idea that it served as a price paid for limited immunity and also as a punishment is a sensible way to understand the word.[57]

### 3.2 *Fjǫrbaugsgarðr as Banishment with Limited Protections in Iceland*

The most familiar passage about lesser outlawry occurs in the assembly procedures section, which defines the limits of movement placed on a *fjǫrbaugsmaðr*. It reads: "When a confiscation court is held for a lesser outlaw, his homes

54 Gösta Åqvist notes that *fjǫrbaugsgarðr* has no parallel in legal traditions outside Iceland, except in laws from Gotland, *Frieden und Eidschwur*, 264–265. This is also noted by Riisøy, "Outlawry: From Western Norway," 123.

55 Gwyn Jones, "Fjörbaugsgarðr," *Medium Ævum* 9 (1940): 155–163.

56 *Grágás Konungsbók*, Þingskapa-þáttr 51, ed. Finsen, 1a.88, trans. Denis et al, 1.92. "þat fe heitir fiorbavgr [...] ef þat fe gelldz eigi þa verðr hann scogar maðr o øll."

57 Jones, "Fjörbaugsgarðr," 155. See also Riisøy, "Outlawry: From Western Norway," 123.

are to be reported. He is to have three homes. It shall not be farther between them than may be traveled one way in one day. He shall be immune at those homes and within bowshot of them in all directions and on the road between them as long as he does not travel by it more than once a month [...]"[58] The next passage outlines the proper way to seek passage for a lesser outlaw, who must leave Iceland within three years after his sentence.[59] This detailed (and probably difficult to enforce) sanction can seem somewhat at odds with the sheer number of offenses that have lesser outlawry named as their sanction in *Grágás*. It is also telling that while so much description is forthcoming, including matters about distances from the road and travel distances, all this description might suggest that the punishment in this precise form was not generally known or accepted. Perhaps the writers sought to codify what was more usually understood as a type of house arrest.[60]

### 3.3 *Offenses Leading to the Sanction of Fjǫrbaugsgarðr*

The offenses that could lead to a sentence of *fjǫrbaugsgarðr* were many. In a passage in the "land-claims" section of Konungsbók, lesser outlawry is the punishment for damaging trees at a cost of five ounce-units or more. It is also the sanction for moving boundary markers.[61] Lesser outlawry is also the sanction for "defamation."[62]

*Fjǫrbaugsgarðr* is the sanction for a variety of failures to abide by duties and conventions expected of all Christians. It is the sanction named for not knowing the pater noster, if you have the capacity to learn it, for example.[63]

58 *Grágás Konungsbók*, Þingskapa-þáttr 52, ed. Finsen, 1a.88. trans. Denis et al, 1.93. "Þa er ferans domr er áttr at fiorbvgs man. þa scal segia til heimila hans. Hann scal eiga þriú heimili. þeirra scal eigi lengra imiðlom vera en fara megi vm dag a anan veg. Hann scal heilagr vera at þeim heimilom oc i örscotz hælgi við a alla vega. oc a götoni a millom heimilana ef hann fer eigi optar en vm sin a manaðe."

59 *Grágás Konungsbók*, Þingskapa-þáttr 53, ed. Finsen, 1a.89–92, trans. Denis et al., 1.93–95.

60 An alternative explanation, that cannot be easily ruled out comes from G. Turville Petre, "Outlawry," *Sjötíu Ritgerðir Helgaðar Jakobi Benediktssyni 20. júlí 1977*, síðari hluti (Reykjavík: Stofnun Árna Magnússonar á Íslandi, 1977), 770. He writes: "The element *-garðr* in the term *fjǫrbaugsgarðr* is puzzling. It is used in some non-legal texts where it seems to mean an area or enclosure outside the hallowed precincts of the assembly from which convicts could exercise their business. That was perhaps the original meaning of the term *fjǫrbaugsgarðr*." Kirsten Hastrup also emphasizes the spatial element in *fjǫrbaugsgarðr* in, *Culture and History*, 140–145.

61 *Grágás Konungsbók*, Landbrigða-þáttr 199, ed. Finsen, 1b.110. trans. Denis et al. 2.129.

62 *Grágás Konungsbók*, Um fullréttisorð 237, ed. Finsen, 1b.181–182, trans. Denis et al., 2.195–196.

63 *Grágás Konungsbók*, Kristinna laga þáttr 1, ed. Finsen, 1a.7, trans. Denis et al., 1.26.

*Fjǫrbaugsgarðr* is also the sanction for marrying within prohibited degrees of kinship[64] and for celebrating a wedding on prohibited days, such as during the period of fasting before Christmas.[65]

*Fjǫrbaugsgarðr* is also the sanction of choice for still murkier areas of deviance, such as poverty and cross-dressing. It is the sanction for a couple marrying with less than 120 ounce-units in legal tender between them (unless the woman is past childbearing age)[66] and for a woman dressing as a man.[67] *Fjǫrbaugsgarðr* is the penalty assigned to a variety of sexual offenses such as for secretly kissing another man's wife.[68] It is also the sanction for having intercourse with a freedman's wife.[69]

### 3.4 *Interpreting Fjǫrbaugsgarðr in Grágás*

I want to concentrate on a few of the less remarked upon features of lesser outlawry in *Grágás* to aid in understanding the limits of what we know about it. I also want to emphasize the diverse uses it seems to have served the *Grágás* compilers and scribes. Part of the wide use of *fjǫrbaugsgarðr* seems to be that there were limited ways to mark distinctions between the severity of different offences.

The compilers of *Grágás* use lesser outlawry to make distinctions between different degrees of harm and punishment. In the section "On homicide," for example, it reads that "It is prescribed that all plots to disfigure carry a penalty of lesser outlawry even if they do not succeed, but full outlawry if they do."[70]

64 *Grágás Konungsbók*, Festa-þáttr 144, ed. Finsen, 1b.31, trans. Denis et al., 2.55. Note that this feature is itself evidence for the presence of canon law in *Grágás* and Icelandic legal thinking as it clearly references legal developments about marriage made in 1215. Agnes Arnórsdóttir, *Property and Virginity*, 83.

65 *Grágás Konungsbók*, Festa-þáttr 148, ed. Finsen, 1b.39. trans. Denis et al., 2.62.

66 *Grágás Konungsbók*, Festa-þáttr 148., ed Finsen, 1b.38, trans. Denis et al., 2.61. This would have been illegal under canon law as interpreted by Gratian, according to which everyone, including slaves, was allowed to marry. See, Anders Winroth, "Neither Slave nor Free: Theology and Law in Gratian's Thoughts on the Definition of Marriage and Unfree Persons," *Medieval Church Law and the Origins of the Western Legal Tradition: A Tribute to Kenneth Pennington*, ed. Wolfgang P. Müller and Mary E. Sommor (Washington D.C.: The Catholic University of America Press, 2012), 105–109.

67 *Grágás Konungsbók*, Festa-þáttr 155, ed. Finsen, 1b.47. trans. Denis et al., 2.69.

68 *Grágás Konungsbók*, Festa-þáttr 155, ed. Finsen 1b.47, trans. Denis et al., 2.69.

69 *Grágás Konungsbók*, Festa-þáttr 156, ed. Finsen 1b.48, trans. Denis et al., 2.70–71. Intercourse with a slave-woman is assinged a penalty of 3 marks, intercourse with a vagrant woman carries no penalty unless she bears a child.

70 *Grágás Kongunsbók*, Vígslóði 108, ed. Finsen 1a.184, trans. Denis et al., 1.169. "Þat er. at manne varðar fiorbavgs garð aliótz rað öll þott eigi comi fram. en scog gang ef fram kømr." A similar situation seems to apply to burnings: Intending to participate in a burning makes one liable for lesser outlawry but once the fire is taken up to burn someone in

The Konungsbók manuscript also features the idea that two lesser outlawry sentences add up to a sentence of full outlawry.[71] This could in part have been a genuine problem about how to address a situation in which the same person was facing multiple summons, especially if it was for different reasons or brought by different complainants, but it also shows how clunky and limited the machinery for justice envisioned by *Grágás* was in some ways.

Both of these features: the idea of adding two lesser outlawry sentences together to make a full outlawry sentence (an idea that is not seen in any of the sagas so far as my research has uncovered) and the idea that a successful plot merited full outlawry, a failed one lesser, suggest that the compilers of *Grágás* were struggling to fit the words and sanctions they knew into existing, I argue often ecclesiastical, ideas of what a lawcode should be and how it should be structured.

One way of understanding lesser outlawry, as presented in *Grágás*, is as a translation of minor excommunication into the idiom of secular sanctions. Minor excommunication, like lesser outlawry, was a less severe sanction, and most interestingly, I think, just as minor excommunication was the sanction for associating with a public excommunicant (i.e. a person under major excommunication), lesser outlawry was sometimes assigned as the penalty for associating with a full outlaw or helping them. The analogy is not a perfect one, and lesser outlawry in *Grágás* is asked to absorb a diverse array of concepts. But in the compilers' efforts to create a hierarchy of sanctions based on severity (lesser outlawry for lesser crimes and full outlawry for greater), we might see influence from ecclesiastical law, which also had a problem of a limited number of sanctions to address a wide scope of misdeeds.

What *fjǫrbaugsgarðr* meant as a legal idea or sanction is, given the sources, vague and open to confusion and contradiction. Sometimes it seems more likely that it refers to a fine, only once is it given anything resembling a definition. Often the word occurs without any way of determining from the context if it meant a fine or a complex sanction involving restrictions on movement and enforced travel. Jones further states that with regard to lesser outlawry: "*Grágás* flatly contradicts the family histories [sagas of Icelanders] and Sturlung sagas, while these two last groups disagree both with each other and internally."[72] Gwyn Jones has argued that the sanction as described in *Grágás* bears little

---

their house, those participating have forfeited their immunity and liable to full outlawry, *Grágás Kongunsbók*, Vígslóði 109, ed. Finsen 1a.184–185, trans. Denis et al, 1.169.

71 *Grágás Konungsbók*, Þingskapa-þáttr 52, ed. Finsen, 1a.89, trans. Denis et al., 1.93. "Ef fiorbavgs maðr gørir fiorbavgs soc oc varðar honom scog gang."

72 Jones, "Fjörbaugsgarðr," 163.

resemblance to practice and concepts as seen in the sagas, although there were forms of temporary banishment in saga sources. Focusing on the lateness of saga manuscripts and the fact that law procedure obsessed sagas like *Njáls saga* adhere most closely to *Grágás* provisions he writes: "Those passages in the sagas which agree even confusedly with *Grágás* law are anachronisms not hard to explain."[73]

Although it seems quite likely, inevitable even, that we should see variation in understandings of *fjǫrbaugsgarðr* across different genres and timescales, the term *fjǫrbaugsgarðr* is also a case where we can see the strain of adapting an existing sanction into one or more writers' ideas about what a lawcode should be and how it should look.[74] I argue that one of the models that the *Grágás* compilers were drawing on was canon law and the few sanctions available in canon law, major and minor excommunication. *Fjǫrbaugsgarðr* within the context of the earliest *Grágás* manuscripts appears to be most useful as a counterpoint or complement to full outlawry. It was a sanction that was useful to mark the difference between relatively minor offences and effects and more devastating ones. Its value and use as a sanction in practice is harder to outline with confidence.

## 4 Outlawry in the Sagas

In this chapter I have been focusing on legal sources, not because they are necessarily more factual or reliable than saga sources, but because they are so often how discussions of outlawry are framed, and they provide more information and suggestions that might allow us to form definitions than saga sources.[75] Moreover, the surviving legal manuscripts are often at least a little earlier than surviving saga manuscripts, particularly for the "outlaw sagas."

Sagas, especially the so-called "outlaw sagas," focus more on the dramatic potential impact outlawry could have on individual lives than on the hypothetical, sometimes highly improbable situations considered in the law books

73 Jones, "Fjörbaugsgarðr," 163.

74 For discussion of layout and other conventions in the production of lawbooks see, Lena Rohrbach, "Matrix of the Law? A Material Study of Staðarhólsbók," *The Power of the Book: Medial Approaches to Medieval Nordic Legal Manuscripts*, ed. by Lena Rohrbach, Berliner Beiträge zur Skandinavistik (Berlin: Nordeuropa-Institut der Humboldt-Universität, 2014), 98–128.

75 Some sagas also present a form of local banishment, called *heraðssekt* or "district outlawry," an idea not formalized in *Grágás* but present in texts such as *Hrafnkels saga* and *Njáls saga*, Jones, "Fjörbaugsgarðr," 161–163.

(if all *Grágás* provisions were followed, we would be forced to imagine a world where every desperate milk stealer was a few steps away from becoming an outlaw). These sagas focus on the consequences for individual, usually rich and talented, people that are sentenced to outlawry.[76]

One of the ideas that adds to the tragedy of the outlaw Grettir's demise in *Grettis saga*, for example, is the idea, confined to his eponymous saga, that if he could have survived as an outlaw for twenty years, he would have been permitted to reenter society as a free man.[77] There is no legal or other literary evidence for this practice. It does add a dramatic edge to an already dramatic and doomed fate, however, and serves to underline the contrast between Grettir's extraordinary powers and tragic fate.

A feature that comes through more strongly in the narrative sources than in the lawbooks is the idea that outlawry was more than the sum of its parts. That there was an absoluteness, stigma, or dread about it that was tied to the sentence itself. In other words, the action or offense that led a person to be outlawed is not as important as the fact of the outlawry itself. It branded a person, not only by limiting the ways that they could act to protect themselves and avoid their enemies (i.e. all of its legal handicaps and loss of property). Outlawry in most of these stories is not just or primarily an inevitable or likely consequence of particular actions, but rather a piece of bad luck or a curse.[78]

The suffering of Gísli and Grettir in their sagas is not to atone for killings, it is rather a symptom of the horrors that outlawry was imagined to bring with

---

76 It is not possible to consider all of the literary approaches to outlawry in this chapter or the scholarship on the so-called outlaw sagas—*Gísla saga*, *Grettis saga*, and to a lesser extent, *Harðar saga* in great detail here. See, Robert Cook, "Grettis saga," *Medieval Scandinavia: An Encyclopedia,* ed. by Phillip Pulsiano et al. (New York and London: Garland, 1993), 241–42; Riti Kroesen, "Gísla saga Súrssonar," *Medieval Scandinavia: An Encyclopedia,* ed. by Phillip Pulsiano et al. (New York and London: Garland, 1993), 227–228; Anthony Faulkes, "Harðar saga," *Medieval Scandinavia: An Encyclopedia,* ed. by Phillip Pulsiano et al. (New York and London: Garland, 1993), 269. For a wide-ranging discussion of outlawry in the *Íslendinga sögur* and an up to date bibliography see, Ahola, "Outlawry in the Family Sagas." As with the legal sources, it can also be useful to compare literary depictions of outlawry from different regions. See, for example, Jones, *Outlawry in Medieval Literature*; and DeAngelo, *Outlawry, Liminality, and Sanctity*.

77 *Grettis saga*, in *Grettis saga Ásmundarsonar, Bandamanna saga, Odds þáttr Ófeigssonar* ed. by Guðni Jónsson, Íslenzk fornrit 7 (Reykjavík: Hið íslenzka fornritafélag, 1936), 77: 244–245.

78 Joonas Ahola divides sagas with outlaw characters into "tragic biographies," "fortunate biographies," and "biographies of pioneering outlawry." All of the major outlaw sagas are "tragic biographies" according to his classification, "Outlawry in the Family Sagas," 105–137.

it—quite independent from whatever actions led to them being outlawed. As mentioned above, in saga sources from this period there is little sense that outlawry was primarily for or about punishing the worst crimes. Those outlawed might have violated certain societal expectations or simply killed the wrong person, but they upheld others and are meant to be figures that are at a basic level, relatable.

A distinct feature of outlaw sagas in particular is their association with and particular interest in landscape features and connections with particular places within Iceland. This is not the focus of this book, but it is still another dimension of outlaw stories that complicates how we understand why they were written, copied, and told. One way of reading them is as a kind of *landnám* (landtaking), a way of inhabiting a place's past through the story of a famous outlaw traveling or hiding in the landscape. In this sense, outlaw sagas can be read as evidence about how audiences related to and discussed a place's past, not primarily about facts of legal punishment.[79]

I want to emphasize the lateness of many of these sources and their continued popularity and copying into a time when the punishment itself was quite different, if not completely absent. The so-called "outlaw manuscript," for example, AM 556 a 4to, which contains versions of *Grettis saga*, *Harðar Saga*, and *Gísla saga*, is usually dated to 1475.[80] This manuscript was produced at a time when outlawry was eclipsed by other sanctions, although it remained a motif for storytelling and history telling.

## 5 Outlawry in the Contemporary Sagas

In contrast with the sagas of Icelanders, outlawry in the contemporary sagas is less dramatic and more common.[81] As there was political excommunication, it is also possible to talk about something that looks like "political outlawry" in the sense that who was outlawed and for what offenses became increasingly a

79 See for instance, Eleanor Rosamund Barraclough, "Inside Outlawry in *Grettis saga Asmundsonar* and *Gísla saga Súrssonar*: Landscape in the Outlaw Sagas," *Scandinavian Studies* 82 (2010): 365–388; Matthías Þórðarson, "Tveir Grettisbústaðir," *Árbók hins íslenzka fornleifafélags* 45 (1936): 49–60; Ahola, "Outlawry in the Family Sagas," 248–64; and Ármann Jakobsson, "*Bárðar saga* as an historical narrative," 53–71.

80 Ahola, "Outlawry in the Family Sagas," 114.

81 In the contemporary sagas it is not uncommon for people to be outlawed in groups, see Heusler, *Zum Isländischen Fehdewesen*, 76–77, 84.

matter of political rivalry and expediency,[82] although such considerations are not absent from the sagas of Icelanders. If outlawry in the sagas of Icelanders is partly about harsh justice, partly about limiting feud, and partly the medieval equivalent of a psychological thriller, outlawry in the contemporary sagas appears to be an occupational hazard for all participants in the conflicts of the age.[83]

The contemporary sagas present a number of cases of what appears to be full outlawry (i.e. the terminology used is *sekr* or *skóggangr* and there is no suggestion of safe houses or return to Island after three years), but passage out of Iceland is permitted and sometimes paid for.[84] This stands in contrast to the Konungsbók stipulation that *skógarmenn* were not to be sustained helped or given passage abroad but fits with the less dramatic types of full outlawry that other passages in *Grágás* mention, particularly outlaws who were *ferjandi*, allowed to be transported out of the country.

## 6 Relationship to State Power and Statelessness

Outlawry is particularly associated with medieval Iceland as a "stateless" society in the period before the 1260s, but it is also a punishment sometimes associated with weak states.[85] Outlawry in this view is seen as an acknowledgement

82 Miller, *Bloodtaking and Peacemaking*, esp. 368–369, note 22. See also, Byock, *Viking Age Iceland*, 232. By the same token, it could be a show of power to protect an outlaw, a point I thank Torfi Tulinius for emphasizing to me.

83 As in the number of outlawries in the wake of the killing of Hrafn Sveinbjarnarson, which are presented matter-of-factly and with little comment. Sturla Þórðarson, *Íslendinga saga*, ed. Kålund, 1.362–369, trans. McGrew, *Sturlunga saga 1*, 46–51: 191–197.

84 In *Íslendinga saga*, Þorbergr was outlawed for the killing of Þórarin Grímsson, but Sighvatr managed to get him a sea passage away from Iceland. Sturla Þórðarson, *Íslendinga saga*, ed. Kålund, 323, trans. McGrew, 33: 158. "hann kom Þorbergi vtan austr i fiordvm." A few decades earlier, Hvamm-Sturla is not able to defend an outlawry case, but he does get passage abroad for his outlawed follower, Þorgeirr. *Sturlunga saga*, ed. Kålund, 1.94, trans. McGrew, *The Saga of Hvamm-Sturla*, Sturlunga saga vol. 1 (New York: Twayne Publishers and the American-Scandinavian Foundation, 1970), 23: 92.

85 Agrarian studies shape my understanding of state power. See, for example, James C. Scott, *Weapons of the Weak: everyday forms of peasant resistance* (New Haven: Yale University Press, 1985); James C. Scott, *Seeing like a state: how certain schemes to improve the human condition have failed* (New Haven: Yale University Press, 1998). Outlaw stories as an expression of popular discontent is a debated issue. The Robin Hood ballads, for example, probably had a largely aristocratic audience in England. See Anthony Faulkes, "Outlaws in Medieval England and Iceland," *Greppaminni, Rit til heiðurs Vésteini Ólasyni sjötugum* (Reykjavík: Hið íslenska bókmenntafélag, 2009), 139.

that some offenders would not and could not be pursued, simply because the resources to search for them did not exist.[86] This idea is also tied to the tendency for outlaws to seek and exist in marginal spaces, like forests, wilderness, and along contested borders.[87] These associations fit well with what we know about Iceland's early political organization, with its emphasis on self-help and the absence of executive power to impose a death penalty.

But outlawry is also a punishment associated with states and state formation, with political power and those able to wield it. Gösta Åqvist brings out this aspect of outlawry in Scandinavian medieval sources. His work focuses on Sweden and the other continental Scandinavian countries, but also draws on Icelandic material (and of course Icelandic laws are thought to be based on early Norwegian provincial codes).[88] Åqvist argues that the development of outlawry in Scandinavian laws of the Middle Ages, although it had ancient roots, is tied to the development of royal power, a trend he sees first in Anglo-Saxon England, where the concept of the king's peace and an increasing role for the king as the only source of clemency for those convicted of crimes that were otherwise unamendable is well documented.[89] Indeed, Åqvist suggests that it was Anglo-Saxon models of lawmaking that influenced the development of law in Norway and Denmark.[90] He argues that crimes that could be atoned for by compensation and subject to private agreements in the past were claimed as the exclusive purview of the king.[91] This construction of outlawry drew on the idea of the "king's peace," the idea that some crimes could only be pardoned by a king, who was responsible for the peace and wellbeing over a particular territory.[92] It can be viewed as a justification for increasing claims for jurisdiction and power. Pardon could be sought for this type of outlawry

86 Maurice Keen, *The Outlaws of Medieval Legend,* 2nd ed. (London and Toronto: Routledge, 1977), 193: "The very existence of the sentence was [...] an implied confession of governmental inability to enforce order."

87 Keen, *The Outlaws of Medieval Legend,* 191–207; Harlan-Haughey, *Ecology of the English Outlaw.*

88 Ari Þorgilsson, *Íslendingabók,* ed. by Jakob Benediktsson, Íslenzk fornrit 1 (Reykjavík: Hið íslenzka fornritafélag, 1968), 2: 6–7, trans. by Siân Grønlie, *Íslendingabók, Kristni saga: The Book of the Icelanders, The Story of the Conversion* (London: Viking Society for Northern Research, 2006), 2: 4–5.

89 It can be traced in both lawcodes and in documentation of individual cases, often in patent rolls from the twelfth and thirteenth centuries. See Hurnard, *The King's Pardon,* 214–250.

90 Åqvist, *Frieden und Eidschwur,* 354–367.

91 Åqvist, *Frieden und Eidschwur,* 229–293.

92 Åqvist, *Frieden und Eidschwur,* 240.

at the hands of the king, often combined with a fine.[93] This development is also seen as an effort to lessen the availability of feud and other types of private conflict resolution to disputants, although whether this led to an absolute reduction in violence is more debatable.

An example of this can be found in the *Frostathing law* in which the king might allow an outlaw to remain in Norway under certain circumstances and on payment of fines: "Now it may come to pass that the king will give an outlaw permission to remain in the land on the request of important men or because of some other circumstance. In such a case he shall buy his peace from the king [on such terms] as the king's mercy may allow, and he shall pay that half [of the atonement] which remains unpaid and [shall pay it] in such installments as, in the opinion of discreet men, he is able [to meet]."[94]

This idea helps to explain the focus on the king in *Járnsíða* and *Jónsbók* (discussed further below), which can be read as an attempt at articulating and strengthening a relatively new idea of kingship, one in which the king had more power than he had had in the past. In other words, *Járnsíða* and *Jónsbók* can be read as sources articulating a new kind of kingship, not just for Icelanders in the wake of their submission to the king of Norway but also in a Norwegian context. This context is that of reforming, reformulating, and strengthening the role of kings in the formation and execution of the law.[95]

Åqvist focuses on continental Scandinavia and his arguments do not, of course, apply exactly to the Icelandic evidence. But his arguments contribute to the conversation about outlawry in the medieval north, which tends to focus on Icelandic exceptionalism and conflict resolution without considering other arguments focusing on outlawry and the state. This is problematic because not only was Icelandic law developed from preexisting codes, not

93 These arguments are not new, but they often do not seem to feature in discussions focused on Iceland, perhaps because Iceland is seen as exceptional and stateless in the period before the 1260s. See, for instance, Gerstein, "The Outlaw as Werewolf," 132.

94 *Ældre Frostathings-Lov*, 5, ed. R. Keyser and P.A. Munch, *Norges gamle love*, 1.122, trans. Larson, *Earliest Norwegian Laws*, 214–215. "Nú kann sá atburðr einnhverr til at geraz at konungr gefr þessum hinum útlaga landzvist með bonærstað höfðingia eða með einhverium öðrum atburðum. þá scal hann sic svá í frið caupa við konung sem konungs er miscunn til oc bæta þann helming bóta er eptir stóð með slícum salastefnum sem scynsamir menn siá at hann megi vel orca."

95 Jørn Øryehagen Sunde, "Daughters of God and Counsellors of the Judges of Men: Changes in the Legal Culture of the Norwegian Realm in the High Middle Ages," *New Approaches to Early Law in Scandinavia*, ed. by Stefan Brink and Lisa Collinson (Turnhout: Brepols, 2014), 131–183.

from whole cloth, surviving Icelandic law manuscripts are also late and likely to show a variety of influences, including influence from newer conceptions of royal power.[96]

At the same time, outlawry existed in Iceland before the submission to the Norwegian crown. It is regularly mentioned in the contemporary sagas and sagas of Icelanders, which, while they do not provide pure access to thirteenth-century Iceland, do most likely preserve basic events and conflicts from the period and these conflicts do contain outlawry, although not perhaps, the same outlawry that we find documentation for in the surviving lawcodes.

## 7 Norwegian Influence and later Icelandic Law Sources

It is tempting to assume that, with the submission of the Icelandic chieftains to the Norwegian king, outlawry as it appears in *Grágás* became irrelevant, but, particularly in medieval contexts, older law was often slow to drift out of use. After *Grágás* our main legal sources about outlawry are codes produced in Norway for Iceland—*Járnsíða* and *Jónsbók*. In these codes, the king, unsurprisingly, has a much bigger role to play in terms of how outlawry is framed, and outlaws are often placed at his mercy.[97] Another feature that changes in these codes is their vocabulary. Whereas *Grágás* tends to use *skógarmaðr* or *sekr* and their variants for full outlaw and *fjǫrbaugsgarðr* for lesser outlawry, in the codes brought from Norway to Iceland the term *útlegð* and variants is generally preferred.[98]

This brief discussion will focus more on *Jónsbók*, which had a much larger impact on the Icelandic legal landscape than *Járnsíða*, which was quickly superseded. *Jónsbók* survives in at least 86 medieval manuscripts while the only medieval witness to *Járnsíða* is AM 334 fol. (Staðarhólsbók). Both of these codes show clear influence from Norwegian legal sources. In them outlawry is often referred to by the term *útlegð* and some provisions seem to be more or less directly borrowed for Norwegian codes and better fit with the geography and topography of Norway than of Iceland.

96 For discussion of the king as an upholder of law in *Egils saga* see, Patricia Pires Boulhosa, *Icelanders and the Kings of Norway: Medieval Sagas and Legal Texts* (Leiden and Boston: Brill, 2005), 195–197.

97 The development and reformulation of Norwegian law under King Magnús Hákonarsón lagabætir (the "law mender") as well as the effects of these changes on the formulation of Icelandic law is a topic that cannot be fully addressed here.

98 KLNM 4.603–608, s.v. "Fredløshed – Island," by Magnús Már Lárusson.

For example, in *Jónsbók* it states that outlaws were not permitted to return unless they came with genuine intelligence of an impending enemy attack.[99] As a practical concern this provision seems implausible, especially in the case of Iceland where the idea of coming "back" becomes ambiguous at best, it is a provision that makes significantly more sense from a Norwegian viewpoint, when such news might reasonably be conveyed and acted upon, and it is clear that the passage stems from the Gulathing laws on coast defense.[100] As a provision in *Jónsbók*, it makes most sense if we consider it in the context of outlawry being used as a way to frame and claim increasing royal jurisdiction and royal control over access to clemency, the shift towards offenses being categorized as *obotamál*, uncompensated-able crimes and the growing role of royal power.[101]

At other times, the geographic realities of Icelanders are taken into account. Section 18 of the of the chapter on personal rights suggests that a man who injures someone or commits some other *wtlegðar werk* "act that leads to outlawry" that others believe was justifiable, should be able to pay compensation and "Þa skal þann mann *at osekíu* flytía vtan til slikrar mískunnar sem konungr vill gera wið hann" [then that man is to be brought un-outlawed to Norway [vtan] to such mercy as the king wants to show him.][102] Here we can see a shifting of responsibility toward the Norwegian king although also an echo of *Grágás* as these men are identified as *feriande* which we might translate either as "to be transported" as Schulman does, or perhaps as "who are allowed to be transported"—in contrast to the *óferjandi* outlaws of Konungsbók.[103] Outlawry is the sanction associated with a variety of offenses, including the possibility of a woman killing a man or another woman (not a feature of *Grágás*).[104] The death penalty (for theft) also became a part of the Icelandic legal landscape at this time.[105]

In later amendments to *Jónsbók*, known as *réttarbœtur*, even more emphasis is placed on the role of the Norwegian king as a source of possible clemency for

99 *Jónsbók*, 4.4, in *Jónsbók: Kong Magnus Hakonsson Lovbog for Island vedtaget paa Altinget 1281 og Réttarbætr: De for Island givne retterbøder af 1294, 1305 og 1314*, Ed. by Ólafur Halldórsson, reprint (Odense: Odense Universitetsforlag, 1970), 40–41, trans, Jana K. Schulman, *Jónsbók, The Laws of Later Iceland* (Saarbrücken, Germany: AQ-Verlag, 2010), 41.

100 *Den eldre Gulatingslova*, 312, ed. Eithun et al, 167–168, trans. Larson, 197.

101 Åqvist, *Frieden und Eidschwur*, 229–293.

102 *Jónsbók*, 4.1, ed. Ólafur Halldórsson, 35, trans. Shulman, *Jónsbók*, 65. Translation modified.

103 *Jónsbók*, 4.1, ed. Óláfur Halldórsson, 35, trans, Schulman, *Jónsbók*, 33. Cf. *Grágás Konungsbók*, Þingskapa-þáttr 55, ed. Finsen, 1a.96, trans. Denis et al., 98.

104 *Jónsbók*, 4.1, ed. Ólafur Halldórsson, 35, trans, Schulman, *Jónsbók*, 33.

105 *Jónsbók*, 10.1, ed. Ólafur Halldórsson, 263, trans. Shulman, *Jónsbók*, 333.

those condemned in Iceland. In 1308 it was decided that offenders seeking the king's mercy had three years to do so. If they did not manage to do so in that time and failed to receive church sanctuary, they could be killed.[106] In a *réttarbót* from 1318 the *hirðstjóri*, the king's legal representative in Iceland, is tasked with deciding which offenders should be sent to Norway and recommended to receive clemency from the king.[107]

Both *Járnsíða* and *Jónsbók*, assert that the law and responsibility for Christian society is shared between the king and the bishop. They present outlawry as something that the king controls and can release people from.[108] In these (slightly) later codes there is a shift in vocabulary and toward the king as a source of both justice and mercy,[109] although older terms and ideas continued to be used in literary production. Indeed, most of the outlaw sagas were probably composed in their extant forms in the fourteenth century; the manuscripts are certainly no earlier than that in most cases.[110]

---

106 *Diplomatarium Islandicum*, 4.9.

107 *Diplomatarium Islandicum*, 2.420.

108 *Járnsíða* "Hákonarbók," 17, ed. R. Keyser and P.A. Munch, *Norges gamle love*, 1.165. "Nv kann sa atburðr einn hverr til at geraz at konongr gefr þessum hinom útlæga manne lanzvist með orðsendingom oc bænarstað goðra manna eða kemr hann a konongs fund og fær grið af konongi, þa skal hann sik sua i frið kaupa við konong sem hans er miskunn til, en bæta þann lut bota sæm eftir stoð með slikum salastefnum sem goðer menn sia at hann mege orka."

109 The idea of the king as a source of mercy for those condemned to outlawry is not a uniquely Nordic one. It is especially well-attested in English medieval legal sources see, Hurnard, *The King's Pardon*.

110 *Gísla saga* is often thought to have been composed in the thirteenth century but the earliest surviving manuscript is from ca. 1400. Emily Lethbridge, "*Gísla saga Súrssonar*: Textual Variation, Editorial Constructions, and Critical Interpretations," *Creating the Medieval Saga: Versions, Variability, and Editorial Interpretations in Old Norse Saga Literature*, ed. by Judy Quinn and Emily Lethbridge (Odense: University Press of Southern Denmark, 2010), 127–128; Emily Lethbridge, "Dating *Gísla saga*: Methodological Problems and Alternative Approaches," *Dating the Sagas: Reviews and Revisions*, ed. by Else Mundal (Copenhagen: Museum Tusculanum Press, 2013), 77–113; and Þórður Ingi Guðjónsson, "Editing the Three Versions of *Gísla saga Súrssonar*," *Creating the Medieval Saga: Versions, Variability, and Editorial Interpretations in Old Norse Saga Literature*, ed. by Judy Quinn and Emily Lethbridge (Odense: University Press of Southern Denmark, 2010), 105–121. *Grettis saga* is often thought to have been written first in the thirteenth century. The earliest surviving manuscripts of the saga are from the fifteenth century, but the figure of Grettir Ásmundarson is mentioned in other earlier sources. Guðvarður Már Gunnlaugsson, " 'Grettir vondum vættum, veitti hel og þreytti': Grettir Ásmundarson og vinsældir *Grettis sögu*," *Gripla* 11 (2000): 38–46, 60–69. The so-called "outlaw manuscript," AM 556 a 4to, which contains versions of *Grettis saga*, *Harðar Saga*, and *Gísla saga*, is usually dated to 1475.

## 8 Outlawry's Afterlife: From Saga to Folklore

Outlawry was is not just a feature of saga storytelling and motif. Long after the timeframe of this thesis, after the Reformation and well into Iceland's time as a Danish possession, the idea of the outlaw remained. Its valence shifted, meaning more and more a person who was not outlawed exactly but, rather, chose to leave society for a life on the margins rather than face harsh punishment within it.[111] The word is no longer *skógarmaðr* og *útlagi* "outlaw" but *útilegumaður* "man outside the law," a person who attempted to live outside of society in unsettled places, usually to avoid punishment. Although such figures were not outlawed in the sense that they were not given a formal sentence of outlawry, the association of them with medieval outlaws is strong, perhaps especially in popular culture.[112]

## 9 Conclusions

Working with the limited sources that we have I hope to have demonstrated several things about outlawry: that it is not portrayed with a lot of consistency even within medieval Icelandic sources from similar periods. In Icelandic legal sources, outlawry was part of a limited range of sanctions: outlawry, lesser outlawry (itself a difficult concept), and fines. Outlawry was a fairly blunt instrument with variable connotations and consequences. It could be a harsh sanction, but it could also be mitigated.

Discussions of outlawry often tend toward short definitions of the sentence and then move to discussion of its use within conflicts, as if the definition was stable and well understood. What I have tried to draw out in this discussion is that outlawry, especially outlawry as it is presented in *Grágás*, was a more diverse sanction and that the ways in which the writers of *Grágás* used both full and lesser outlawry may reflect their own particular concerns in presenting a comprehensive lawcode rather than an anthropologically or historically reliable portrait of outlawry.[113] *Grágás* presents many ideas about outlawry, not

111 Turville-Petre, "Outlawry," 775–776. "In later times the outlaw takes to the wilderness to avoid penalty." He also says that later outlaws tended to have even more supernatural powers attributed to them "they come to resemble the elves and the huldufólk (the Hidden People)." See also, Hastrup, *Culture and History*, 142–145.

112 Briem, *Útilegumenn*. On Fjalla-Eyvindur (Jónsson) see also, Þorsteinn Bjarnarson, "Fjalla-Eyvindur og niðjar hans," 91–96.

113 Many caution against reading *Grágás* as a stable reflection of a legal system. See for instance, Gunnar Karlsson, "Goðar and höfðingjar in Medieval Iceland," *Saga-Book* 19

a single definition. It is important not to put too much weight on any one passage or provision, not least when it only appears in one manuscript. I also want to highlight that part of the complexity comes from a legal world in which the number of possible offenses was vast and the number of sanctions available (at least in written codes) small.

The next chapter offers a way of understanding some of outlawry's frustrating and elusive qualities. Rather than focusing on outlawry as an independent sanction, I argue for the possibility that outlawry was in many ways, particularly by the thirteenth century and later, a derivative sanction, based on Christian excommunication and drawing some of its power and sometimes its mechanics from this sanction, which never quite lost its overtones of damnation.

---

(1977): 360–361; and Orri Vésteinsson, *The Christianization of Iceland: Priests, Power, and Social Change 1000–1300* (Oxford: Oxford University Press, 2000), 6.

CHAPTER 3

# Outlawry as Secular Excommunication

Scholars have often observed, but rarely tried to explain, that the secular punishment of outlawry in northern Europe and the ecclesiastical sanction of excommunication share many characteristics, both in general and in their details. In this chapter, I argue that this is not a coincidence, but rather that the idea of outlawry in Icelandic medieval society was inspired by and derived from the canonical concept of excommunication. This is a difficult argument to make and one that cannot be proven in a strict sense. My argument is based on a detailed comparison of how outlawry and excommunication, respectively, functioned and were applied, if not in reality, then at least in the minds of the writers of sagas and lawbooks. I also consider carefully the material philology of the manuscripts that preserve the Icelandic texts we have that discuss outlawry and excommunication, noting that they were typically copied in the thirteenth century and later.

Outlawry did not develop in a vacuum. Writers and jurists in the twelfth, thirteenth, and later centuries had to consider outlawry as part of a larger legal landscape, a landscape in which the sanction of excommunication and its related punishment of unconsecrated burial were unmistakably present. Any pre-Christian ideas of outlawry would have been confronted continuously with the ideas of excommunication being presented by the current Church. It is reasonable that under these circumstances, outlawry would absorb features from the developing concept of excommunication, since the two sanctions, as we will see, were constantly contrasted and compared with each other and used in similar situations in lawcodes. My analysis will focus on evidence from Iceland and Norway, but I will also reference English sources, in which similar parallels between outlawry and excommunication have been drawn and from whence influence on Norway and Iceland cannot be ruled out.

I present my argument in four sections. First, I trace how previous scholars have addressed the similarities between outlawry and excommunication. Second, I present my understanding of the Icelandic lawbooks as sources, particularly *Grágás*; I will argue that we should approach the preserved texts of this lawbook as texts from a particular point in time, namely when they were put down on parchment in the thirteenth century. Third, I will compare outlawry as it appears in the Icelandic legal and literary sources with canonical excommunication. Fourth, I argue that outlawry was used as a sanction for

 | DOI:10.1163/9789004461468_005

breaches of Christian law more frequently than we might expect. I also emphasize the ways in which the laws treated outlawed men as excommunicants.

## 1 Previous Scholarship

Scholars have noted that excommunication and outlawry shared many features. Maitland, for example, referred to excommunication as "ecclesiastical outlawry."[1] Liebermann, who edited many of the Anglo-Saxon laws, was struck by the similarities between the two sanctions in some of his texts to the point that he suggested that the framing of outlawry in these texts was done by foreign clerics who had no other way of thinking about outlawry other than through the lens of excommunication.[2] Building on Liebermann's observations, Gösta Åqvist suspected that the compiler of the *Consiliatio Cnuti*, a text associated with the Anglo-Danish King Cnut/Knútr: "saw in the outlawry expression a direct correspondence to the canonical concept of excommunication."[3] Lára Magnúsardóttir, working with Old Norse evidence, suggested the possibility that the secular concept of outlawry and the word *útlegð* was used to translate excommunication into an intelligible form for readers of the vernacular, at least in the twelfth century.[4] Heidi Anette Øvergård Beistad, discussing the time in Iceland after the introduction of *Jónsbók*, suggests that it was rather with the introduction of uncompensatable crimes at this time that "the church's sanction [excommunication] received a worldly counterpart."[5]

1 Frederick Pollock and Frederic William Maitland, *The History of English Law before the Time of Edward I*, 2nd ed., 2 vols. (Cambridge: Cambridge University Press, 1898), 1.478.

2 Felix Liebermann, *Die Gesetze der Angelsachsen*, 3 vols. (1903–1916; repr., Aalen, Germany, 1960), 3.308, 330, 334.

3 Åqvist, *Frieden und Eidschwur*, 254. "In dem *utlag*-Ausdruck eine direkte Entsprechung zu dem kanonischen *excommunicatio*-Begriff zu sehen."

4 Lára Magnúsardóttir, *Bannfæring og kirkjuvald*, 46. "Hugsanlegt er að þörfin fyrir skýr lagahugtök hafi getið af sér norræna orðasambandið útlegð í kristni í merkingunni bannfæring á tólftu öld, með hugtakanotkun veraldlegu laganna að fyrirmynd." [It is possible that that need for clear legal concepts led to the coining of the Old Norse phrase 'outlawed in Christindom,' to mean excommunication in the twelfth century with the secular legal concept [i.e. of outlawry] as a model.]

5 Heidi Anette Øvergård Beistad, discussing the time in Iceland after the introduction of *Jónsbók*, suggests that it was rather with the introduction of uncompensatable crimes at this time (1281) that "kirkens sanksjon hadde dermed fått et verdslig motsvar," [the church's sanction [excommunication] received a worldly counterpart.], "Kirkens frihet: Biskop Arne Torlaksson som Islands reformator," (Master's thesis. NTNU, Trondheim, 2008), 55–56.

Scholars are more likely to observe rather than explain the similarities between the two sanctions. Perhaps this is because many writers focus primarily on either canon law or on local, often vernacular, lawcodes from an individual region. In this chapter I account for the similarities by arguing that there was not simply a chance resemblance, but rather direct intellectual influence of excommunication on outlawry. In this, I follow some of the arguments made over a century ago – and largely undiscussed in the context of Scandinavian laws – by Eduard Eichmann, who focused his research on the laws of high medieval Germany. Eichmann emphasized the connections between secular and ecclesiastical laws, arguing that many provisions in secular laws, not least those concerning outlawry, only make sense when interpreted in the light of contemporary canon law.[6]

Hinrich Siuts, coming from a perspective of folklore, has argued that outlawry derived from excommunication in northern Europe. He argues that "excommunication and outlawry shared not only a formal parallelism, due to the dependence of outlawry on excommunication, but also an inner parallelism, which in both of them were based on common foundations and roots—in folk belief about the presence of the dead."[7] As he signals already in the title of his book, *Bann und Acht und Ihre Grundlagen im Totenglauben*, which refers to beliefs about the dead, he sees the roots of both sanctions in a common belief that people banished from society whether by the Church or other authorities were, in essence, dead.[8] By this argument, both outlaws and excommunicants exited the world of the living until they were reintegrated back into society. Siuts focuses especially on rituals, such as the ringing of bells and closing of doors, associated with banishment from society and attested in sources about both excommunication and outlawry.[9]

Siuts focuses on a relatively limited source base for his discussion of excommunication, particularly documents from church councils, the *Decretum* of

6 Eduard Eichmann, *Acht und Bann im Reichsrecht des Mittelalters* (Paderborn: Ferdinand Schöningh, 1909), 3: "Viele Bestimmungen des mittelalterlichen weltlichen Rechts können nur im Zusammenhange mit dem kirchlichen Rechte ihre Erklärung finden." [Many provisions in medieval secular laws can only be understood when seen in comparison with canon law.]

7 Hinrich Siuts, *Bann und Acht und Ihre Grundlagen im Totenglauben* (Berlin: Walter de Gruyter, 1959), 144. "So zeigte sich bei Bann und Acht nicht nur eine formale Parallelität, bedingt durch die Abhängigkeit der Acht vom Bann, sondern auch eine innerliche, die in der beiden gemeinsamen Grundlage und Wurzel, den Volksanschauungen vom Dasein der Toten, begründet war."

8 Siuts, *Bann und Acht*, 80–144.

9 Siuts, *Bann und Acht*, 80–144.

Burchard of Worms, and the work of Regino of Prüm.[10] These sources, especially Regino, do discuss rituals for excommunication. It is difficult to assume a sustained, consistent set of rituals employed across hundreds of years, however. It is also difficult to say how often and to what degree such rituals were performed, especially if we consider how often they can be traced to a few written sources such as Burchard's *Decretum*.[11]

Siuts's attempt to account for the similarities between the sanctions as part of a common, long-standing set of folk beliefs is unconvincing. He is too ready to find ancient remnants in sources that are demonstrably themselves not ancient, such as Scandinavian lawcodes, whose manuscripts are in general not earlier than the thirteenth century. Nor does Siuts address the later developments in excommunication or outlawry in the twelfth and later centuries to any extent (although he does consider the development of excommunication in the early Church). I agree with Siuts's conclusion that outlawry was dependent on excommunication, but I reach it from a different reading of the evidence, and also for a more restricted chronological and geographical scope.

## 2 The Legal Sources, Reading *Grágás*

My argument is based on interpretation of the legal source material from medieval Iceland, especially the early vernacular law manuscripts collectively known as *Grágás*. It can be difficult to determine when and why these texts were produced and how people used them. Although there are early stories about the development of law in Iceland and in Scandinavia, the manuscripts of legal sources that survive are generally not earlier than the thirteenth century.

According to Ari Þorgilsson's *Íslendingabók* laws were first brought to Iceland from Norway by Úlfljótr in the early tenth century.[12] Ari also writes that at the General Assembly (Alþingi) of 1117 men decided that all the laws needed to be written down, a task to be completed at the farm of Hafliði Másson, according

10 Siuts, *Bann und Acht*, 6–13, 81–103.

11 As discussed in chapter 1. For a cautionary perspective on the overuse of the concept of "ritual" to explain medieval societies and texts see, Buc, *The Dangers of Ritual*. Burchard's *Decretum* appears to be a common source for rituals and descriptions of rituals associated with excommunication, including in Anglo-Saxon and, as I argue in chapter 1, Icelandic sources.

12 Ari Þorgilsson, *Íslendingabók*, ed. Jakob Benediktsson, 2: 6–7, trans. Grønlie, *Íslendingabók*, 2: 4–5.

to dictation of Bergþórr Hrafnsson, who was then the lawspeaker, and other wise men.[13] These early laws do not survive. It is possible, indeed probable, that a group of men learned in law under the leadership of Hafliði Másson put Icelandic customs down in writing at Breiðabólstaðr in 1117/1118,[14] but it is methodologically unwise to equate this Hafliðaskrá with either Konungsbók or Staðarhólsbók of *Grágás* – the two quite different versions of the text that have been preserved only in thirteenth-century manuscripts. The earliest manuscript fragment of Icelandic law is AM 315 d fol., a fragment of the land claims section dated to 1150–1175.[15] The two codices often referred to as *Grágás*, Konungsbók and Staðarhólsbók, were both produced in the mid- to late-thirteenth century.[16] Most of the surviving legal manuscripts from Scandinavia were produced in the mid- to late thirteenth century and later. The earliest surviving codes from Norway are the provincial lawcodes of the Gulathing and Frostathing.[17] The earliest surviving Swedish and Danish lawcodes, mostly of regional laws, are from the early to mid-thirteenth century.[18] These codes are firmly in the period after the 1150s when canon law was undergoing continuous codification and elaboration.

This is not to imply that every bit of law in these thirteenth-century manuscripts was brand new. Patrick Wormald has argued more broadly that medieval codes were not necessarily or always primarily produced to be useful as law texts or reference works, but had value at least as much as physical objects. He also argues that in the context of much medieval legal writing, people perceived old law as good law. This meant that lawbooks that preserved old law, even if it was irrelevant (or not particularly old) had value not tied to their

13 Ari Þorgilsson, *Íslendingabók*, ed. Jakob Benediktsson, 10: 23–24, trans. Grønlie, *Íslendingabók*, 10: 12.

14 Hans Henning Hoff, presents an imaginative but ultimately misguided hypothesis about Hafliði's possible knowledge of Roman law, acquired while in the Varangian guard in Constantinople, to account for the strong influence from Roman law visible in the two major *Grágás* manuscripts. Given that these manuscripts are at least 150 years younger than the no longer extant *Hafliðarskrá*, it seems just as likely that the Roman influences were introduced or strengthened later. *Hafliði Másson und die Einflüsse des römischen Rechts in der Grágás*. Ergänzungsbände zum Reallexikon der Germanischen Altertumskunde, vol. 78 (Berlin and Boston: De Gruyter, 2012), 129–175.

15 Hans Fix, "Laws," *Medieval Scandinavia: An Encyclopedia,* ed. by Phillip Pulsiano et al. (New York and London: Garland, 1993), 384–385.

16 Introduction to, *Grágás,* trans. Denis et al., 1.13–16.

17 KLNM 5.559–565, s.v. "Gulatingsloven (Gtl.)," by Trygve Knudsen; KLNM 4.656–661, s.v., 559-565, "Frostatingsloven," by Trygve Knudsen.

18 KLNM 10.228–233, s.v. "Landskabslove," by Stig Iuul and Jan Liedren.

practical use in current disputes.[19] In a Scandinavian context this is perhaps the best way to explain the tendency to attribute laws to St. Olaf, even laws that were likely written much later.[20]

A variety of scholars suggest that the *Grágás* manuscripts preserve laws that were at one time or another recognized as valid or customary but that were not necessarily reflective of the customs and rules in force at the time that any given manuscript was produced.[21] Moreover, many of the legal manuscripts of early Iceland are not preserved as discrete copies of an individual text. The Staðarhólsbók manuscript (AM 334 fol.), which contains one of the two early versions of *Grágás*, for example, also contains the only early copy of *Járnsíða*, the first of the codes sent from Norway to Iceland to replace previous law, including the *Grágás* text that precedes it in the manuscript.[22] This complicates any attempt to read the preserved manuscripts of *Grágás* as active legal documents, but it is also important to remember that codes like *Grágás* did not cease to be relevant or useful once they had been superseded. Parts of the Christian laws section of *Grágás* continued to be copied in the fifteenth century.[23]

We do not know precisely who made or commissioned the manuscripts of *Grágás* or why. The general consensus is that they were made for personal use

19 Patrick Wormald, *The Making of English Law: King Alfred to the twelfth century* (Oxford and Malden, Mass.: Blackwell, 1999), 3–263; Patrick Wormald, *Legal culture in the early medieval West: law as text, image and experience* (London: The Hambledon Press, 1999), 1–44.

20 Many laws in the earliest surviving Norwegian codes are explicitly attributed to St. Olaf, but in most cases, it is impossible to say whether they actually stemmed from him or were simply associated with him and thereby gained more authority.

21 Konrad Maurer, *Island von seiner ersten Entdeckung bis zum Untergange des Freistaats* (Munich: C. Kaiser, 1874), 471; introduction to, *Grágás*, trans. Denis et al., 1.ii; and Patricia Pires Boulhosa, "Layout and the Structure of the Text in *Konungsbók*," *The Power of the Book: Medial Approaches to Medieval Nordic Legal Manuscripts*, ed. by Lena Rohrbach, Berliner Beiträge zur Skandinavistik (Berlin: Nordeuropa-Institut der Humboldt-Universität, 2014), 94.

22 Rohrbach, "Matrix of the Law?" 99.

23 There are at least four copies of the Christian laws section of *Grágás* from the fourteenth century: AM 346 fol., AM 347 fol., AM 351 fol., and AM 135 4to. The traditional argument is that Árni's Christian lawcode was first accepted only in the diocese of Skálaholt, and that the Christian laws in *Grágás* remained in use in the diocese of Hólar until 1354. This claim is based on a letter of King Magnús Eriksson from the year 1354, which specifies that all of Iceland should use the same Christian law, that which held over the southern diocese of Skálaholt. *Diplomatarium Islandicum,* 3.98. More recent scholarship argues that this assumption is inaccurate and that Árni's Christian laws were in force throughout Iceland from 1275, a view that I share. See, Magnús Lyngdal Magnússon, "Kátt er þeim af kristinrétti," 43–90; and Lára Magnúsardóttir, *Bannfæring og kikjuvald*, 303–305.

by individuals. Patricia Boulhosa emphasizes that the "private" nature of these manuscripts does not preclude their preserving laws that were generally recognized as valid or customary.[24] These different points of departure emphasize the intractable problem of how to estimate what *Grágás* is, whose voices it speaks in, or whose agenda it speaks for. Thomas McSweeney, to cite one example, has suggested that one way of reading *Grágás* is to consider it as a nostalgic image of how society was in the past, before the civil chaos and royal interference that ended the Sturlung period.[25] Gwyn Jones suggests a similar view, calling the compilers of *Grágás* "legalistic romancers," although he makes the claim with no particular reference to an ideal past.[26] There will probably never be complete consensus about the nature of *Grágás* as a law text, but it is undeniable that the manuscripts are from the second half of the thirteenth century.

Moreover, there is evidence to suggest that the manuscripts of *Grágás*, particularly Konungsbók, were not conceived of as complete representations of the law at any given time but rather were intended, even at the time of their creation, to refer to a wider group of texts and manuscripts, an idea that Helgi Skúli Kjartansson suggests in his discussion of the use of Latin terms, especially *usque* in the *Grágás* manuscripts.[27] Or the idea, suggested by Lena Rohrbach, that some legal manuscripts were prepared at least in part to aid in the compilation and codification of new laws.[28]

These approaches address *Grágás*, or the manuscripts of *Grágás*, as products of a particular context. They do not preclude the possibility that these manuscripts contain provisions that were generally accepted and followed by many people in Iceland, but nor do they assume that *Grágás* is primarily statute law provisions that were generally agreed upon and followed. Moreover, especially in early medieval societies, such formal law codices existed alongside other mechanisms for social regulation, including informal agreements, mediated settlements, and feuding.[29] Lawcodes were not and should not be

---

24 Patricia Pires Boulhosa, "Ideals and Aspirations: Democracy and Law-Making in Mediaeval Iceland," *The Secret History of Democracy*, ed. by Benjamin Isakhan and Stephen Stockwell (London: Palgrave Macmillan, 2011), 92–104.

25 McSweeney, "Law and Fiction in Medieval Iceland: The Story in the *Grágás* Manuscripts," American Society for Legal History's pre-conference workshop, 2014.

26 Jones, "*Fjörbaugsgarðr*," 161.

27 Helgi Skúli Kjartansson, "Quousque? Um latínuglósur í Grágásarlögum," *Heimtur, Ritgerðir til heiðurs Gunnari Karlssyni sjötugum*, ed. by Guðmundur Jónsson et al. (Reykjavík, 2009), 201–214.

28 Rohrbach, "Matrix of the Law?" 125.

29 See, for example, Paul Hyams, *Rancor and Reconciliation in Medieval England* (Ithaca and London: Cornell University Press, 2003). The argument is frequently made about medieval

taken as a complete reflection of the law either in general or at the time they were produced. It is impossible to be certain about precisely why and to what ends any one manuscript was produced or the ways in which it was subsequently employed (or ignored). There is no one answer to the question of what these lawcodes were. Within these limitations, I base the following arguments on the texts that these manuscripts contain and the way that they present excommunication and outlawry.

## 3 Similarities between Excommunication and Outlawry

In a Scandinavian medieval context, basic features of excommunication and outlawry were similar. They both deprived affected individuals of their standing as members of the community. Both were designed for systems that lacked strong executive power and enforcement and relied on community enforcement, being largely ineffective without it.

If we compare details concerning excommunication from canon law texts and the material about outlawry in *Grágás*, other similarities emerge. As discussed in chapter 1, excommunication could be contagious. The traditional penalty from as early as the third century C.E. for associating with or aiding an excommunicant was excommunication.[30] In the ninth century, some writers began to try and soften this provision, suggesting that forty days of penance, for example, should be the penalty for willingly associating with an excommunicated person.[31] In 1078 Pope Gregory VII issued the canon *Quoniam multos* which provided that wives, children, or other dependents, including servants, could still speak with their excommunicated family member without incurring the sentence themselves, but a person's social equals could not.[32]

In vernacular Scandinavian codes of the thirteenth century, directly helping an outlaw could give rise to a sentence of outlawry for the person helping. In *Grágás* this is often not full outlawry but rather the "lesser outlawry" sentence of *fjǫrbaugsgarðr*.[33] This keeps it in parallel with minor excommunication as

Iceland, probably most strongly by William Ian Miller, *Bloodtaking and Peacemaking*, 179–299.

30 Vodola, *Excommunication*, 16–17.

31 Vodola, *Excommunication*, 17.

32 Vodola, *Excommunication*, 24.

33 *Grágás Staðarhólsbók*, Vígslóði 382, ed. Finsen 2.402, trans. Denis et al., 1.238: If men meet an outlaw and "they barter with him or have any other kind of exchange, or give him advice so that he is closer to saving his life than he was before, that is assistance for him and the penalty is lesser outlawry. Anything men do or any advice men give so that

the sanction for aiding an excommunicant. A similar provision occurs in the Norwegian Frostathing Law in the section on The Law of Personal Rights: "If a man gives food or shelter to an outlaw or conveys him or guides him, he shall lose all his rights and shall suffer the same form of outlawry as the other who did the deed […] But even though he harbors one whose outlawry has been published in the [district], if he does not know him, he does it unwittingly and may defend himself with a threefold oath."[34] These lawcodes do not suggest an entirely uniform approach, however. Perhaps strangest is a provision in the older Gulathing Law that allows an outlaw fleeing by boat to be thrown an oar or other piece of boating equipment and no more.[35] This passage defies easy

---

an outlaw is closer to saving his life than he was before is assistance to him, no matter whether whatever is deemed assistance is large or small." *Grágás Konungsbók,* þingskapa-þáttr 73, ed. Finsen 1a.122–123, trans. Denis et al., 1.121. "The chieftain to whose assembly group the man prosecuted belongs is to be called on to form [a panel] of twelve to give a verdict on whether that man had shared living quarters with the outlaw or not and thereby given him assistance." *Grágás Konungsbók,* þingskapa-þáttr 59, ed. Finsen 1a.108, trans. Denis et al. 1.108. "If men are outlawed at a spring assembly and are sustained between the time the confiscation court is held for them and the time their outlawry is reported at Lögberg, the penalty is lesser outlawry and the summons in that suit is to be made locally and the chieftain to whose assembly group the man prosecuted belongs is to be called on to form a panel of twelve. But such sustaining of men who are outlawed at a spring assembly carries a penalty only for those who hear of his outlawry." Ignorance could be a defence: *Grágás Konungsbók,* þingskapa-þáttr 77, ed. Finsen, 1a.127, trans. Denis et al., 1.125. Sometimes the penalty for assisting an outlaw was dependent on the timing of when such assistance was given. *Grágás Konungsbók,* þingskapa-þáttr 55, ed. Finsen, 1a.94–95. trans. Denis et al., 1.97: "If a confiscation court has not been held, he is to have the testimony given in the Quarter Court which should have been given in the confiscation court if it had been held. Now, as soon as anyone has been prosecuted for assisting this outlaw in the manner now told and that testimony has come before the Quarter Court, [or, possibly, confiscation court], the penalty is full outlawry for anyone who assists that outlaw thereafter, and such people are to be prosecuted before the Fifth Court; but prosecution of those who had assisted him prior to that remains as rehearsed earlier." See also, *Grágás Staðarhólsbók,* Vígslóði 380, ed. Finsen 2.397–398, trans. Denis et al., 380; 1.236. The sanction for allowing an outlaw that one had previously condemned go free was outlawry. A similar provision is also in *Grágás Konungsbók,* Vígslóði 110, ed. Finsen, 1a.189. trans. Denis et al., 1.171. "A man is not required to kill an outlaw, unless he was the one who got him condemned, even if he happens to meet him to speak to, as long as he does not capture him and gives him no saving advice."

34 *Ældre Frostathings-Lov (IV),* 41, ed. R. Keyser and P.A. Munch, *Norges gamle love,* 1.170. trans. Larson, *Earliest Norwegian Laws,* 274. "Ef maðr ell mann útlagan eðr húsar. flytr eða forer. þá er sá útlagr oc úheilagr slícre útlegð sem hinn er vercit vann […] En þá at hann ale mann þann er hann cann eigi oc er lýst innan fylkis. þá er honum óvísa vargr. þá scal hann hafa ryrir ser lýritar eið."

35 *Den elder Gulatingslova,* 153, ed. Eithun et al., 110, trans. Larson, 129: "Nv rennr mannzbane til skips. þa ma maðr at usecku skiota út efter hanom ár. æða austker. æða styrí. æða

interpretation, not least because the scenario imagined seems rather unlikely, but it cautions against the idea that there was a uniform response to the issue of helping outlaws in different lawcodes.

The offense of knowingly hosting an outlaw or providing him with help was also sanctioned with a fine in some codes, particularly in *Jónsbók* and in early Norwegian codes.[36] In *Jónsbók* the provision reads that: "If someone, whether a householder or any other man, houses and shelters an outlaw or eats or drinks with him, then he is fined one mark to the king for one night, and two marks for two nights. But if the outlaw is with him for three nights, provided that he was declared an outlaw within the host's district, then the host is fined thirteen marks to the king, unless he did not know that the other had been outlawed when he offered him shelter. The charge against the host shall never be greater than the other's was when he was declared an outlaw. And the sheriff is legally required to publish his outlawry at the assembly on the same day as he learns that he has committed the act of an outlaw."[37] In this passage helping an outlaw is more or less synonymous with hosting an outlaw, the offense growing as the days passed.

The emphasis on hospitality and sharing, particularly sharing food with an outlaw, is a repeated theme in these texts. In the older Gulathing Law the role of an outlaw's wife is specifically addressed: "A wife may with impunity provide her husband with food for five nights after the judgment has befallen him. If he remains longer on his own invitation, let her go to her neighbors and report that he [her husband] is staying on his own invitation; then she is blameless."[38] Here, as in *Quoniam multos*, being a dependent of an outlaw is explicitly addressed. As in the canon, a wife is still expected to provide food to her outlawed husband and, so long as she declares that he stays at his own invitation, she is not implicated with him in the sanction. It is not accidental that these provisions about sustaining an outlaw focus not just on help, but also on the acts of eating with and sharing with an outlaw, of being in communion with him or her. Eating a meal in these cases is, I argue, a deliberate parallel

---

skutpilíu. æða einhvern grip þeírra. oc eigi fleiri. En ef hann gerír meira at. þa flytr hann utlagan mann. oc líggr hanom við .xl. marca."

36 *Den elder Gulatingslova*, 152, 202, ed. Eithun et al., 110, 125–126, trans. Larson, *Earliest Norwegian Laws*, 129, 145–146. *Ældre Frostathings-Love*, 12, ed. R. Keyser and P.A. Munch, *Norges gamle love*, 1.123., trans. Larson, *Earliest Norwegian Laws*, 217.

37 *Jónsbók*, 4.6, ed. Ólafur Halldórsson, 42–43., trans, Schulman, *Jónsbók*, 45.

38 *Den elder Gulatingslova*, 203, ed. Eithun et al., 126, trans. Larson, *Earliest Norwegian Laws*, 146. "kona ma føða bonda sínn netr .v. at u/secku. siðan domr kemr a hendr hanom. en ef hann sítr þar lengr slímu setr. þa scal hon ganga til granna sínna. oc segia til at hann sítr þar slímu setr. þa er hon usecc."

with the communion of the Eucharist that excommunicants were forbidden from sharing.

### 3.1 *Legal Formulations*

Another similarity comes from the manuscripts themselves, from the fact that we are comparing different types of written law. The ways of presenting legal material in text were drawn from Latin models (the production of legal texts was not particularly earlier in Norway or the other Scandinavian countries than in Iceland.) At a more specific level, the idea of presenting hypothetical legal situations with an anonymous N.N. for *nescio nomen* "I do not know the name," as is done in Staðarhólsbók, is a clear adoption of the tools of Latin law into *Grágás*.[39] A striking application of the tools and methods of Latin legal writing occurs in the way that *Grágás* presents and uses lesser outlawry.

### 3.2 **Lesser Outlawry in *Grágás* and Minor Excommunication**

As discussed in chapter 2, Icelandic lesser outlawry is a difficult sanction to understand fully, not least because the same word, *fjǫrbaugsgarðr*, covers a wide range of sanctions, including fines and banishment. In *Grágás*, however, lesser outlawry sometimes takes on a function similar to minor excommunication. I suggest, although definitive proof is impossible, that the way in which lesser outlawry is used in *Grágás* was inspired by the sanction of minor excommunication. This fits chronologically with the development of minor excommunication as a sanction and is the best available explanation for the use of the sanction in *Grágás*, when it is unattested in this format in almost all other sources.

Canonists increasingly made a distinction between major and minor excommunication, especially in the thirteenth century. The influential Goffredus of Trano (d. 1245), for example, separated the two sanctions in the mid-thirteenth century as discussed in chapter 1.[40] We do not know precisely when or how quickly such knowledge reached Iceland, but Goffredus's work was available there by the early fourteenth century,[41] and it is also worth bearing in mind

39 For examples of this usage see *Grágás Staðarhólsbók*. Um fiárleigor 249, 250; Vígslóði 277, 283; ed. Finsen, 2.281, 282, 305–308, 315, trans. Denis et al., 1.207–208, 210, 213. See also, introduction to *Grágás*, trans. Denis et al., 1.19; and Rohrbach, "Matrix of the Law?" 123.

40 Gottofredo da Trani (Goffredus Tranensis), *Summa super titulis Decretalium* (Lyon, 1519. Reprint Aalen: Scientia, 1968), 491–492, Title 539. Available at: http://works.bepress.com/david_freidenreich/17. See also, Hans Walther, *Lateinische Sprichwörter und Sentenzen des Mittelalters in alphabetischer Anordnung* (Göttigen: Vandenhoeck und Ruprecht, 1967), 5.573 (32696).

41 Fol. 19v of AM 544 4to (Hauksbók) contains a fragment of a translation into Old Norse-Icelandic of Goffredus's *Summa decratalium*, discussing interactions with

that canon law concepts were often in general recognized use before they were given an explicit definition by canonists.

This adoption is all the more likely if we consider Gwyn Jones's argument about how the meaning of *fjǫrbaugsgarðr* changed over time. He argues that the concept of lesser outlawry did not exist in early Iceland (870–1030). He suggests that the word *fjǫrbaugsgarðr* meant a type of sanctuary, not necessarily for a defined period of time or associated with a court of confiscation. He bases his reasoning on the contradictions and different uses of *fjǫrbaugsgarðr* in different sagas and law texts as well as its use in *Njáls saga*, one of the few sagas in which *fjǫrbaugsgarðr* resembles the sanction outlined in *Grágás*.[42] *Fjǫrbaugsgarðr* is a particular, difficult case. It is not the only place that influence from canon law appears in the secular laws. Perhaps the clearest point of overlap occurs in the treatment of dead outlaws.

## 3.3 *Burial in Consecrated Ground*

As discussed in chapter 1, although it was not an intrinsic part of the sanction, excommunicants were often denied burial in consecrated ground. It was possible for them to be posthumously absolved and reburied in the churchyard, but it seems clear that this was a potential consequence of excommunication that most people were at pains to avoid.[43] Consecrated burial features in some of the earliest preserved sources from Iceland, including the Icelandic Homily Book (ca. 1200), which emphasizes that churches are a place for *sáttar fundr* "a meeting for reconciliation" between God and men and that "when a person dies, their body should be brought to church and buried there, and there clerics (*kennimenn*) give their soul unto God with frequent prayers and masses for the soul."[44] This suggests that the practice of consecrated burial was familiar from quite soon after the conversion of Iceland, particularly if we consider that

excommunicants, i.e. minor excommunication. Finnur Jónsson (ed.), *Hauksbók*, 1.187. See also, Elizabeth Ashman Rowe, "Literary, Codicological, and Political Perspectives on Hauksbók," *Gripla* 19 (2008): 57. This same passage is also in AM 351 fol. (Skálholtsbók eldri), which in addition has a passage from Raymond of Penyafort's *Summa*. Westergård-Nielsen, introduction to, *Skálholtsbók Eldri*, 20.

42 Jones, "*Fjörbaugsgarðr*," 155–163.

43 Marafioti, "Unconsecrated Burial and Excommunication," 86–99; Vodola, *Excommunication*, 38–39; and Nilsson, *De sepulturis*, 242–290. See also, chapter 1, pages 13–15.

44 *The Icelandic Homily Book*, ed. de Leeuw van Weenen, 45r: "Þa es maþr andasc, þa skal líkam hans til kirkio féora oc þar grafa. oc skolo þar kenemen fela á hende goþe aond hans meþ oftlegom beonom og sælo saongom." (orthography simplified from the diplomatic edition); *Íslensk Hómilíubók*, ed. Sigurbjörn Einarsson, Guðrún Kvaran and Gunnlaugur Ingólfsson, 148.

it is likely that the Icelandic Homily Book is based on earlier vernacular copies. Archeological records also suggest that consecrated burial or at least burial at churches began to be practiced in Iceland soon after the conversion.[45]

The earliest surviving Icelandic and Norwegian lawcodes forbid consecrated burial not only to excommunicated persons and the unbaptized, but also to various criminals and in some cases specifically outlaws.[46] The longest passage about burial and the most often cited reads as follows in the Konungsbók manuscript of *Grágás*: "There are four classes of corpse not to be buried at church. The first is the corpse of someone who dies unbaptized. The second is the corpse of a full outlaw who may not be sustained or given passage; it is not to be buried at church unless the bishop with jurisdiction in that Quarter permits. But if the bishop permits it, the body may be taken to church. The third corpse not to be buried at church is of someone who willfully inflicts on himself the injuries that cause his death, unless he afterwards repents and confesses to a priest, and then he is to be buried at church [...] The fourth corpse not to be buried at church is of anyone the bishop sees fit to ban from burial at church."[47] These bodies are also not to receive services for the dead.[48] This passage does not suggest, and certainly does not prove, that outlaws were automatically excommunicated.[49] Rather it suggests that the default treatment of full outlaws after death was not to permit them church burial, although the final authority was left with the bishop, who could make his own determination. In Konungsbók there is also a provision that if a man had no right to enter a church while he was alive, his body is not to be taken into church.[50] Outlaws

45 Orri Vésteinsson, *The Christianization of Iceland: Priests, Power*, 45–57.

46 Discussed in more detail by Nilsson, *De sepulturis*, 228–290.

47 *Grágás Konungsbók*, Kristinna laga þáttr 2, ed. Finsen, 1a.12, trans. Denis et al., 1.30. "Fiogur ero lik þav er eigi scal at kirkio grafa. þat er lik eitt. ef maþr andazk öskirþr. annat er skogar manz lik. þess er öæll er. oc öferiandi. þat scal oc eigi at kirkio grafa. nema byskop sa lofi er yfir fiorþvngi þeim er. En ef byskop lofa. oc scal þa til kirkio færa. Þat er lik it þriþia er eigi scal at kirkio grafa. ef maþr viþr a ser verk þav er honvum verþa at bana. sva at hann vildi vnnit hafa. nema hann fáe iþrvn siþan. oc gangi til scriptar við prest. oc scal þa grafa hann at kirkio ... þat er lik it .iiij. er eigi scal at kirkio grafa ef byskop vill bannat hafa at grafa at kirkio. þat lik er eigi a at kirkio lægt."

48 *Gragás Konungsbók*, Kristinna laga þáttr 2, ed. Finsen, 1a.12. trans. Denis et al, 1. 30. "oc syngva eigi liksong yfir."

49 Cf. Kirsten Hastrup, *Culture and history*, 139: "Finally, according to *Kristinna laga þáttr*, the Christian law by which the original law was supplemented some time after the acceptance of Christianity (AD 1000), a *skogarmaðr* was automatically excommunicated and might not be given a Christian burial."

50 *Grágás Konungsbók*, Kristinna laga þáttr 2, ed. Finsen, 1a.8. trans. Denis et al., 1.27. "eigi scal þess manz lik i kircio bera er eigi atti kircio genkt. meþan hann lifþi."

were almost certainly not permitted in churches (see the section below, outlaws at the church door), but this might also be a reference to excommunicants, who are never directly mentioned in *Grágás*, at least in the major manuscripts.

Surviving Icelandic laws are more explicit than the Norwegian ones concerning outlaws as a specific group with regards to burial. In the older Frostathing law it reads: "Every Christian shall be buried at the church and his body must normally be brought to the church within five nights, unless he was by intent his own banesman or was separated from the Christian faith [i.e. was excommunicated] while he was still living; but if he lost his life through negligence, he shall be buried at the church."[51] The older Gulathing law on burial mentions a category of offenders *udaða menn*, whom we might think of as outlaws, which it further breaks down into different types of offenders. It reads "every man who dies shall be brought to church and buried in hallowed earth, excepting only *udaða menn*, traitors, murderers, truce breakers, thieves, and men who take their own lives."[52] This list details more specific actions that barred a person from church burial, but *udaða menn*, are listed first, as the overarching category before the more specific offenders. As discussed above, the precise meaning of *udaða menn*, beyond the general sense of "criminals" is not entirely clear, but here, given that it demanded unconsecrated burial, it seems likely to have been a category of severe, socially disruptive crimes.

In the Kristinna laga þáttr in *Grágás*, not only were certain bodies forbidden consecrated burial, bringing such bodies for burial in consecrated ground was also a punishable offense. Also in the Konungsbók manuscript we find: "If a man takes a body to church which had no right to church burial, the penalty is lesser outlawry, unless he can get a verdict that he thought that man had the right to church burial, and he must have it taken away within a fortnight of the end of the assembly, and atone to the church for the desecration with twelve ounce-units."[53] Here not only is compensation required

51 *Ældre Frostathings Lov*, 2.15, ed. R. Keyser and P.A. Munch, *Norges gamle love*, 1.135–136., trans. Larson, *Earliest Norwegian Laws*, 232. "Kristin mann huærn skal at kirkiu grafa oc til kirkiu hafa fort lik innan fim natta nauðsynia laust. nema þan er ser banar sealfr at sinum vilia eða hann hafe veret fra kristni skilder meðan hann uar lifs. En ef vaða verk værðr þa ma at kirkiu grafa." (translation modified).

52 *Den elder Gulatingslova*, 23, ed. Eithun et al., 46, trans. Larson, *Earliest Norwegian Laws*, 51. "Þat er nu þvi nest at mann hvern scal til kirkíu føra er dauðr verðr. oc grava i iorð helga. nema udaða menn. drottens svica. oc morðvarga. tryggrova. oc þiova. oc þa menn er sialver spilla ond sínní."

53 *Grágás Konungsbók*, Kristinna laga þáttr 2, ed. Finsen, 1a.11–12. trans. Denis et al., 1.30: "Ef maþr ferir lik þat til kirkio er eigi atti at kirkio legt. oc varþar þat fiorbavgs garþ. nema hann geti þann quid. at hann hygði at sa maþr ætti kirkio legt. oc scal hann fra hafa fært á xiiij. nottom envm næstvm eptir þing lávsm. oc bæta lavstinn kirkionni xij. avrvm."

even (or perhaps only) in cases of ignorance of the full facts about a body, the compensation is paid to the church. It seems likely that the reference is to the precise church building that has been wronged or desecrated by a body that should not have been permitted to be buried within its consecrated ground. It is a bit as if the church building becomes a wronged individual person, although other interpretations are possible. It is not only outlaws that could bring this defilement but also other criminals and, notably, suicides. There is a strong Christian tradition that those who commit suicide should not be granted consecrated burial.[54]

AM 173 c 4to, a mid-fourteenth century manuscript that contains part of the Christian laws section of *Grágás* and some of Árni's Christian laws, contains a formula that seems to refer to this same provision. It reads "[I name witnesses to witness] that I summon N.N. because he carried or caused to be carried to church the body of that man N.N. when he had no right to church burial. I claim that he owes a fine of three marks for that and should atone to the church for its desecration with twelve ounce-units. I summon it to the assembly."[55] Here compensation is demanded both for the offense and in compensation to the church, in this case seemingly the individual building violated.

The Staðarhólsbók manuscript of *Grágás* considers the possibility that a body found in the wilderness might be that of an outlaw and thus not required to be brought for burial. It reads: "If a man finds a body in the countryside, he is to cover the corpse so that beasts do not prey upon it and tell the man who lives nearest and who has two serving men over and above himself. And this man is to bring it to church as soon as possible, or else he is fined three marks, unless they know of no one not under legal penalty missing and think it is the

54 Suicide was grounds for denial of prayers for the dead in Gratian's *Decretum* C. 23 q. 5 c. 12 (second recension), ed. Friedberg, 1.935. In C. 13 q. 2 c. 16 (second recension) of the *Decretum* those whose sins have not been forgiven are also said not to benefit from burial in "holy places:" "a sacris locis non iuuantur post mortem quibus peccata dimissa non sunt." This passage is attributed to St. Augustine in the *Decretum* (also in the *Decretum* of Burchard of Worms and in the *Decretum* of Ivo of Chartes), but according to Friedberg it is actually a combination of texts from Gregory the Great's *Dialogues* and might also be traced to the Council of Tribur, Gratian, *Decretum*, ed. Friedberg, 1.726. The *Decretum* of Gratian itself is not as focused on consecrated burial or its denial as such as the the Nordic lawcodes seem to be. The major commentators on the *Liber extra* (the decretalists) all include suicide as grounds for unconsecrated burial. See Nilsson, *De sepulturis*, 260–267. In Archbishop Eilifr's statute of 1320 only a bishop is permitted to posthumously absolve suicide victims, and hence allow posthumous reburial in consecrated ground, *Norges gamle love*, 3.247.

55 *Grágás* AM 173 c 4to, ed. Finsen, 3.278–279. trans. Denis et al., 1.203.

body of an outlaw" in which case it seems that the body should be left or buried at the spot.[56]

Unconsecrated burial was also something that at least one provision in Konungsbók suggest a person could specifically demand when prosecuting cases involving someone who violated a woman and was killed on account of this offense. It reads: "If a man has killed a man on account of a woman for whom he has the right to kill, he is to summon the dead man […] 'I claim that all his goods are under penalty. I claim that he fell with forfeit immunity,' and if he wishes to state it in these terms, that he has no right to church burial."[57] This is notable both for its mention of the denial of church burial and the suggestion that this was something that the person prosecuting such a case was entitled to have some say over, it was not a requirement or automatic consequence as articulated in this passage.

Árni Þorláksson's Christian laws for Iceland, accepted at the Alþingi in 1275, show influence from Norwegian models, in this case specifically the newer Christian laws for the Gulathing law province.[58] On burial it reads: "Every Christian man who dies shall be buried in consecrated ground but not in the church unless the bishop has given permission. Wrongdoers should not be buried in consecrated ground, namely, traitors, murderers, trucebreakers, *griðníðingar* ("peace or sanctuary breakers,") condemned thieves, *flugu menn* ("assassins, hired killers,") excommunicants, public robbers, those who die under church ban, and those who kill or harm themselves by their own hand unless they did so unintentionally."[59] This code is moving away from a focus on

56 *Grágás Staðarhólsbók*, Kristinna laga þáttr 7, ed. Finsen, 2.9, trans. Denis et al., 1.198.

57 *Grágás Konungsbók*, Vígslóði 90, ed. Finsen, 1a.165, trans. Denis et al., 1.155. "Ef maðr hefir vegit man vm kono er hann avigt vm. Oc scal hann stefna enom davða manne […] tel ec sect fe hans allt. Tel ec hann ohælgan hafa fallit oc eiga eigi kirkio lægt af hann vill sva at queþa."

58 On the use of Norwegian lawcodes in Árni's Christian law see, Magnús Lyngdal Magnússon, introduction to, "Kristinréttur Árna frá 1275: Athugun á efni og varðveizlu í miðaldahandritum," (Master's thesis, University of Iceland, 2002), 76–137, and *Norges gamle love*, 5.850–852, which contains a table of correspondences between different late thirteenth-century Christian lawcodes from Norway, including the Kristinréttr Árna.

59 Árni Þorláksson, "Kristinréttur Árna," chap. 18, ed. Magnús Lyngdal Magnússon, 163. See also, *Kristinréttur*, 11, in *Járnsíða og Kristinréttur Árna Þorlákssonar*, ed. Haraldur Bernharðsson, Magnús Lyngdal Magnússon, and Már Jónsson, 156. "[H]vern mann cristinn sem deyr scal iarþa ikirkio garþi vigðvm. en eigi ikirkio nema byscops se lof til. Vdaða menn scal eigi ikirkio garði grafa. sem erv drotins svikar. morðingiar. trygrofa. griðniðingar. þiofar dæmðir. flugu menn. bannsættir menn. oc opinberir ransmenn. oc þeir sem dæyia i forboþi heilagrar kirkio. oc þeir sem hendr leggia asic oc tyna sialfvm ser nema *uaða uerc værþi." (orthography simplified).

outlaws and suicides and instead gives a more exhaustive list of those not to be buried at church including both those under excommunication *bannsettir menn* and those who died *í forboði heilagrar kirkju* (under minor excommunication?). Árni's terminology is different from *Grágás*, indeed this passage is derived from the Gulathing law, and the terms that he uses for excommunication are those seen also in the bishops' sagas. It is possible that one of these terms meant major excommunication and one minor, but it is difficult to be certain that Árni was making this precise distinction.[60] Outlaws are not here given specific mention. Perhaps the provisions from *Grágás* about outlaws still held, although perhaps outlaws were deemed a less important concern than these other offenders. Árni's law also provides that a bishop must *hreinsa* "clean" any grave in a churchyard that had been occupied by the body of an excommunicant.[61] This "cleaning" is to be done with *vigðo vatni* "holy water."[62] This provision suggests that it was self-evident that excommunicants should not receive consecrated burial, although no such "cleaning" is specified in connection with the graves of other criminals that could be denied consecrated burial in the same code.

At the end of the thirteenth century, it seems that provisions for denying offenders convicted of certain secular crimes consecrated burial was seen as a custom that was acceptable to continue, in part because it might serve as a deterrent to future offenses. In a statue attributed to Bishop Árni Þorláksson (d. 1298) it is stipulated that everyone, including those notorious for their bad conduct, should be buried in the churchyard so long as they showed at or near the time of their death, that they were "reconciled with the Holy Church" with the exception of those who, "according to the custom of the land should not be buried at church" the statue then switches from Old Norse-Icelandic to Latin and specifies that these were people "such as thieves and brigands, who were condemned to death for their evil doing, as a deterrent to others."[63]

60 According to some writers the bar for being denied consecrated burial was pretty low, with some suggesting that even those not taking yearly confession be denied it, Nilsson, *De sepulturies*, 264. Interdict forbid consecrated burial to all those in the area under it, Nilsson, 291.

61 Árni Þorláksson, "Kristinréttr Árna," chap. 12, ed. Magnús Lyngdal Magnússon, 158: "Sva hit sama scal ok hreinsa þar sem bannsettr maþr hefir verit grafinn ikirkio garþi."

62 Árni Þorláksson, "Kristinréttr Árna," chap. 12, ed. Magnús Lyngdal Magnússon, 158.

63 *Diplomatarium Islandicum*, 2.27. "at þeir se j sætt uid heilaga kirkiv at fra teknum þeim sem eptir landz sid ero eigi at kirkiu grafnir sicut fures et latrones qui pro suis sceleribus morte condempna[n]tur. Et hoc ad terrorem." The statue appears in a number of manuscripts, including several important fourteenth-century codices such as AM 350 fol. (Skarðsbók) and AM 671 4to.

This passage of Latin is probably derived from Gratian's *Decretum* (C. 13 q. 2 c. 31) or the ordinary gloss on this text, which discuss who and whom should be permitted consecrated burial.[64] Here is further evidence that denial of consecrated burial to certain secular offenders was seen as an established custom in Iceland by the end of the thirteenth century.

Clearly burial was an important concern in these laws. There are as many stipulations about burial as there are for baptism. The bookends of a Christian life were defended, and preventing improper persons from being buried in consecrated ground occupied significant space in the Christian laws. There are differences between early Norwegian and Icelandic codes, with Icelandic codes addressing outlaws as a specific category of persons (or rather non-persons) and the limits and contagious dangers of their existence in more detail. What makes the *Grágás* provisions odd is that the number of offenses that could lead to outlawry was both diverse and extensive, and, at least by the thirteenth century, the likelihood of an outlawry being almost purely political was high. This holds even if we assume that only full outlaws were forbidden consecrated burial.

Bertil Nilsson has suggested that these provisions in *Grágás* were translating outlawry into Christian idiom in the sense that "all those guilty of serious violent crimes of the sort that the canonists would classify under the category *excommunicatio latae sententiae* [excommunication that fell automatically for committing a deed, like assaulting a cleric, that by its very nature was against the Church and Christian community, these offense required no prior warning to cease the behavior, the behavior itself was deemed anti-Christian enough to merit automatic sanction] and thus forbidden church burial, are fit under the category *skóggangr*."[65] This is an interesting suggestion but it assumes, as do other suggestions about translating excommunication into the vernacular cited above, that a major difficulty of crafting a vernacular Christian lawcode was a lack of vocabulary. Perhaps this was the case, but given the length, diversity, and amount of descriptive material present in *Grágás*, it seems unlikely that the reason that excommunication *latae sententiae* was not mentioned specifically was that it implied the same offenses that would lead to full outlawry.

64 Gratian, *Decretum*, C. 13 q. 2 c. 30; Gloss. Ord. Ad C. 23 qu. 5 c. 11, ed. *Corpus Juris Canonicii*, vol. 1 *Decretum Gratianii, emendatum et notationibus illustratum, Una cum glossis* (Rome, 1582), col. 1776. http://digital.library.ucla.edu/canonlaw/index.html (last accessed 27 April 2020).

65 Nilsson, *De Sepulturis*, 278: "Sålunda innefattas i begreppet *skóggangr* alla dem som gjort sig skyldiga till grövre våldsbrott av det slag som enligt den kanoniska rätten ledde till *excommunicatio latae sententiae* och därmed följande begravningsförbud."

It seems more likely that the Christian laws were formulated to define membership in Christian society (through burial and baptism) and that those formulating these laws were in little doubt that full outlaws, at least, were outside of those boundaries.

## 3.4 *Outlawry and the Soul*

Burial in consecrated or unconsecrated ground could serve as a proxy or indirect statement about the likely status of a person's soul. Excommunication as effective damnation seems to have been a common early medieval understanding, particularly when combined with such a visible dislocation from Christian society as unconsecrated burial.[66] As mentioned in chapter 1, however, the connection between unconsecrated burial, excommunication, and damnation was neither absolute nor universal. The idea of consecrated burial was itself an idea that developed over centuries, focused on the idea of burial *ad sanctos*, near the graves of Christian martyrs and saints.[67] Over time, however, it is clear that at least in northern Europe consecrated burial came to be seen as a Christian norm that conferred potential benefits on the souls of the dead.[68]

It is difficult to pinpoint precisely when excommunication became firmly linked to burial in unconsecrated ground. The precedent for the idea is old, as we have seen in the provision from Pope Leo I, but the establishment of Christian graveyards and the expectation that everyone in a community would be buried in consecrated ground and hence the construction of unconsecrated burial as a punishment is a development that is harder to trace precisely. The idea seems to be firmly established in Iceland by the time of the earliest surviving Icelandic legal codes, but it has been suggested, for example, that in early Anglo-Saxon England, the connection between excommunication and unconsecrated burial was not yet universally established, even as the idea of

66 See further discussion in chapter 1, esp. pages 13–15.

67 Effros, "Beyond Cemetery Walls," 1–6; Peter Brown, *The Cult of the Saints: Its Rise and Function in Latin Christianity* (Chicago: University of Chicago Press, 1981).

68 Although this idea coexisted with a contradictory view that held that only prayers, fasting, and alms could aid the souls of the dead. See, Nilsson, *De sepulturis*, 37–41. Pope Gregory the Great maintained that grave sinners that died without being absolved would derive no benefit from burial *ad sanctos* (his precise phrasing is *in ecclesiis* "in churches"). Gregory the Great, *Dialogues*, ed. by Adalbert de Vogüé and Paul Antin, *Grégoire le Grand: Dialogues, tome III (livre IV)*, Sources chrétiennes 265 (Paris: Les Éditions du Cerf, 1980), 176 (book 4.52). As mentioned above, this is cited but misattributed in the *Decretum* of Gratian, see Gratian, *Decretum*, ed. Friedberg, 1.726.

being buried in a *clænum* "clean," i.e. consecrated, grave seems to have become increasingly important.[69]

In Anglo-Saxon sources, particularly those produced later than the eleventh century, there seems to be a clear connection between unconsecrated burial, excommunication and the consequences of these sanctions for the afterlife although the evidence discussed by Nicole Marafioti suggests that in some early Anglo-Saxon sources the connection between unconsecrated burial and excommunication was weaker than it was in later sources.[70] Even given these caveats, much of the Anglo-Saxon evidence points to a strong association between unconsecrated burial as a sign that an offender was, if not damned outright, nevertheless denied the protections and privileges of the Christian community. The connection is not absolute, but there were strong associations between denial of consecrated burial and the likely status of a person in the afterlife.

Control over who could be buried in consecrated ground mattered. In *Grágás* there is at least official deference to the bishop as arbiter over who could be buried in consecrated ground. But the fact that outlaws, even when found dead in the wilderness, were by default forbidden burial in consecrated ground suggests that at least in certain Icelandic sources, particularly *Grágás*, outlaws were strongly associated with excommunication and its consequences, particularly unconsecrated burial, as were more diverse criminals in the earliest Gulathing and Frostathing lawcodes, even if the legal foundation for such a blurring was canonically shaky by the thirteenth century.

Saga sources also sometimes depict outlaws as prohibited from buried in consecrated ground (although some of these outlaws are portrayed as part of a half pagan world under conversion).[71] One example of this occurs in *Fóstbræðra saga*. One of the foster brothers of this saga, the unruly Þorgeirr, dies an outlaw, is not given Christian burial, and indeed becomes a *draugr* or revenant after his death.[72] His foster brother Þormóðr by contrast dies redeemed, in

69 For further discussion of the laws surrounding consecrated burial in Anglo-Saxon England and particularly the idea of a consecrated grave as *clænum* "clean" see, Marafioti, "Unconsecrated Burial and Excommunication," 55–123, esp. 92.

70 Marafioti, "Unconsecrated Burial and Excommunication," 55–123.

71 Cf. Marion Poilvez, "The Inner Exiles: Outlaws and Scapegoating Process in *Grettis saga Ásmundarsonar* and *Gísla saga Súrssonar*," (Master's thesis, University of Iceland, 2011), 47–48.

72 *Fóstbræðra saga*, in *Vestfirðinga sögur, Gísla saga Súrssonar, Fóstbræðra saga, Þáttr Þormóðar, Hávarðar saga Ísfirðings*, ed. by Björn K. Þórólfsson and Guðni Jónsson, Íslenzk fornrit 6 (Reykjavík: Hið íslenzka fornritafélag, 1943), 17: 208–213. (of the main text, not the *Flateyjarbók* version.)

the retinue of St. Olaf (King Olaf Haraldsson) at the battle of Stiklastaðir.[73] In *Grettis saga*, Glámr cannot be buried in the church yard because men cannot lift him.[74] Grettir himself, however, is said to have been buried as a Christian, despite living as an outlaw before his death, suggesting he gained some posthumous clemency.[75]

Outlawry is sometimes understood (and in some sources is depicted as) a torturous and difficult sanction, one marked by bad dreams, sleeplessness, and haunting.[76] Many have associated outlawry also with animals, supernatural beings, and monstrousness.[77] I would like to suggest that the strong association with damnation was another reason for the dread of outlawry. Dead outlaws were often, especially in Icelandic legal sources, denied Christian burial and by association, denied entry into heaven.

### 3.5 *Outlaws at the Church Door*

There is also evidence that outlaws were among those people who were forbidden entry into churches and thus would have been denied church burial according to the *Grágás* provision that denies it to anyone who could not have entered a church when living. In *Íslendinga saga*, there was an otherwise little-attested Guðmundr inn seki "the outlaw" in the following of Eyjólfr Kársson at Rauðasandr in the Westfjords. Eyjólfr and his men fell into conflict with Gísli Markússon and "there were many opportunities in their neighborhood for quarrels about sheep pastures and so on. Gísli thought Eyjólf's followers played fast and loose with the women, which he thoroughly disliked."[78]

At Christmas of 1217 Eyjólfr and his men were in the church when Gísli decided to attack. The passage reads as follows: "Gísli was told that they were

73 *Fóstbræðra saga*, ed. Björn K. Þórólfsson and Guðni Jónsson, 24: 259–276.

74 *Grettis saga*, ed. Guðni Jónsson, 32: 111–113.

75 *Grettis saga*, ed. Guðni Jónsson, 84: 269–270. Perhaps his suffering during his life as well as the dubious tactics of those who had him killed made this acceptable. It is worth noting that the saga compiler mentions the final resting place of Grettir specifically. See also, Haki Antonsson, *Damnation and Salvation in Old Norse Literature* (Cambridge: D.S. Brewer, 2018), 127–128.

76 This is certainly the case in the best-known outlaw sagas, in which Gísli and Grettir in particular suffer from disturbing dreams and sleepless fear of the dark respectively.

77 Jacoby, *Wargus, vargr 'Verbrecher' 'Wolf'*; Breen, "'The Wolf is at the door' Outlaws, Assassins," 31–43. Gerstein, "Germanic Warg: The Outlaw as Werewolf," 131–156; Merkelbach, "Monstrosity, Familial Disruption, and the Cultural Relevance of the Outlaw Sagas," 103–137; and Poilvez, "The Inner Exiles."

78 Sturla Þórðarson, *Íslendinga saga*, in *Sturlunga saga*, ed. Kålund, 2.323, trans. McGrew, 33: 158. "Varþ þeim margt til i bygdar-lagi, vm fiar-beitir ok annat. Gisla þotti fylgdar-menn Eyiolfs glepja conur, þær er honum gaz eigi at."

in the church, and sent a man to lock the church up. Eyjólf was inside, but Guðmund was outside in the passageway (*í skotinu*) for he had then no right to go to church. Gísli and his men ran to their weapons and went toward the church. Eyjólf asked them for quarter (*griða*), but they refused. Guðmund came out of the passageway and surrendered to Gísli. Gísli said he would accept this, and called his homeman, whom Guðmund had earlier treated badly by trifling with his wife, to kill Guðmund. They took him up to the yard and there killed him."[79]

In a similar situation, Aron Hjǫrleifsson, outlawed and, according to *Guðmundar saga A*, being sheltered at Oddi by Haraldr Sæmundarson, hid not in the church itself but rather, in the *kirkjuskot*,[80] the same vestibule or passageway Guðmundr the outlaw was resigned to. A similar situation plays out in *Grettis saga*, when Grettir brings bones to a church but he himself does not or cannot enter, instead leaving the bones *í forkirkju*, in the vestibule of the church.[81] In all these cases, outlawry is presented as incompatible with entry into the church building.

These sources suggest that there was a consensus that outlaws were not permitted to seek sanctuary within churches. The practices of sanctuary in the medieval Church could be complicated;[82] I have elsewhere argued that sanctuary practices in the contemporary sagas were heavily tied to the idea of the

79 Sturla Þórðarson, *Íslendinga saga*, ed. Kålund, 2.323–324, trans. McGrew, 33: 158 (Translation modified). "Þa var Gisla sagt, at þeir voro i kirkiv. Þa sendi hann til mann at læsa kirkiunni; var Eyiolfr þar, enn Gvdmundr i skotino, hann atti eigi kirkiv-gengt. Gisli ok hans menn liopv til uopna ok foro til kirkiv; bað Eyiolfr þa griþa, enn þess var varnat. Gvdmunðr gekk ut or skotino ok færþi Gisla havuð sitt, enn Gisle letz þiggia munðo, ok kvadi heima-mann sinn, þann er Gvdmundr hafði aðr illa leikit ok glapit cono firir, at hann skylldi drepa hann. Þa leiddv þeir hann vpp vm garð ok drapv hann þar."

80 *Guðmundar saga A*. *Guðmundar sögur Biskups I: Ævi Guðmundar Biskups, Guðmundar saga A*, ed. by Stefán Karlsson. Editiones Arnamagnæanæ, Series B, vol. 6. (Copenhagen: The Arnamagnæan Commission, 1983), 232. "ok var hann þar ikirkiu skote. um stund."

81 *Grettis saga*, ed. Guðni Jónsson, 66: 216.

82 On medieval sanctuary see, William Chester Jordan, "A Fresh Look at Medieval Sanctuary," *Law and the Illicit in Medieval Europe*, ed. by Ruth Mazo Karras, Joel Kaye, and E. Ann Matter (Philadelphia: University of Pennsylvania Press, 2008), 17–32.; Richard H. Helmholz, *The ius commune in England* (Oxford and New York: Oxford University Press, 2001), 17, 26–28; Karl Shoemaker, *Sanctuary and Crime in the Middle Ages, 400–1500* (Bronx, NY: Fordham University Press, 2011); Sverrir Jakobsson, "Heaven is a Place on Earth: Church and Sacred Space in Iceland," *Scandinavian Studies* 82 (2010): 1–20.; and Norman Maclaren Trenholme, "The Right of Sanctuary in England," *The University of Missouri Studies* 1 (1903): 1–31. For a broad legal perspective on sanctuary in Iceland see, Sveinbjörn Rafnsson, "Um grið og griðastaði á Sturlungaöld," *Saga* 54.2 (2016): 90–107.

church building as a safe zone or space for groups as much as for individuals.[83] Outlaws were not automatically excommunicated, but they did lose a variety of legal protections, including, at least according to these narratives, the right to seek sanctuary. This example of cooperation and overlap, of outlaws losing the privileges of a member of the Christian community, are a feature of both legal and literary sources.

## 4 Cooperation between Legal Systems

Medieval Scandinavia was a legally plural culture in the sense that there were at least two systems of law that were generally recognized, Church law and local law.[84] The two systems were not necessarily clearly defined as separate, and local law also addressed Church matters. Much of the earliest surviving legal material in Old Norse-Icelandic focuses on the minimum requirements for membership in and maintenance of a Christian society, for example requirements about baptism, burial, and maintaining church buildings.[85] Even the parts of these lawcodes not explicitly concerned with Christian practice address Christian concepts about, for example, marriage.

There is increasing debate about how unusual and how old the local, usually vernacular, lawcodes of medieval Scandinavia are. Some suggest that much of the material of medieval Scandinavian lawcodes is to be found in or can be traced to canon and Roman law sources from continental Europe or trace specific provisions to Latin legal sources.[86] Of course, it is also possible

83 Elizabeth Walgenbach, "Church Sanctuary in the Contemporary Sagas," *Íslensk klausturmenning á Íslandi á miðöldum*, ed. by Haraldur Bernharðsson (Reykjavík: Miðaldastofa Háskóla Íslands og Háskólaútgáfan, 2016), 103–117.

84 On legal pluralism see, John Griffiths, "What is Legal Pluralism?" *Journal of Legal Pluralism and Unofficial Law* 24 (1986): 1–55.; Richard J. Ross and Philip J. Stern, "Reconstructing Early Modern Notions of Legal Pluralism," *Legal Pluralism and Empires, 1500–1850*, ed. by Richard J. Ross and Lauren Benton (New York: NYU Press, 2013), 109–141.; J.H. Elliott, "A Europe of Composite Monarchies," *Past and Present* 137 (1992): 48–71.

85 The first section of both of the earliest manuscripts of *Grágás* is the *Kristinna laga þáttur*, the section on Christian laws. introduction to *Grágás: Lagasafn íslenska þjóðveldisins*, ed. by Gunnar Karlsson et al., xix.

86 On the topic generally see, Per Andersen, Ditlev Tamm and Helle Vogt (eds.), *How Nordic are the Nordic Medieval Laws?: Proceedings from the first Carlsberg Conference on Medieval Legal History*, 2nd ed. (Copenhagen: DJØF Publishing, 2011); and Per Andersen, Kirsi Salonen, Helle I.M. Sigh, and Helle Vogt (eds.) *How Nordic Are the Nordic Medieval laws? Ten Years After; Proceedings of the Tenth Carlsberg Academy Conference on Medieval Legal History 2013* (Copenhagen: DJØF Publishing, 2014). There is a growing literature on the influence of Roman and canon law on medieval vernacular lawcodes produced in the

to overstate the similarities and ignore the interpretive work of translating canon and Roman law concepts and terms into another language and context. Moreover, much of the early law material that has survived concerns topics that the Church had a particular investment in, such as baptism and marriage, so these portions are more likely to show extensive influence from continental Latin sources.

It can be difficult to decide what is evidence of influence versus what is evidence for cooperation between two relatively independent jurisdictions. As discussed in chapter 2, secular leaders and secular laws were sometimes keen to punish excommunicants, particularly those that stayed defiant. In many high medieval German contexts, unrepentant excommunicants (especially heretics) were made outlaws after remaining excommunicated (i.e. having not sought to be reintegrated into the church) for six weeks.[87] Later Anglo-Saxon laws associated with King Cnut/Knútr considered harboring either an excommunicant or an outlaw an unamendable crime that only the king could pardon.[88]

Similar provisions can be found in the oldest Norwegian codes. In one provision in the Frostathing law excommunicated persons are given three months to reform their ways before they are made outlaws: "If the bishop excommunicates a man he shall have three months to reform in the matter. And that men may not be further tangled into his misfortune, the bishop's bailiff shall summon him before a thing and declare him an outlaw, unless he brings his case to a proper conclusion there and at once. And let the bishop have all his chattels and the king the right to buy the property."[89] This law, in addition to

north, see, Sveinbjörn Rafnsson, "Grágás og Digesta Iustiniani," *Sjötíu Ritgerðir Helgaðar Jakobi Benediktssyni 20. júlí 1977*, síðari hluti (Reykjavík: Stofnun Árna Magnússonar á Íslandi, 1977), 720–732. Vadum, "Bruk av kanonistisk litteratur i Nidarosprovinsen;" Joel Anderson, "Disseminating and Dispensing Canon Law in Medieval Iceland," *Arkiv för nordisk filologi* vol. 128 (2013): 79–95; Sigurður Líndal, "Um þekkingu Íslendinga á rómverskum og kanóníiskum rétti;" Lára Magnúsardóttir, *Bannfæring og kirkjuvald*; and Hoff, *Hafliði Másson und die Einflüsse des römischen Rechts*, 177–373; Walgenbach, "*Si quis suadente* and Excommunication;" Winroth, "The Canon Law of Emergency Baptism;" and Anders Winroth, "Goffredus och Västgötalagen," 183–188.

87 Eichmann, *Acht und Bann im Reichsrecht des Mittelalters*; Brian A. Pavlac, "Excommunication and Territorial Politics in High Medieval Trier," *Church History* 60 (1991): 24.

88 Hurnard, *The King's Pardon*, 1; II Cnut, 66.

89 *Ældre Frostathings-Lov (III)*, 21, ed. R. Keyser and P.A. Munch, *Norges gamle love* 1.154. trans. Larson, *Earliest Norwegian Laws*, 254. Translation revised. "Ef biskup bannsætr mann þa skal hann hafa .iij. manaða frest at leiðretta mal sitt. En at mænn vefizt eigi længr i hans vgiptu þa stefni biskups armaðr honum þing oc gere hann utlægan nema hann leiðrette þar þegar mal sitt oc hafe biskup allt fe hans en konungr landkaup."

being rather similar to the Carolingian model mentioned above, justifies the outlawry as a way of preventing further corruption, highlighting the ways in which excommunication could be seen as contagious. This also neatly splits the confiscation of the outlaw's property between the king and the bishop, suggesting a split jurisdiction but also that the sanction was a joint effort rather than a conflict between jurisdictions.

In Árni's Christian laws (Kristinréttr Árna Þorlákssonar) if a child was not baptized within four or five nights and subsequently died, the person responsible was made an outlaw ("vtlægr") along with all of his property, of which half went to the king and half the bishop.[90] This is not the *skóggangr* of the *Grágás* codes, indeed it is clearly from a Norwegian model,[91] but it still suggests a strong secular sanction for a failure of what was presented as a basic Christian duty for all members of a community.

Secular sanctions for offenses that harmed the Church features in many medieval secular lawcodes. It appears frequently in Anglo-Saxon legal material. Elaine Treharne cites, for example, II Cnut. 39 in which a person who kills a cleric is made both an outlaw and an excommunicant: "If anyone slays a minister of the altar, he shall be an outlaw from both God and men, *utlah wið God and wið menn*, unless he make amends to the best of his ability by pilgrimage and likewise to the kin."[92] It is likely that this passage does refer to a dual punishment of excommunication and outlawry (in addition to suggesting a particular Anglo-Saxon interpretation of the idea expressed in the canon *Si quis suadente*). It requires also a dual recompense offered both to the kin (probably with money) and to God (with a pilgrimage) and in this way defers to both "laws."

Treharne cautions that the evidence can be difficult to interpret and emphasizes that these dual punishments are found "with regard to crimes that are

90 Árni Þorláksson, "Kristenréttur Árna," chap. 8, ed. Magnús Lyngdal Magnússon, 154. See also Árni Þorláksson, *Kristenréttur*, 1, ed. Haraldur Bernharðsson et al., 146. "helldr hann lengr oc deyr barn heiðið. þa er hann vtlægr oc allt fé hans. ahalft konungr en halft byscop."

91 Similar texts appear in: Nyere Gulatings kristenrett I, *Norges gamle love*, 2.310–311, 2.327–328; Nyere Borgartings kristenrett I, *Norges gamle Love*, 2.293–294; Nyere Borgartings kristenrett II, *Norges gamle Love*, 4.161–162; and Erkebiskop Jons kristenrett, *Norges gamle love*, 2.341–342. A marginal notation in the earliest manuscript of Kristinréttr Árna (AM 49 8vo) identifies "Gula þings boc" as a source, Árni Þorláksson, "Kristenréttur Árna," chap. 8, ed. Magnús Lyngdal Magnússon, 153.

92 Dorothy Whitelock, M. Brett, and C.N.L. Brooke (eds.), *Councils and Synods, with other documents relating to the English Church A.D. 871–1204*, 2 vols. (Oxford: Clarendon Press, 1981), 1.491, cited by Treharne, "Formula for excommunication," 193, note 39.

anti-clerical or anti-Christian (such as sexual sins, incestuous relationships or mistreatment of church property), not crimes such as murder of a layman or theft."[93] As mentioned previously, laws associated with King Cnut/Knútr list harboring an excommunicated person or an outlaw as a crime that cannot be atoned for, but could be pardoned by the king.[94] We might compare these cases to the evidence Bryan Carrella evaluates from an early Anglo-Saxon legal source. According to her arguments, a Latin document associated with the Kingdom of Northumbria (in northern England) called for a joint punishment of excommunication and outlawry as early as the eighth century. According to this text, certain offenders lost the protection of "both" laws, that is to say both the secular laws and the laws of the Church: they were both outlawed and excommunicated.[95]

A focus on offenses perceived as anti-clerical or anti-Christian being sanctioned by both the Church and secular leaders appears in some early Norwegian laws. In the Eidsivatings law, it is said that a person who commits incest "has given up property and freedom, land and chattels to go to a heathen land never to come where there are Christian men."[96] It is impossible to classify this sanction as either Church law or local law: it is both and encompasses both sanctions. It is blunt and unsophisticated but contains elements of both the banishment characteristic of outlawry and the casting out from Christian society of excommunication. The softer, medicinal features of excommunication are not present.

The assumption is often made that the offenses being sanctioned by both bishop and king were those that would harm society or that dual sanctions were often employed only for crimes perceived as particularly grave. Before we imagine this too strongly to be mostly or exclusively about atrocity or terrible crimes, however, I refer to an example from an, admittedly later, bishop's saga, that of the Icelandic Bishop Laurentius of Hólar (1267–1331). This saga was probably produced in the mid fourteenth-century, about 70 or 80 years later than the lawcodes I have been analyzing. This saga is about, among other things, conflicts between the canons of the cathedral of Niðaróss and the archbishop. The canons are excommunicated but stubbornly resisting the bishop until King Hákon gives them two choices—beg the archbishop's mercy and

93 Treharne, "Formula for Excommunication," 195.

94 II Cnut, 66.

95 Carella, "The Earliest Expression for Outlawry," 111–143.

96 *Eidsivatings law,* 52, ed. R. Keyser and P.A. Munch, *Norges gamle love,* 1.392. "hann hefer firigort fe oc friði lannde oc lausum oyri fare a lannd heiðit. oc koma alldri þar sem cristnir menn ero firi."

submit to his judgement or be outlawed from Norway.[97] This seems to be an example of this law at work, suggesting moreover that the archbishop had very little muscle to enforce his judgements. (Although this ultimatum did not actually end the conflict, it did allow for King Hákon to put himself on the side of the archbishop and the saga hero, Laurentius, at least for purposes of the saga.) Whether or not this is law in practice, and there are reasons to be doubtful, this episode shows a situation in which the king is involved in a dispute within the Church hierarchy and in which his voice has power.

## 5 How Independent Were Secular and Church Law?

The level of cooperation and perhaps especially the use of "secular" sanctions for breaches of church law raises a different question: how interdependent or separate was the Christian law from secular local law? There is some evidence that the systems in Iceland were seen as distinct, perhaps especially in the provision that Church law would be honored over secular law when the two came into direct conflict that is articulated in Kristinréttr Árna, whose earliest manuscript is from around 1300.[98] Although the *Grágás* manuscripts contain a distinct section devoted to Christian laws, they give more or less no details about how these laws might have been enforced, and the procedures concerning witnesses and judges seem to follow the secular forms as far as we can judge, although in isolated cases the bishop's judgement is referenced, as in the case of who may be buried in consecrated ground.[99] The issue of the independence of church law was of course a developing feature of high medieval laws in many places, not least in Iceland.[100] By the end of the thirteenth century many

97 *Lárentíus saga*, ed. Guðrún Ása Grímsdóttir, 16: 255. (the A text).

98 The text can be found in Árni Þorláksson, "Kristinréttr Árna," chap. 16, ed. Magnús Lyngdal Magnússon, 162. It is also printed in *Diplomatarium Islandicum*, 2.1. The provision is dated to 1253, although it has been suggested that this pronouncement was "probably not wholly real." introduction to *Grágás*, trans. Denis et al., 1.5.

99 The Christian laws section, Kristinna laga þáttr, of the earliest *Grágás* manuscripts also circulated and was copied in later medieval manuscripts long after the introduction of Kristinréttr Árna Þorlákssonar in 1275. Winroth, "Canon Law of Emergency Baptism," 204.
On bishops having the power to make decisions about consecrated burial see, *Grágás Konungsbók*, Kristinna laga þáttr 2, ed. Finsen, 1a.12, trans. Denis et al., 1.30.

100 In Iceland much of the conflict centered around the rights surrounding church benefices called *staðir*. For discussion of *staðir* and the so-called *staðamál* see, Magnús Stefánsson, *Staðir og staðamál: Studier i islandske egenkirkelige og beneficialrettslige forhold i middelalderen I*. Historisk institutt. Universitetet i Bergen, Skrifter 4 (Bergen: Historisk institutt,

church officials, including Icelandic bishops demanded significant rights over jurisdiction, but in earlier codes the distinctions between secular and ecclesiastical justice can be difficult to pin down, not least if we remember that in the earliest stages of the Christianization of Iceland, many chieftains (*goðar*) were also ordained priests.[101]

Anglo-Saxon, Norwegian, and later Icelandic lawcodes frequently split fines between the king and the bishop for a range of offenses that harmed the Church.[102] The practice is clearly related to the frequent division of power outlined in these same lawcodes, with God giving spiritual power to the bishops and earthly power to kings.[103] The degree that we can assume separate jurisdictions in this environment of bishops writing laws for kings and chieftains ordained as priests is an issue that requires further investigation, but at least some studies suggest caution about assuming that ecclesiastical officials, even before the Gregorian reforms, were entirely subsumed into secular legal traditions.[104]

---

2000); and Helgi Þorláksson (ed.) *Church Centres: Church Centres in Iceland from the 11th to the 13th Century and their Parallels in other Countries* (Reykholt: Snorrastofa, 2005).

101 Orri Vésteinsson, *The Christianization of Iceland*, 78.

102 For an Anglo-Saxon example see, Marafioti, "Secular and Ecclesiastical Justice," 774–775. In the oldest Gulathing law, a householder who failed for three years to hold an "ale feast" is said to forfeit his property—half to the king and half to the bishop. *Den elder Gulatingslova*, 7, ed. Eithun et al., 36, trans. Larson, *Earliest Norwegian Laws*, 40; If a man fails to pay tithe for three winters his property is also forfeit in the same code—half to the king and half to the bishop, *Den elder Gulatingslova*, 8, ed. Eithun et al., 36–37, trans. Larson, *Earliest Norwegian Laws*, 41; The property of a woman convicted of practicing sorcery is also split between the king and the bishop. *Den elder Gulatingslova*, 28, ed. Eithun et al., 50–51, trans. Larson, *Earliest Norwegian Laws*, 56–7. As is that of men who fail to defend a sodomy accusation, *Den elder Gulatingslova*, 32, ed. Eithun et al., 54–55 trans. Larson, *Earliest Norwegian Laws*, 60. For failure to baptise a child before it dies, Kristinréttr Árna divides a person's property between the king and the bishop. Árni Þorláksson, "Kristenréttur Árna," chap. 8, ed. Magnús Lyngdal Magnússon, 154.

103 As, for example, in *Jónsbók*, 2, Um Vǫld Konungs ok Biskups, ed. Ólafur Halldórsson, 19, trans. Schulman, 27: "Nú af því að guðs miskunn sér til þess hversdagliga þǫrf útǫluligs lýðs ok ýmiss fjǫlmennis, þá hefir hann skipat sínum tveim þjónum at vera augsýniliga hans umboðsmenn at halda þessa heilaga trú ok hans heilagt lǫgmál […] Eru þessir .ii. annarr konungr en annarr biskup." Helle Vogt, *The Function of Kinship in Medieval Nordic Legislation* (Leiden and Boston: Brill, 2010). The idea is a general European one, Eichmann, *Acht und Bann im Reichsrecht*, 5–7; R.I. Moore, "Postscript: The Peace of God and the Social Revolution," *The Peace of God: Social Violence and Religious Response in France around the Year 1000*, ed. by Thomas Head and Richard Landes (Ithaca and London: Cornell University Press, 1992), 309.

104 Marafioti, "Secular and Ecclesiastical Justice," 774–805; Sverre Bagge, "Kirkens jurisdiksjon i kristenrettssaker før 1277," *Historisk tidsskrift* 60 (1981): 133–159.

## 6 Outlawry for Offenses against Christian Law

Icelandic sources sometimes display instances in which there is no sense of distinct jurisdiction between offenses punished by the Church and those by laymen. The idea of using outlawry to sanction breaches of Church law, for example, appears in *Grágás*. The Staðarhólsbók manuscript states that: "If a priest discloses anyone's confession without what his diocesan thinks legitimate excuse, the penalty is lesser outlawry. Nine of the priest's neighbors are to be called at the assembly."[105] The most striking thing about this is that ecclesiastical discipline, while deferring in some ways to the Church hierarchy, relies on the mechanisms of secular justice to sanction offenders although, of course, breaking the confessional could have consequences in secular society as well.

A more ambiguous provision, this one about incest, is found in *Grágás*. It specifies not a specific sanction but rather notes that "It is lawful for bishops to ask leave of the Law Council men to decide the penalty to be imposed on people who have fallen into major incest."[106] This is evidence for an interdependent legal system with competing sources of authority. The bishop is being deferred to in one sense, but is also put in a position in which he had to seek leave of the law council to proceed with the sanctioning of a breach of Church law.

In *Grágás* there is no discussion about the status of lesser outlaws relative to Church privileges. *Fjǫrbaugsgarðr,* unlike *skóggangr* is not addressed specifically with reference to consecrated burial or ability to enter churches, suggesting that those sentenced to *fjǫrbaugsgarðr* did not lose these privileges. The main connection between *fjǫrbaugsgarðr* and the laws of the Church in *Grágás* is the use of this sanction for breaches of church law.

This might be explained in part by the limited number of legal mechanisms available in relatively remote Iceland. The thirteenth century was a firmly Christian period but also a time when the role of Church law was, as ever, under negotiation. Regardless of how we explain it, the *Grágás* sources are comfortable with the idea of sanctioning breaches of Church law with what is

105 *Grágás Staðarhólsbók*, Kristinna laga þáttr 16, ed. Finsen, 2.25, trans. Denis et al., 1.200: "Ef prestr rýfr script at manne. sva at byscopi þeim þickir navðsynia lavst er sa prestr er þa undir. oc varðar þat fiör bavgs garð. scal queðia til ix. heimils bva hans a þingi."

In canon law, the penalty was deposition. This was laid down at Lateran IV (canon 21) at the same time that confession for all those who had reached the age of reason was mandated once a year. Hinschius, *System des katholischen Kirchenrechts*, 4.127. The canon was incorporated into the *Liber extra*, X 5. 38. 12, ed. Friedberg, 2.887–888.

106 *Grágás Skálholtsbók*, 9 ed. Finsen, 3.20. trans. Denis et al., 2.281.

at least nominally a secular sanction: outlawry. Part of this might be because bishops were present at the Alþingi and seem to have both needed and sought confirmation for important Church policies and legal changes at this venue, perhaps not least because it was the most reliable way to spread information across the country.[107] The use of sanctions like outlawry for offenses against the church has parallels in other early lawcodes.

In the earliest preserved Frostathing lawcode (Codex Resenianus from ca. 1260–1270), a variety of offenses against the Church are punished with outlawry.[108] Marrying within the prohibited degrees or "a woman who has taken the veil and given herself to God" is cause for outlawry, the person is outlawed ("vtlægzt"); it would also have merited excommunication.[109] Marrying within the prohibited degrees is sanctioned with lesser outlawry in the Konungsbók manuscript of *Grágás*.[110] Before a man and wife could separate they were required to see the bishop, although at least in the article as it survives in Konungsbók, it is not clear what possible grounds for a separation might be.[111]

In the Frostathing law, the idea of being outlawed for violating Church law more generally is also present: "if a man is outlawed for breach of church law and he makes atonement before the outlawry becomes effective, there are no dues to the king. But if he is declared an outlaw at the thing, a payment is due the king for restoring his rights before he may return to peace and security. Fines are also due [the king] from those who associate with him, except that, when he is taken before the bishop to do penance, men may be with him without fear of penalty and also after the period has expired which the bishop set for him to atone for his guilt abroad. And the kingsmen shall not promise protection within the land to anyone who the bishop's bailiff has declared an outlaw for breach of church law. If he returns, having done the penance that he was to perform abroad, let him call a thing, and let him produce a writ from the bishop or from the chapter, […] and let him be restored to his personal rights: but first the king must be paid for annulling the outlawry ("*skogar*

107 The clearest example of this is the approval of Kristinréttr Árna Þorlákssonar by the Alþingi (with modifications), *Árna saga biskups*, ed. Guðrún Ása Grímsdóttir, 32: 49.

108 On the manuscripts of the Frostathing lawcode see *Norges gamle love*, 4.393–394, 449, 489–490, 503–504, 673.

109 *Ældre Frostathings-Lov (III)*, 3, ed. R. Keyser and P.A. Munch, *Norges gamle love*, 1.148–149. trans. Larson, *Earliest Norwegian Laws*, 246–247. "su kona er vil hefir tekit oc sik guði gefet."

110 *Grágás Konungsbók*, Festa-þáttr 144, ed. Finsen, 1b.31. trans. Denis et al., 2.55. "En ef frænd semi er nanare en at v. manne oc .vi. manne. þa varðar fiorbavgs garð samforin nema þav geti biarg quiþ þan at hann visse eigi frændsemina þa er hann gecc at eiga kono."

111 *Grágás Konungsbók*, vm hiona scilnað 150, ed. Finsen, 1b.42–43. trans. Denis et al., 2.64–65.

*kaup*")."[112] This passage is not easy to interpret. It displays a sense of jurisdiction that is difficult to pin down, although it is clear that it envisions secular and Church authorities working together. Outlawry comes close to an excommunication, although it is not one, in part or indeed mostly because secular authorities could not excommunicate. Like an excommunication, this outlawry could be temporary, after a period set by the bishop, and the stipulation that men accompanying someone who is to do penance are themselves blameless, a provision that echoes the idea that both excommunication and outlawry could be contagious in many circumstances. The king, however, is just as involved as the bishop. An outlaw under this provision could return after the time stipulated by the bishop but also had to pay a fee to the king, the *skogar kaup*, or payment to end or avoid outlawry. It is difficult to be certain if this period away is best understood as an exile, outlawry, or simply a type of pilgrimage to atone for offenses. Regardless, this passage underscores the close proximity we find between excommunication and outlawry in many legal sources.

## 7 Conclusions

Outlawry as formulated in surviving lawcodes in Scandinavia is influenced and shaped by the sanction of excommunication. It borrows some of its dreadfulness from the threat of damnation that often, especially in early medieval contexts, went hand in hand with a sentence of excommunication. Outlawry and excommunication are often presented together. One pattern that often appears in the sources is a sentence of excommunication followed, after a defined period, by outlawry. We see this in Carolingian, Anglo-Saxon, and Norwegian legal sources. This suggests a certain confluence between the two sanctions. In

112 *Ældre Frostathings-Lov* (*III*), 24, ed. R. Keyser and P.A. Munch, *Norges gamle love*, 1.155–156., trans. Larson, *Earliest Norwegian Laws*, 255–256: "En ef maðr gerer til vtlægðar i kristnum rette oc gengr hann til ifirbota fyr en utlægð kemr a hond honum þa a konungr ecki a þui. En ef hann verðr vtlægr gor a þingi þa a konungr landkaup aðer en hann kome i frið oc settir af þeim er i samuist eru með honum nema þa er hann er fluttr til ifirbota til biskups þa skolu mænn vera sektlaust með honum oc sua siðan stefna su er liðin er biskup lagðe firir hann at boeta gloep sin vttan landz. En konungs mænn mego þeim engom landzuist loeyfa er biskups armaðr gerer vtlægan vm kristin rett. Nu kemr hann aptr oc hefir int skript sina þa er hann skilldi vttan landz inna þa kanne hann þing oc hafa þar rit biskups eða staðarens ef biskup er eigi heima. eða ef hann er frafallen oc lata gera sit ilændan. en konungr hafe aðr skogar kaup. En ef manni er su sok eegen af konungs hendi at hann uar eigi ilændr gor siðan hann uar vtlægr gor. þa skal hann abyrgiazt vitni sin innan .y. vettra at hann uar ilændr gor oc hafe siðan eins eiði firir ser at þat er or vatta abyrgð. Ok enge a at gefa sok vm samuist siðan .x. uettr eru liðnir."

some other sources there does not even appear to be a gap between the two sentences, both falling more or less simultaneously, a possibility made comprehensible, in part, by the concept of automatic excommunication that fell as soon as a forbidden action was performed.[113]

The lawcodes discussed here, as emphasized above, are complex sources—they are unlikely to document the precise legal realities of one particular time or reflect the experiences of ordinary people to any large extent. But they are the sources that we have. The surviving legal evidence is quite removed from the pre-Christian period in Iceland, written at a time when bishops and other church officials were referred to without particular comment and sat in the *lǫgrétta* at the Alþingi.[114]

Outlawry in Icelandic law, especially in the *Grágás* manuscripts, has many of the same consequences as excommunication. Full outlaws could not, absent episcopal intervention, be buried in consecrated ground, nor could they enter churches. Moreover, granting hospitality to outlaws was itself grounds for outlawry. Harboring offenders as grounds for sanction is not a deeply radical or unprecedented idea, it is not unique to excommunication, but the depiction of harboring an outlaw as a type of communion with outlaws and the contagious nature of the sanction is similar. No explicit comparison with excommunication occurs within *Grágás*. Indeed, *Grágás* never uses the term excommunication or the most common Old Norse-Icelandic translations of the word. In *Grágás* and other Icelandic sources, however, outlawry often has the same practical and legal consequences as excommunication.

These observations are not about what was canonically possible or justifiable, but rather reflect the compromises and interpretations that we see being made in the sources themselves. These point to an effort not only to make outlawry more like excommunication, but also an effort to have outlaws treated as excommunicants by the local church in Iceland, an effort that seems to have succeeded, at least to a point. I argue that when we see the idea of outlaws as unable to enter church spaces or receive Christian burial, that the direction of influence is clear. Ecclesiastical legal ideas were shaping outlawry, how it was understood and, at least to a degree, practiced. This idea competes with another possible explanation, the one suggested by Maitland, Lára Magnúsardóttir, and Liebermann, that excommunication was spoken about in terms of outlawry to make it more understandable to vernacular, local audiences.

113 *Si quis suadente* excommunication, discussed above pages 18–19.

114 Iceland's two bishops were members of the *lǫgrétta* from soon after there were bishops in Iceland.

What the cooperation shows is the writers about outlawry adapting both the patterns and the consequences of excommunication to shape and define outlawry. Outlawry surely existed in early, pre-Christian Iceland, but the pictures that we are presented of it are inextricably tied up in ideas of excommunication and perhaps also royal power. This influence appears both in how the sanction is presented and in its consequences. I suggest that Maitland got it backwards: by the thirteenth century, at least, outlawry was "secular excommunication."

The issue of offenses against Christian society being sanctioned with outlawry is a feature of what I would like to consider local canon law, it sets material punishment for offenses that were seen as harming the social fabric. It also raises real questions about the extent to which the vernacular codes, especially *Grágás*, can be understood as independent, separate witnesses to a distinct legal tradition. This argument has been raised before in questions of "How Nordic are the Nordic Medieval laws." One of the things that I would like to emphasize is that assessing the degree of "Nordicness" might be a misleading point of focus. These laws were local, adapted to local conditions, including geography and weather considerations—The Christian laws section of *Grágás*, for example, makes provision for the possibility of using snow or ice for emergency baptism and makes careful provision for who has responsibility for conveying the dead for burial, including from offshore islands or fisherman's huts—but they were still influenced by or rather based around the structures and ideas of canon law at different stages of its development.[115]

It is difficult to say how pressing some of the offenses that *Grágás* and these other codes concern themselves with were. There is a good deal of discussion in the codes about the bookends of a Christian life, baptism and burial, and the ways in which they had to be properly stewarded. It is hard to say, and seems unlikely, that the failure to baptize a child, especially a child thought unlikely to live long, which is usually one of the first offenses listed in Nordic Christian laws, was a problem of frequent concern. No sources suggest an Alþingi filled with negligent baptisers.[116] What the provision did was present a united front of joint sanctions, often supported by both the king and the bishop. That some offenses against Christian law were punished with outlawry points to local understanding of Church law and how best to enforce it and possibly also a colloquial understanding of outlawry as a type of excommunication.[117]

115 *Grágás Kónungsbók*, Kristinna laga þáttr, ed. Finsen, 1a.5–6, 7–12. Trans. Denis et al, 1.23–26, 28; Winroth, "Canon Law of Emergency Baptism," 203–220.

116 Winroth, "Canon Law of Emergency Baptism," 203–220.

117 Cf. Lára Magnúsardóttir, *Bannfæring og kirkjuvald*, 46.

The degree of interweaving and overlap of Christian laws and supposedly secular terminology such as *fjǫrbaugsgarðr* as a sanction for offenses such as breaking the confessional raises questions. One interpretation suggested in different ways by both Lára Magnúsardóttir and Bertil Nilsson is the possibility that terms for excommunication were translations of ecclesiastical terminology into the existing vocabulary of outlawry.[118] One problem with this argumentation is that it assumes that the vocabulary of outlawry was older and more widely understood. This cannot be proven based on the surviving manuscript sources. Moreover, it does not consider the issue of *fjǫrbaugsgarðr*, the term often used in *Grágás* to sanction both secular crimes and unmistakably ecclesiastical offenses.

It is possible that the Anglo-Saxon and Norwegian evidence, which suggests a close alignment between excommunication and outlawry, with outlawry often following on the heels of excommunication, represents a completely different pattern than that displayed in Old Norse-Icelandic sources. But it is also possible, and I argue much more likely, that the influence and the direction of influence is the same in both cases. Especially given that the concepts appear to converge to the degree that they do in both sets of data. One of the features that these sources, particularly the variety of lawcodes and their particular preoccupations, bring into focus is that there was a considerable amount of local variation and interpretation of the sanction of excommunication. Some of these codes associated it more strongly with outlawry or with more ambiguous sanctions like *fjǫrbaugsgarðr* than others.

In the chapters that follow, I examine the legal problems and interpretive power of outlawry as a legal concept shaped by excommunication in saga sources. Chapter 4 centers on the conflict between Bishop Guðmundr Arason and the chieftain Kolbeinn Tumason, a conflict that drew on differing interpretations of law and Christian community. Chapter 5 focuses on stories about the outlaw hero Aron Hjǫrleifsson, a friend to Bishop Guðmundr who found himself a precarious and marginalized outlaw but was "redeemed" to become a member of King Hákon Hákonarson's court and return, no longer an outlaw, to Iceland.

118 Lára Magnúsardóttir, *Bannfæring og kirkjuvald*, 46; Nilsson, *De sepulturis*, 278; and Liebermann, *Die Gesetze*, 1.432–434.

CHAPTER 4

# Excommunication and Outlawry in Sturla Þórðarson's *Íslendinga saga*

In this chapter I argue that Sturla Þórðarson (1214–1284) in his *Íslendinga saga* depicts excommunication and outlawry as similar weapons deployed in an ongoing struggle. The biggest difference between the two is often whether the person using them is a cleric or a secular chieftain. Sturla presents a typical picture of what I referred to in chapter 1 as "political excommunication" and also a picture of "political outlawry." In Sturla's narration the rivals Kolbeinn Tumason and Guðmundr Arason deploy these punishments as part of wider power struggles, not to mark atrocities or heresy. Indeed, as presented in the saga, there are few meaningful differences between excommunication and outlawry except which side of the conflict inflicts them. Sturla's understanding of law was deep and sophisticated for his time and context, and he chose to present outlawry and excommunication as similar within his narrative.

Before making these arguments in more detail, I first argue that we can read *Íslendinga saga* as the work of Sturla Þórðarson and product of the late thirteenth century. In the second section of this chapter I provide a detailed account of the conflict between Bishop Guðmundr and Kolbeinn, which took place in the early thirteenth century, as narrated in *Íslendinga saga*. The next section analyzes the portrayal of both excommunication and outlawry in this saga, focusing on the ways that Sturla engages (or does not engage) with contemporary legal thinking. The final section compares the narration of the conflict in *Íslendinga saga* with the late-twelfth-century conflict between Thomas Becket and Henry II. I focus particularly on *Thómas saga Erkibiskups*, which survives in at least two Old Norse-Icelandic versions. It is likely that this story, which spread to Iceland and became popular soon after the archbishop's death, influenced the way that the conflict between Guðmundr and Kolbeinn was constructed in *Íslendinga saga*.

 | DOI:10.1163/9789004461468_006

## 1 *Íslendinga saga* and Sturla Þórðarson

*Íslendinga saga* is one of the contemporary sagas, preserved as part of the *Sturlunga saga* compilation.[1] It is most often attributed to Sturla Þórðarson, a member of the Sturlung family powerful in west Iceland.[2] Sturla was the poet and writer Snorri Sturluson's nephew.[3] Sturla became a chieftain in western Iceland, and was allied with Snorri until Snorri was killed in 1241. He continued to be politically active in Iceland but was forced into exile in Norway in 1263.[4] It was there that King Hákon's son, Magnús, commissioned Sturla to write a biography of his late father, now preserved as *Hákonar saga Hákonarsonar*.[5] Sturla returned to Iceland in 1272 and was made *lǫgmaðr* "lawman." According to at least some accounts, Sturla Þórðarson brought the lawcode *Járnsíða* to Iceland

1 KLNM 17.355–359, s.v. "Sturlunga saga," by Jakob Benediktsson. Úlfar Bragason, "Sagas of Contemporary History (Sturlunga saga): Texts and Research," *A Companion to Old Norse-Icelandic Literature and Culture*, ed. by Rory McTurk (Oxford: Blackwell, 2007), 427–446; Peter Hallberg, "Sturlunga saga," *Medieval Scandinavia: An Encyclopedia,* ed. by Phillip Pulsiano et al. (New York and London: Garland, 1993), 616–618; R. George Thomas, introduction to *Sturlunga saga 1: The Saga of Hvamm-Sturla and The Saga of the Icelanders*, trans. by Julia McGrew (New York: Twayne Publishers and The American Scandinavian Foundation, 1970), 31–45; and Stephen Norman Tranter, *Sturlunga Saga: The rôle of the Creative Compiler* (Frankfurt am Main: Peter Lang, 1987). Citations in this chapter refer to Kristian Kålund's edition of 1906–1911, *Sturlunga saga efter membranen Króksfjarðarbók udfyldt efter Reykjafjarðarbók* 2 vols. (Copenhagen and Kristiania, 1906–1911). I also give references, by chapter and page number, to Julia McGrew's (not always satisfactory) translation.

2 *Íslendinga saga* is attributed to Sturla Þórðarson in a preface that is itself preserved along with the saga in the *Sturlunga* compilation. *Sturlunga saga,* ed. Kålund, 1.119–120, trans. McGrew, 55.

3 Sturla was a son of Snorri's brother Þórðr by his concubine Þóra. Marlene Ciklamini, "Sturla Þórðarson," *Medieval Scandinavia: An Encyclopedia,* ed. by Phillip Pulsiano et al. (New York and London: Garland, 1993), 613–614. For more on Sturla's life see, Guðrún Ása Grímsdóttir and Jónas Kristjánsson (eds.), *Sturlustefna, ráðstefna haldin á sjö alda ártíð Sturlu Þórðarsonar sagnaritara 1984* (Reykjavík: Stofnun Árna Magnússonar á Íslandi, 1988); Marlene Ciklamini, "Biographical Reflections in 'Íslendinga saga:' A Mirror of Personal Values," *Scandinavian Studies* 55 (1983): 205–221; and Jón Viðar Sigurðsson and Sverrir Jakobsson (eds.), *Sturla Þórðarson: Skald, Chieftain and Lawman* (Leiden and Boston: Brill, 2017).

4 Guðrún Ása Grímsdóttir, "Sturla Þórðarson," *Sturlustefna, ráðstefna haldin á sjö alda ártíð Sturlu Þórðarsonar sagnaritara 1984*, ed. by Guðrún Ása Grímsdóttir and Jónas Kristjánsson (Reykjavík: Stofnun Árna Magnússonar á Íslandi, 1988), 19. For more on the possible reasons for this exile see, Magnús Stefánsson, "Drottinsvik Sturlu Þórðarsonar," *Sturlustefna, ráðstefna haldin á sjö alda ártíð Sturlu Þórðarsonar sagnaritara 1984,* ed. by Guðrún Ása Grímsdóttir and Jónas Kristjánsson (Reykjavík: Stofnun Árna Magnússonar á Íslandi, 1988), 147–183.

5 KLNM 6.51–53, s.v. "Hákonar saga Hákonarsonar," by Knut Helle; Paul Schach, "Hákonar saga gamla Hákonarsonar," *Medieval Scandinavia: An Encyclopedia,* ed. by Phillip Pulsiano et al. (New York and London: Garland, 1993), 259–260.

on this same return journey.[6] He was compelled to return to Norway to answer accusations that he was neglecting his duties but did not fall entirely out of royal favor.[7] It is most often thought that Sturla composed *Íslendinga saga* near the end of his life, sometime in the period between 1271 and 1284.[8] He died on Fagurey in Breiðafjǫrðr in 1284.

In this discussion I especially emphasize Sturla's connections to clerics and clerical learning. Sturla, as an illegitimate son with no secure inheritance, may well have been trained for a career in the priesthood,[9] and his brother was Óláfr hvítaskáld "the white poet," a court poet who also became a sub-deacon. Óláfr composed poems about Archbishop Thomas Becket and also about the outlaw Aron Hjǫrleifsson (a figure discussed in more detail in chapter 5) as well as a grammatical treatise.[10] Sturla's (and Óláfr's) father Þórðr Sturluson, was a friend and supporter of Bishop Guðmundr; Sturla was twenty-three years old when Guðmundr died in 1237, and it is likely that the two met in person, perhaps in 1231.[11] Þórðr's views are likely to have colored Sturla's perspective although it is unsafe to assume that Sturla was a mindless partisan of the bishop.

In this chapter I assume that the attribution of *Íslendinga saga* to Sturla is accurate. Perhaps more importantly, I assume that there is an authorial voice to be found in *Íslendinga saga*. We do not have an autograph copy of the manuscript, and there are differences between the different surviving copies of the *Sturlunga* compilation.[12] Moreover, it is probable that Sturla was working with existing sources to shape his narrative, particularly a saga of Bishop

6 Guðrún Ása Grímsdóttir, "Sturla Þórðarson," 20; Guðrún Ása Grímsdóttir, "Um sárafar í Íslendinga sögu Sturlu Þórðarsonar," *Sturlustefna, ráðstefna haldin á sjö alda ártíð Sturlu Þórðarsonar sagnaritara 1984*, ed. by Guðrún Ása Grímsdóttir and Jónas Kristjánsson (Reykjavík: Stofnun Árna Magnússonar á Íslandi, 1988), 196–197. For discussion of the law text brought to Iceland by Sturla see, Boulhosa, "Narrative, Evidence and the Reception of Járnsíða," 223–232.

7 Guðrún Ása Grímsdóttir, "Sturla Þórðarson," 20.

8 Guðrún Ása Grímsdóttir, "Sturla Þórðarson," 27; Guðrún Nordal, "*Sturlunga saga* and the context of saga-writing," *Introductory Essays on Egils saga and Njáls saga*, ed. by John Hines and Desmond Slay (London: The Viking Society for Northern Research, 1992), 1–14; and Úlfar Bragason, "In the Scriptorium of Sturlunga's Compiler," *International Scandinavian and Medieval Studies in Memory of Gerd Wolfgang Weber*, ed. by Michael Dallapiazza et al. (Trieste: Edizioni Parnaso, 2000), 471–482.

9 Guðrún Ása Grímsdóttir, "Sturla Þórðarson," 11.

10 Lauren Goetting, "Óláfr hvítaskáld Þórðarson (Ólhv)" [Skaldic Poetry Database] http://www.abdn.ac.uk/skaldic/db.php?id=157&if=default&table=skalds accessed 22.1.2016.

11 Guðrún Ása Grímsdóttir, "Sturla Þórðarson," 31.

12 The two major medieval manuscripts of *Sturlunga saga*, AM 122a fol. (Króksfjarðarbók) and AM 122b fol. (Reykjarfjarðarbók) are from the fourteenth century.

Guðmundr.[13] Despite these caveats, *Íslendinga saga* presents a coherent narrative voice and perspective on events that is susceptible to analysis though it is colored by personal and political loyalties. We cannot be certain that any individual turn of phrase is Sturla's, but there is enough consistency in the text to assume that it represents a coherent point of view toward the events being narrated.[14]

## 2 Narration of the Conflict

The conflict between the chieftain Kolbeinn (and later his brother Arnórr) and Bishop Guðmundr dominates the first third of *Íslendinga saga*, covering roughly the period between 1203 when Guðmundr was elected Bishop of Hólar and Guðmundr's death in 1237.[15] Kolbeinn was the most powerful chieftain in the northern quarter in Iceland in the early thirteenth century; Guðmundr was the bishop he appointed to Iceland's northern see.[16]

### 2.1 *First Steps in the Conflict (1203–1207)*

The two men's quarrel began soon after Guðmundr's consecration when Kolbeinn decided to prosecute a priest, Ásbjǫrn, "to death and outlawry" for an old claim about money, which some claimed was unjust.[17] Ásbjǫrn sought the help of Bishop Guðmundr. Guðmundr was prompt in his assessment: the priest should not be subject to prosecution by Kolbeinn. Guðmundr came to the court "with staff and stole," i.e. symbols of his episcopal authority, and

13 Sturla Þórðarson seems to have been at the very least aware of *Guðmundar saga dýra*, a version of *Guðmundar saga góða*, and *Hrafns saga Sveinbjarnarsonar*. He was probably also aware of *Þórðar saga kakala* and *Þorgils saga skarða*. KLNM 17.357, s.v. "Sturlunga saga," by Jakob Benediktsson.

14 On Sturla's authorial perspectives see particularly Hans Jacob Orning, "Sturla Þórðarson's Two Perspectives on Thirteenth-Century History: Royal Chronicler vs. Icelandic Chieftain," 148–155; Theodore M. Andersson, "Sturla Þórðarson's Narrative Personalities," 156–67, Ármann Jakobsson, "A Personal Account: The Official and the Individual in *Hákonar saga Hákonarsonar*," 192–199; and Helgi Þorláksson, "The Bias and Alleged Impartiality of Sturla Þórðarson," 200–211, all in the volume: *Sturla Þórðarson: Skald, Chieftain and Lawman*, ed. by Jón Viðar Sigurðsson and Sverrir Jakobsson (Leiden and Boston: Brill, 2017).

15 The dates provided throughout this account are taken from Jón Jóhannesson, Magnús Finnbogason and Kristján Eldjárn's edition, *Sturlunga saga* vol. 1 (Reykjavík: Sturlunguútgáfan, 1946).

16 Sturla Þórðarson, *Íslendinga saga*, ed. Kålund, 1.251. trans. McGrew, 12: 127–128.

17 Sturla Þórðarson, *Íslendinga saga*, ed. Kålund, 1.276, trans. McGrew 20: 134. "til davþa oc vtlegþar." (translation modified).

forbade Kolbeinn and his men to sentence Ásbjǫrn.[18] Guðmundr was here following canon law, which reserved judgement of clerics to their bishops, seeking to prevent them from being subject to secular courts and their sanctions.[19]

Kolbeinn and his followers prosecuted Ásbjǫrn anyway. In response, Guðmundr forbade all religious services to Kolbeinn and those who gave evidence or swore oaths against Ásbjǫrn.[20] This looks like the first stage in the process that led to excommunication by a bishop's sentence in canon law, which required a warning to mend behavior before the full sentence could be invoked.[21] It was a clear message to Kolbeinn to drop the suit or risk full excommunication. It is also notable that the sentence extended to everyone involved in the prosecution, not just Kolbeinn, who had brought the suit.

Kolbeinn, in a neatly parallel response, summoned the men of the bishop's household for associating with the priest that he had outlawed, emphasizing that outlawry too, could be contagious.[22] After this action, Guðmundr excommunicated Kolbeinn. According to the saga "The bishop was so angry at this [that Kolbeinn was prosecuting the men of his household for outlawry] that he excommunicated Kolbeinn."[23] After this first standoff others helped them to reach a reconciliation, one that stipulated that Guðmundr would have self-judgement to decide the fine and penance. With advice from Iceland's other bishop, Páll of Skálaholt, and the chieftain Sæmundr Jónsson at Oddi, Guðmundr decided to fine Kolbeinn twelve hundreds of *vaðmál*.[24] Kolbeinn only paid half of this fine, however, saying that others who had already pledged money in the case should pay the rest.[25]

The next incident began when a cleric was taken away from his monastery and maimed (the motives behind this action remain unspecified in the

---

18 Sturla Þórðarson, *Íslendinga saga*, ed. Kålund, 1.276, trans. McGrew, 20: 134. "við staf oc stolv."

19 Anne J. Duggan, "Clerical Exemption in Canon Law from Gratian to the Decretals," *Medieval Worlds* 6 (2017): 78–100. DOI 10.1553/medievalworlds_no6_2017s78.

20 Sturla Þórðarson, *Íslendinga saga*, ed. Kålund, 1.276, trans. McGrew, 20: 134. "fyrir-bavd biskup Kolbeini oc ollvm þeim, er i þessvm domi hofðv verit oc þar havfðv æiðvm, vitni æða vætti borit, alla gvðs þionostv."

21 Vodola, *Excommunication*, 5–7; 31. X 2. 28. 26, *Liber extra*, ed. Friedberg, 2.418–419.

22 Sturla Þórðarson, *Íslendinga saga*, ed. Kålund, 1.277, trans. McGrew, 20: 134. "Vm havstið eptir væitir Kolbeinn biskupi heimsocn oc stefnir huscorllvm hans skoggangs stefnvm vm samneyti við prestinn."

23 Sturla Þórðarson, *Íslendinga saga*, ed. Kålund, 1.277, trans. McGrew, 20: 134. "Varð við þetta biskup sva stygr, at hann bann-setr Kolbein."

24 This was a standardized quality of woolen cloth often used as currency in coin-poor Iceland. See, KLNM 19.409–412, s.v., "Vadmål," by Marta Hoffmann.

25 Sturla Þórðarson, *Íslendinga saga*, ed. Kålund, 1.277, trans. McGrew, 20: 134.

narration).[26] The men responsible for the attack on this unnamed monk were Sigurðr Ormsson and Hallr Kleppjárnsson, who were chieftains in the northern quarter. They also took money from an unnamed farmer and held it as a ransom. Here, based on subsequent events, we can assume that Sigurðr and Hallr were excommunicated *latae sententiae* for their blatant physical attack on a cleric.[27] Sigurðr and Hallr, after delaying and in the case of Hallr attempting to settle the matter with the maimed cleric directly, put themselves at the mercy of the bishop's judgement on the Feast of St. Mauritius (22 September) in 1206.[28]

Kolbeinn, who had not wanted to be involved in any direct negotiations with the bishop, came into association with Hallr and Sigurðr before they had settled with the bishop. Bishop Guðmundr "held Kolbeinn in excommunication" for associating with Sigurðr and Hallr (even though that case had subsequently been settled). Kolbeinn's excommunication on the basis of his interactions with Sigurðr and Hallr confirms that Hallr and Sigurðr were in fact excommunicated because of their violence towards the monk.[29] Sturla reports that Kolbeinn and his followers ignored their sentence of excommunication.

That winter, before Christmas in 1207, the bishop excommunicated Kolbeinn again, or perhaps reiterated his previous sentence.[30] He gave the reasoning that Kolbeinn was excommunicated because of his associations with Sigurðr and Hallr and also because he had not fully paid the fine of twelve hundreds previously imposed on him.[31] This is simply too many excommunications to be correct under canon law, especially if it implies that the first excommunication was never actually lifted because the full fine was not paid. It does, however, follow the idea that association with an excommunicated person could be grounds for excommunication.[32]

In the spring of 1208 Kolbeinn gathered a force to ride to the see at Hólar, where he summoned all of the men in the bishop's household for outlawry, according to Sturla, "most of them for small cause."[33] At this same time, Bishop

26 Sturla Þórðarson, *Íslendinga saga*, ed. Kålund, 1.277, trans. McGrew, 20: 134.

27 Helmholz, "'Si quis suadente,'" 425–438; Vodola, *Excommunication*, 28–29; Walgenbach, "The Canon *Si quis suadente*," 155–185; and Lára Magnúsardóttir, *Bannfæring og kirkjuvald*, 78–104, 153–154.

28 Sturla Þórðarson, *Íslendinga saga*, ed. Kålund, 1.277, trans. McGrew, 20: 134.

29 Sturla Þórðarson, *Íslendinga saga*, ed. Kålund, 1.277, trans. McGrew, 20: 135. "callar biskup Kolbein i banni af samneyti við þa Sigurð."

30 Sturla Þórðarson, *Íslendinga saga*, ed. Kålund, 1.277–278, trans. McGrew, 20: 135.

31 Sturla Þórðarson, *Íslendinga saga*, ed. Kålund, 1.278, trans. McGrew, 20: 135.

32 See above, page 8.

33 Sturla Þórðarson, *Íslendinga saga*, ed. Kålund, 1.278, trans. McGrew, 20: 135. "flestvm fyrir litlar sakir."

Guðmundr read the sentence of excommunication over Kolbeinn in the vernacular. Sturla explains that this was done so that everyone could understand it in case there was any doubt at this point in the conflict. Many documents related to pastoral care emphasize the need to use the vernacular so that there is no ambiguity about who is being sanctioned and why.[34]

According to the saga, Kolbeinn recited several poems about the harshness of Guðmundr, specifically focused on his zeal in excommunicating people, and was very angry.[35] There were rumbles of an open, violent confrontation, but a temporary settlement was reached in which both parties agreed to submit the case to the archbishop in Norway, although it is less clear in the narration if this results in an actual intervention from the archbishop or simply leads to a status quo ante bellum for the time being. Kolbeinn and his men dropped the outlawry cases, and Guðmundr removed the excommunication from everyone under it.[36]

## 2.2 Phase Two of the Conflict, Escalation (*1208*)

This unsteady peace did not last very long. It was later in the same year that a wayward cleric fell on the bishop's mercies and reignited the conflict. Skæringr, an acolyte notable for only having one arm (which meant he was technically ineligible to *be* a cleric),[37] fathered a child on a woman out of wedlock. Her brother sought out Kolbeinn to take up the case. Skæringr himself sought out the bishop's aid. The bishop attempted to make a settlement, offering compensation (twice that generally stipulated for such cases) to the aggrieved parties. Kolbeinn would have none of this and prosecuted Skæringr for outlawry.[38] Sturla highlights the stakes of this sentencing by referring to Skæringr here not by his name but rather as *klærcinn*, "the cleric."[39]

34 Sturla Þórðarson, *Íslendinga saga*, ed. Kålund, 1.278, trans. McGrew, 20: 135. It was standard to insist on the use of the vernacular to make certain that the excommunication, as well as the reasons for it, was understood. Burchard, *Decretorum libri xx*, 11.3, fol. 145.

35 Sturla Þórðarson, *Íslendinga saga*, ed. Kålund, 1.278, trans. McGrew, 20: 135–136.

36 Sturla Þórðarson, *Íslendinga saga*, ed. Kålund, 1.279, trans. McGrew, 20: 136: "Gafv þeir Kolbeinn þa vpp sectir allar, enn biskup toc þa alla or banni." McGrew's translation is not accurate here and has been modified. She seems to have been misled by the use of Kolbeini in the dative rather than the nominative Kolbeinn in the edition by Jón Jóhannesson et al. (eds.), *Íslendinga saga, Sturlunga saga* vol. 1, 20: 246.

37 This would have made him unable to be a cleric without a papal dispensation. See, Hinschius, *System des katholischen Kirchenrechts*, 1.14–16. A discussion of clerical ranks from the lowest minor orders (porter, lector, exorcist, and acolyte) and ending with the pope is preserved in Old Norse-Icelandic in Stock. Perg nr. 5 fol., a manuscript from about 1360, *Diplomatarium Islandicum*, 3.152.

38 Sturla Þórðarson, *Íslendinga saga*, ed. Kålund, 1.279, trans. McGrew, 20: 136.

39 Sturla Þórðarson, *Íslendinga saga*, ed. Kålund, 1.279, trans. McGrew, 20: 136.

The bishop responded by putting Kolbeinn and those who participated in the summoning of Skæringr for outlawry under ban.[40] Kolbeinn, unfazed, planned for and carried out a court of execution to confiscate Skæringr's property, a standard part of the procedure for an outlawry case.[41] Guðmundr excommunicated Kolbeinn and the other men involved in the confiscation court. Kolbeinn, in turn, brought a suit against six of Guðmundr's followers for aiding Skæringr.[42] Kolbeinn and Guðmundr are portrayed here as punishing each other's followers for a very similar offense: that of associating with men who were either excommunicated or outlawed. The word used in Old Norse-Icelandic for both instances is *samneyti*, the same word that is used to translate and discuss how association with an excommunicated person can itself lead to excommunication.[43]

A mutually paralyzed standoff developed between the two sides. Neither man would accept the authority of the other to judge the men each was protecting. Guðmundr allowed the men outlawed by Kolbeinn to live as free men and attend church services.[44] At the same time, Kolbeinn ignored the sentence of excommunication on himself and his followers. They had priests say mass for them as if nothing had happened, and the local priests obliged, perhaps having little choice in the matter, even after Guðmundr had also excommunicated the priests themselves for disobedience (*vhlydni*).[45]

Neither side would give in, but neither side is portrayed as quite secure. The outlawed men would not leave the bishop's side for fear that, as outlaws who could be killed with impunity, they would not last long outside Guðmundr's protection.[46] The spiritual position and physical security of the excommunicated men, though harder to judge, was also uncertain.

40 Sturla Þórðarson *Íslendinga saga*, ed. Kålund, 1.279, trans. McGrew, 20: 136–137. The term used here is *forbodar*.

41 Sturla Þórðarson, *Íslendinga saga*, ed. Kålund, 1.279, trans. McGrew, 20: 137.

42 Sturla Þórðarson, *Íslendinga saga*, ed. Kålund, 1.280, trans. McGrew, 20: 137.

43 As discussed in chapter 1, continuing to associate with and especially to help an excommunicated person was often grounds for the excommunication of the person helping or associating with the offender, page 8. A similar principle often applied to outlaws as well, as discussed above, pages 47–49 and 72–75.

44 Sturla Þórðarson, *Íslendinga saga*, ed. Kålund, 1.280, trans. McGrew, 21: 137: "Hann mat engis sect manna þeira, er Kolbeinn hafði sekta, let þa ganga i kirkior sem frialsa menn."

45 Sturla Þórðarson, *Íslendinga saga*, ed. Kålund, 1.280, trans. McGrew, 21: 137. He uses two terms, *bannaði* and *bannsetti*. *Óhlyðni* and its lexical variants are the usual Old Norse translation for the Latin term *contumancia*, or defiant disobedience to church directives. See Lára Magnúsardóttir, *Bannfæring og kirkjuvald*, 56–64.

46 At least according to *Grágás Konungsbók*, Þingskapa-þáttr 55, ed. Finsen, 1a.96, trans. Denis et al., 1.98. Note that this provision specifies that it was in force not just in Iceland but anywhere.

The tensions between Guðmundr and Kolbeinn did not improve when Bishop Guðmundr decided to remove precious objects, including relics and books, from a church building at Mǫðruvellir in an area for the most part controlled by Kolbeinn's supporters.[47] Guðmundr claimed that he was protecting the Church from defilement and further injury. His opponents called it simple robbery, further proof that the bishop could not be trusted.[48]

Kolbeinn and other northern notables then planned to attack the bishop at his see. On the latter feast of the Virgin Mary (8 September) in 1208, the conflict came to a head. Kolbeinn's forces gathered around Guðmundr at Hólar.[49] According to Sturla, efforts were made to reach a settlement, but Guðmundr insisted that he would not abandon the men outlawed by Kolbeinn to the axe, and Kolbeinn also refused a compromise.[50] Kolbeinn, goaded on by those who pointed out that his honor was at stake, would not allow the bishop and his followers to simply ride away, so he attacked. A battle (*Víðinesbardagi*) ensued with fatalities on both sides. Among the dead was Kolbeinn, killed by a stray rock.[51] Sturla claims that Kolbeinn remained conscious long enough to swear an "oath of reconciliation" and receive last rites.[52] Later accounts even suggest that this was when Kolbeinn composed the hymn "Heyr himna smiður."[53]

### 2.3 *Phase Three of the Conflict, the Bishop Driven from His See*

Kolbeinn's death did not end the conflict. There were more bodies and blame to be accounted for. Bishop Guðmundr offered to submit the matter to the archbishop. But the other parties did not accept this. Some men, especially Ogmundr sneis, who was in the uncomfortable position of being related to

47 Sturla Þórðarson, *Íslendinga saga*, ed. Kålund, 1.281, trans. McGrew, 21: 138.

48 Sturla Þórðarson, *Íslendinga saga*, ed. Kålund, 1.281, trans. McGrew, 21: 138.

49 Sturla Þórðarson, *Íslendinga saga*, ed. Kålund, 1.281–282, trans. McGrew, 21: 138–139.

50 Sturla Þórðarson, *Íslendinga saga*, ed. Kålund, 1.281–282, trans. McGrew, 21: 138–139.

51 Rocks were frequently used as weapons in thirteenth-century Icelandic battles because weapons were expensive and relatively rare. In the 1220s Aron Hjǫrleifsson justified his use of a dead enemy's weapons on the grounds that there were too few weapons available because of poverty. *Guðmundar saga B*, ed. Stefán Karlsson, 159.

52 Sturla Þórðarson, *Íslendinga saga*, ed. Kålund, 1.282, trans. McGrew, 21: 139.

53 This is usually considered the oldest surviving psalm in Old Norse-Icelandic. It was made much more widely known after being placed in the Icelandic Psalm book in 1945 and gained even more visibility (including on youtube) when set to music composed by Þorkell Sigurbjörnsson. Guðrún Þórhallsdóttir, "Bragur og breytingar: Kolbeinn og himnasmiðurinn," lecture given 4.2.2016 at the University of Iceland. The oldest manuscripts that preserve this psalm are AM 657 c 4to and AM 396 4to, both from the mid-fourteenth century. See Finnur Jónsson (ed.), *Den Norsk-Islandske Skjaldedigtning: A, Tekst efter håndskrifterne*, 2 vols. (Copenhagen: Gyldendal, Nordisk forlag, 1912–1915), 2.39–40.

both Guðmundr and Kolbeinn, offered property to help reach a settlement.[54] Many propertied farmers were forced to pay fines, which they did with bad grace and grumbling, saying that "it was all pillage and robbery."[55] Despite these grumblings, the bishop remained resident at Hólar during this time.

Even after this settlement some men associated with the bishop continued to cause trouble—burning a farm, wounding some men, and killing a priest, causing further mistrust.[56] Sturla is careful to say that the bishop had forbidden them to do this, but they, of course, were still associated with him by the people who suffered at their hands. The bishop for his part reminded the unhappy farmers who had fought with Kolbeinn that they were still excommunicated because of their refusal to adhere to the agreements and pay the fines they still owed.[57] Some men went to the Dalir region to seek the help of Sighvatr Sturluson in the matter.[58]

Sighvatr and three others, including his brother, the writer and politician Snorri Sturluson, began to plan a new attack against the bishop in the north.[59] At this point in the narrative, Sturla gives these plans an ominous cast by mentioning that at this time a man in Skagafjǫrðr and another in the Westfjords had ominous dreams that portended bloody conflict. These dreams, as is common in *Íslendinga saga*, are reported partly in verse form.[60]

That spring (1209) a force of about 700 men attacked the bishop at his see. The bishop was outnumbered, and some of his men deserted him during the night while the attackers waited. According to Sturla some joined the opposing forces, and some simply left. The next day many of the bishop's men fled to the church because they thought it unlikely that they would receive mercy in defeat.[61] Those that remained put up such a defense as they could. Some men

---

54 Sturla Þórðarson, *Íslendinga saga*, ed. Kålund, 1.283, trans. McGrew, 21: 140.

55 Sturla Þórðarson, *Íslendinga saga*, ed. Kålund, 1.284, trans. McGrew, 21: 140: "kalla þeir þetta allt hernaþ oc ran."

56 Sturla Þórðarson, *Íslendinga saga*, ed. Kålund, 1.284, trans. McGrew 21: 140–141.

57 Sturla Þórðarson, *Íslendinga saga*, ed. Kålund, 1.284, trans. McGrew 21: 141: "Biskup kallar bændr i sama banni, sem aðr þeir sættvz, þviat þeir villðv ecki giallða þat, er þeir hofðv fest oc svarit, oc villdv allt i mot honum."

58 Sturla Þórðarson, *Íslendinga saga*, ed. Kålund, 1.284, trans. McGrew, 21: 141.

59 Sturla Þórðarson, *Íslendinga saga*, ed. Kålund, 1.285–286, trans. McGrew, 23: 141–142.

60 Sturla Þórðarson, *Íslendinga saga*, ed. Kålund, 1.285–286, trans. McGrew, 23: 142. For further discussion of dreams in *Íslendinga saga* see, Robert J. Glendinning, "Saints, Sinners, and the Age of the Sturlungs: Two Dreams from *Íslendinga saga*," *Scandinavian Studies* 38 (1966): 83–97; and Robert J. Glendinning, *Träume und Vorbedeutung in der Islendinga Saga Sturla Thordarsons: Eine Form- und Stiluntersuchung* (Bern and Frankfurt: Herbert Lang, 1974).

61 Sturla Þórðarson, *Íslendinga saga*, ed. Kålund, 1.287, trans. McGrew, 24: 143.

were killed inside buildings, and the blood of a man killed in the churchyard spilled onto the church.[62]

The bishop was given two choices by the attacking forces, led by Arnórr Tumason, Kolbeinn's brother: either he release his enemies from excommunication and thereby ensure that some of his men would be given quarter, or they would kill all of his men and force him out of his see in humiliation (although not kill him).[63] The bishop found neither of these choices acceptable, he agreed to read a *miserere* over the excommunicated men who were dying, but said that they were not more absolved than before.[64]

According to Sturla, immediately after this prayer, Snorri Sturluson invited Bishop Guðmundr to stay with him. Guðmundr agreed and left Hólar with Snorri the same day, leaving a church full of men hoping for mercy behind him.[65] Arnórr and his allies went, armed, to the church building and encouraged those inside to come out, or they would either attack or starve them out.[66] The bishop's men still in the church are then said to have come out, all unarmed "because they did not want the church to be defiled by them or their blood."[67] Several of the men are summarily killed, including one immediate cause of the quarrels, the cleric Skæringr. He was beheaded on the spot. Sveinn Jónsson, another of the bishop's men, was killed while singing the Ave Maria.[68]

### 2.4 *Phase Four of the Conflict: Consequences*

The men who died as outlaws (that is the men whom the bishop had been protecting) were buried in a hole with no masses, while the dead among the other

62 Sturla Þórðarson, *Íslendinga saga*, ed. Kålund, 1.287, trans. McGrew, 24: 143: "Þar voro fleiri menn drepnir, en svmir i husvm inni; einn drapv þeir i kirkio-garðinvm, sva at blodit ravt a kirkiona."

63 Sturla Þórðarson, *Íslendinga saga*, ed. Kålund, 1.286–287, trans. McGrew, 24: 143–144. For further discussion of *grið* see, Guðrún Nordal, *Ethics and Action in Thirteenth Century Iceland* (Odense: Odense University Press, 1998), 192–198; KLNM 5.463–467 s.v., "Grið," by Arne Bøe, Magnús Már Lárusson, Gerhard Hafström, and Elias Wessén; and KLNM 5.467–470 s.v., "Griðamál og trygðamál," by Arne Bøe and Poul Meyer.

64 Sturla Þórðarson, *Íslendinga saga*, ed. Kålund, 1.287, trans. McGrew, 24: 144: "hann las yfir þeim miserere, oc segir þeim at þa voro þeir eigi lavsari enn aðr." The *miserere* is taken from one of the so-called penitential psalms, Psalm 50 under the Vulgate numbering. For futher discussion of these psalms see, Clare Costley King'oo, *Miserere Mei: The Penitential Psalms in Late Medieval and Early Modern England* (Notre Dame IN: University of Notre Dame Press, 2012).

65 Sturla Þórðarson, *Íslendinga saga*, ed. Kålund, 1.287, trans. McGrew, 24: 144.

66 Sturla Þórðarson, *Íslendinga saga*, ed. Kålund, 1.287–288, trans. McGrew, 24: 144.

67 Sturla Þórðarson, *Íslendinga saga*, ed. Kålund, 1.288, trans. McGrew, 24: 144.

68 Sturla Þórðarson, *Íslendinga saga*, ed. Kålund, 1.288, trans. McGrew, 24: 144.

force, who are explicitly identified as unreconciled excommunicants dying "without repentance or absolution," were buried in the churchyard.[69] Sturla reports this as a deliberate mockery of the bishop saying that: "they said it was just what the bishop would have done, because he had let outlawed men go to church."[70] The attacking chieftains also took some of the bishop's men into their followings, picking and choosing whom they liked.[71]

Bishop Guðmundr, now with Snorri and likely at Reykholt, attempted to govern his see remotely, mostly by letter. Guðmundr insisted that the excommunicated men be reburied outside the churchyard and that no masses be said in the church building, desecrated as it was by killing and the bodies of excommunicated men.[72] It is said that "The bishop did not let one of Kolbein's men who had fallen impenitent [i.e. excommunicated] remain buried in the church for a month."[73] Guðmundr's new chief enemy in the north, Arnórr Tumason, Kolbeinn's brother, paid little attention to the bishop's scruples. According to Sturla, he demanded that masses be said in the church because he could not bear that it should be empty and masses said outside in a tent.[74] He also instructed the priests to lift the excommunication, clearly usurping Guðmundr's authority and showing his own power in the north. Furthermore, Arnórr forced four men, two of them priests, to prove by ordeal of hot iron that they had not killed Kolbeinn.[75]

This section of the text also contains a lament for the Church in the north that is of a very different tone than the surrounding, more matter of fact text. It reads that: "Miserable and sorrowful were Christians then. Some priests gave up singing the Mass from fear of God; some performed the offices from fear of the chieftains; but some of their own will. The head church, the mother, sat in sorrow and affliction, and some of her daughters joined her, although some exulted in her affliction."[76] This shift, which is stylistically quite distinct from

69 Sturla Þórðarson, *Íslendinga saga*, ed. Kålund, 1.288, trans. McGrew, 24: 144. "an iðran oc lavsn."

70 Sturla Þórðarson, *Íslendinga saga*, ed. Kålund, 1.288, trans. McGrew, 24: 144. "oc collvðvz þat allt licia eptir biskupi, er hann let seca menn i kirkio ganga."

71 Sturla Þórðarson, *Íslendinga saga*, ed. Kålund, 1.288–289, trans. McGrew, 24: 145.

72 Sturla Þórðarson, *Íslendinga saga*, ed. Kålund, 1.289, trans. McGrew, 25: 145.

73 Sturla Þórðarson, *Íslendinga saga*, ed. Kålund, 1.288, trans. McGrew, 24: 145.

74 Sturla Þórðarson, *Íslendinga saga*, ed. Kålund, 1.289, trans. McGrew, 25: 145.

75 Sturla Þórðarson, *Íslendinga saga*, ed. Kålund, 1.289, trans. McGrew, 24: 145: "IIII goþir menn, prestar II oc leic-menn II, voro til iarns færdir vm þat, at þeir hæfdi eigi vnnit a Kolbeini, oc vrðv allir vel skirir vm þat mal." All of them come through the ordeal innocent.

76 Sturla Þórðarson, *Íslendinga saga*, ed. Kålund, 1.289–290, trans. McGrew, 25: 146: "Avmlig oc hormvlig kristni var þar þá at sjá. Svmir prestar logðv messo-song fyrir hræzlv sacir við gvð, svmir fromdo fyrir hræzlo við hofþinga, svmir at sinvm sialf-villia. Hofuð-kirkian,

the surrounding text, may derive from a written source such as an early saga about Guðmundr; it emphasizes that at this point in the conflict, Guðmundr was unable to hold onto any control over the northern churches, which were entirely controlled by Arnórr and his followers. It is a sign that Sturla's sympathies in the conflict were with Guðmundr and his cause, implying that not just Guðmundr, but all Christians and the mother Church in the north suffered from the chieftain's actions.

It is also at this juncture in the narrative that Archbishop Tore of Niðaróss added his voice to the fray. In a letter (only preserved within the saga) he expressed his displeasure. He told Sigurðr, Arnórr, and others involved that only the pope could absolve them given their offenses, and demanded that all parties come to Norway to see him in person.[77] Arnórr and Guðmundr prepared to sail to Norway in 1213 (about three years after the letter had arrived). Arnórr sailed that year, but Guðmundr became too ill and sailed the following year.[78] The saga gives no report of any meetings with the archbishop or other similar details. We only learn that Bishop Guðmundr spent his first year in Norway at Vík, in the east with Bishop Nikolaus Árnason of Oslo, who was himself a contentious figure in his struggles with Norwegian royal power.[79]

When Guðmundr arrived back in Iceland from Norway in 1218, he reestablished a household at Hólar. He also started a school and maintained a large household. This calm interlude did not last even a year, however. Arnórr, also back in the country, kidnapped Bishop Guðmundr one night and removed him from Hólar.[80] He also threatened to burn down the school, students and all. Guðmundr spent a winter and summer as a prisoner in Arnórr's household, kept almost constantly guarded in a storage room and suffering quite miserably according to Sturla, who details some of his physical afflictions.[81]

Eyjólfr Kársson eventually rescued the bishop the next year in a daring plot.[82] Despite hostility, the bishop continued his residence in the north, although not firmly based at Hólar, with a large and hungry following. He

---

modirin, sat i sorg oc svt, oc svmar dætrnar meðr henni, en svmar gleymdv yfir hennar harmi."

77 Sturla Þórðarson, *Íslendinga saga*, ed. Kålund, 1.291–293, trans. McGrew, 26: 147–148.

78 Sturla Þórðarson, *Íslendinga saga*, ed. Kålund, 1.297, trans. McGrew, 31: 152–153.

79 Sturla Þórðarson, *Íslendinga saga*, ed. Kålund, 1.297, trans. McGrew, 31: 153. Nikulás Árnason was the bishop of Oslo from 1190–1225. See, *Diplomatarium Norvegicum* 17 B, Tillæg til Syttende samling *Den norske Kirkes Erkebiskoper og Biskoper indtil Reformationen* (Christiania, 1913), 17 B.241.

80 Sturla Þórðarson, *Íslendinga saga*, ed. Kålund, 1.332, trans. McGrew, 36: 165.

81 Sturla Þórðarson, *Íslendinga saga*, ed. Kålund, 1.332, trans. McGrew, 36: 166.

82 Sturla Þórðarson, *Íslendinga saga*, ed. Kålund, 1.333–334, trans. McGrew, 36: 166–167.

became peripatetic, without an established residence. He was usually followed by a miscellaneous group of poor people. Many local notables hesitated to host him because of the expense.[83]

### 2.5 *Part Five, Miracles and Endings*

At this stage in the narrative (in the year 1219) Sturla decides to incorporate accounts that suggest that Guðmundr had special access to the supernatural. Evidence for such powers appear earlier in the *Prestsaga Guðmundar* that is also a part of *Sturlunga saga*, but these are the first clearly miraculous events to be mentioned after Guðmundr has been made bishop. These powers could take on a rather vindictive cast. Guðmundr predicted bad things for a priest who did not want to accommodate his request for a place to celebrate the latter feast of the Virgin Mary (a day for which he had a special affinity),[84] and the next year on the feast day the man's house and goods burned to cold coals.[85] The bishop also contributed positively in some areas. He cleansed a farmstead that was severely haunted, for instance, and in general we get a glimpse of the kinds of actions that fit with the bishop's reputation as a saint, although the saga is not particularly focused on miraculous situations.[86]

Why does Sturla foreground these supernatural elements at this point in the narrative, as well as insert the tonally discordant lament for Christians in the north? We cannot be certain, and it is of course possible that one or more of these passages was inserted during copying, but they provide, after the end of the conflict with Kolbeinn, a picture of Christianity in danger and the bishop as a saint with unmistakable powers, making an implied argument that Guðmundr retained or even had enhanced spiritual powers after having lost the struggle for firm temporal control over the north.

The bishop continued to live in the north with a large household. He made himself an unwelcome guest despite whatever reputation he may have already had for miraculous powers. People did not want him to stay, and they certainly did not want him to stay twice, probably especially because of his large

83 *Grágás* is rather vague on the responsibilities or limits on responsibilities for hosting bishops. See the *Konungsbók* version, which only mentions that horses were to be provided on the day the bishop left and that householders had to lend him horses if asked. *Grágás Konungsbók*, Kristinna laga þáttr 5, ed. Finsen, 1a.19–20, trans. Denis et al., 1.36.

84 The cathedral at Hólar was dedicated to the Virgin Mary, which partly explains the focus on her feast days in the narration. Cormack, *The Saints in Iceland*, 194.

85 Sturla Þórðarson, *Íslendinga saga*, ed. Kålund, 1.334–335, trans. McGrew, 37: 167.

86 Sturla Þórðarson, *Íslendinga saga*, ed. Kålund, 1.335, trans. McGrew, 37: 168.

following of poor and itinerant people.[87] Some of the northern farmers, feeling put-upon by Guðmundr's large and hungry following, sought help from Arnórr and Sighvatr to prevent the bishop and his followers from imposing on them any more than they already had.

The northern chieftains obliged with an attack on the bishop (known as *Helgastaðabardagi*). The attack occurred just outside the church at Helgastaðir, which Guðmundr had just consecrated. Sturla here foregrounds the cost of feeding the bishop's following, mentioning that men said that the chieftains had come and "slammed the doors shut now on the storehouses of the Reykjadalers."[88]

The bishop was successfully driven out of the north again after this clash at Helgastaðir. The bishop ended up all the way in the south at Oddi, as a guest of the chieftain Sæmundr.[89] Arnórr and his allies wanted to protect the north from Guðmundr and "the men of the district then as before wanted to make him [Guðmundr] an outlaw from his episcopal wealth."[90] Arnórr was intermittently, though never totally successful at this task until his death (of sickness) in 1221.[91]

The conflicts with the northern farmers and the demanding bishop never really ceased until Guðmundr died in 1237. Even after Arnórr Tumason died, others continued to resist the bishop. Tumi Sighvatsson, a son of Sighvatr Sturluson, who had been a friend of Kolbeinn Tumason and was related to him by marriage,[92] for instance, physically took over the see at Hólar, living in the bishop's quarters.[93] He took this extreme step in part because he knew that he could get support from disgruntled northern farmers and in part because his father refused to give him an inheritance of his own. The takeover, however, was not long successful: the bishop's men returned a few months later, on the

87 Ívarr of Múli received the bishop one time but was not thrilled at the imposition and planned for a battle when he heard that the bishop planned to visit him again. Sturla Þórðarson, *Íslendinga saga*, ed. Kålund, 1.335, trans. McGrew, 37: 168.

88 Sturla Þórðarson, *Íslendinga saga*, ed. Kålund, 1.337, trans. McGrew, 37: 169: "enða skellr þar nv lass firir bvr þeira Reykðæla."

89 Sturla Þórðarson, *Íslendinga saga*, ed. Kålund, 1.337–339, trans. McGrew, 37: 168–171.

90 Sturla Þórðarson, *Íslendinga saga*, ed. Kålund, 1.350, translation modified, trans. McGrew, 40: 181. "Heraðsmenn villdv þa enn sem fyrr utlaga hann af sino goðs."

91 Sturla Þórðarson, *Íslendinga saga*, ed. Kålund, 1.351, trans. McGrew, 41: 182. Guðmundr was at Hólar when Arnórr died.

92 On Sighvatr's friendship with Kolbeinn Tumason see, Sturla Þórðarson, *Íslendinga saga*, ed. Kålund, 1.275, trans. McGrew, 18: 133.

93 Sturla Þórðarson, *Íslendinga saga*, ed. Kålund, 1.352, trans. McGrew, 42: 182–183: "Tvmi sez nv a staðinn at Holvm með sveit sina, sva sem þat væri hans födvr-leifð."

Feast of St. Blaise (3 February 1222), killed Tumi, and forced his followers to surrender.[94]

The bishop did not, or at least is not portrayed as, resorting to excommunication as a way to chastise his enemies in these later years. Sturla gives only one further example of excommunication connected with the bishop, in what appears to be an isolated incident that is swiftly settled.[95] This might be explained by a variety of factors other than narrative choices, however. Guðmundr was sometimes ill, sometimes more or less under house arrest and not as politically active after the mid twelve-twenties (he also spent time in Norway). He was usually not present personally at þings and the general range of his activities and influence was curtailed.[96] No excommunications attributed to Guðmundr were done by letter. He seems to have excommunicated personally, usually in the vernacular. Guðmundr did continue to serve as something of a protector of outlaws at least according to accounts concerning Aron Hjǫrleifsson, who was outlawed after fighting for the bishop on Grímsey, a topic discussed at more length in chapter 5.

As the saga continues, the narrative focus shifts away from Guðmundr and toward the south, with focus on even larger quarrels and growing Norwegian influence. Other, later, texts that narrate the conflict between Guðmundr and the northern chieftains survive in sagas of Bishop Guðmundr, most probably written in connection with the attempt to canonize him in the fourteenth century. They are more explicitly hagiographical and are more interested in Guðmundr's miracle-working powers than on his power struggles.[97] The

94 Sturla Þórðarson, *Íslendinga saga*, ed. Kålund, 1.352–353, trans. McGrew, 42.183–184. Sturla reports that the bishop was angry that his men had killed Tumi and not brought him back with them to the island of Málmey, whence the bishop had retreated.

95 The last excommunication associated with Bishop Guðmundr in *Íslendinga saga* occured after the killing of Jón Birnuson (who had killed the priest Knútr), which was done at Hólar just outside the church, which was also bloodied. Kolbeinn ungi, one of the killers, who was holding Guðmundr as a virtual prisoner at the time, quickly reached a settlement with the bishop. Guðmundr lifted the excommunication from Kolbeinn and Kleppjárn Hallsson and the two agreed to compensate the man's relatives, the bishop, and the church, Sturla Þórðarson, *Íslendinga saga*, ed. Kålund, 1.416, trans. McGrew, 76: 237.

96 One year after Christmas, Bishop Guðmundr is taken ill and spends the rest of the winter at Hvammr with Þórðr Sturluson. Sturla Þórðarson, *Íslendinga saga*, ed. Kålund, 1.390, trans. McGrew, 62: 215. Later, the bishop is virtually under house arrest at Hólar, attended by a small group of clerics and not allowed to receive donations, Sturla Þórðarson, *Íslendinga saga*, ed. Kålund, 1.415, trans. McGrew, 76: 237. He spent the final period of his life at Hólar, blind and ill, before he died in 1237, Sturla Þórðarson, *Íslendinga saga*, ed. Kålund, 1.488–490, trans. McGrew 118–119: 302–304.

97 Stefán Karlsson dates all the complete sagas of Bishop Guðmundr to the fourteenth century, Stefán Karlsson, "Guðmundar sögur biskups," *Medieval Scandinavia: An Encyclopedia,*

conflict between Guðmundr and the northern chieftains remains a compelling and under-studied story that can help us to understand the role of excommunication and outlawry in medieval Iceland. In his narration of the conflict Sturla engages often with both Iceland's vernacular laws and their concepts of outlawry as well as ideas developing within canon law in the twelfth and early thirteenth centuries.

## 3 Sturla's Use of Vernacular and Canon Law

### 3.1 *Engagement with Vernacular Law*

We have every reason to suppose that Sturla was an expert in Iceland's vernacular laws. We need only point to his role as lawman "lǫgmaðr" and likely direct involvement in the production or at least transmission of the lawcode *Járnsíða* for confirmation.[98] Sturla shows an easy familiarity with vernacular laws, although not the same zeal for procedural details present in, for example, *Njáls saga*.[99]

Sturla frequently mentions outlawry, excommunication and other legal ideas such as confiscation courts (*féránsdómr*), but as is usual in sagas, never defines them. He makes no reference to *fjǫrbaugsgarðr* of the type defined in *Grágás*. Outlawry as it appears in *Íslendinga saga* also appears more frequently to be a sentenced inflicted on (small) groups rather than on individuals. It is also possible and indeed likely that Sturla's ideas were influenced by Norwegian legal concepts. The legal vocabulary in *Íslendinga saga* sometimes adopts Norwegianisms, although this usage could potentially derive from later copyists.[100]

### 3.2 *Engagement with Canon Law*

Sturla engages frequently with the claims and assertions of canon law in his narration. He addresses the *privilegium fori*, the consequences of violence

---

ed. by Phillip Pulsiano et al. (New York and London: Garland, 1993), 245–246. See also, KLNM 5.542–543, s.v., "Guðmundar saga biskups Arasonar," by Björn Sigfússon.

98 Boulhosa, "Narrative, Evidence and the Reception of Járnsíða," 223–232. Sturla was *lǫgmaðr*, from 1272–1283.

99 On Sturla Þórðarson's education see, Jón Viðar Sigurðsson, "The Education of Sturla Þórðarson (and the Icelandic Elite)," *Sturla Þórðarson: Skald, Chieftain and Lawman*, ed. by Jón Viðar Sigurðsson and Sverrir Jakobsson (Leiden and Boston: Brill, 2017), 20–30.

100 The text uses *sekr*, *skógarmaðr*, the Norwegian *útlagi*, and their lexical variants. Agneta Breisch suggests that *útlagi* is used more when Norway is being discussed and the *skóggangr* forms when Iceland is under discussion, *Frid och fredlöshet*, esp. 130–148.

against clerics, ordeal, and excommunication.[101] The clearest driver of the conflict between Kolbeinn and Guðmundr, as presented in *Íslendinga saga*, is the issue of the *privilegium fori*, according to which Church officials demanded jurisdiction over a larger sphere and the exclusive right to try their own in ecclesiastical courts according to canon law rather than subject them to the secular courts. We see this clearly in Sturla's narrative when clerics, whose conduct is less than exemplary, are nevertheless protected by Guðmundr on the basis that as clerics they should not be judged and punished by secular rulers or judges.[102]

Sturla presents excommunication as a political weapon, mostly adhering to an older conception of the sentence as one brought orally against individuals by a bishop. He touches on some of the mechanics of how the sentence was designed to operate, sometimes including the need for a warning and the use of the vernacular in communicating excommunication sentences. He makes no distinction between major and minor excommunication as such, but if we consider that those under excommunication in *Íslendinga saga* were banned from church buildings and forbidden consecrated burial, it seems that we are to understand *bannfæring* in *Íslendinga saga* as major excommunication.

Since the establishment of the penalty of excommunication *latae sententiae*, or "automatic excommunication" in the twelfth century (in 1139, at the second Lateran council), those who assaulted clerics were automatically excommunicated.[103] *Íslendinga saga* contains multiple accounts of clerics being killed or wounded, not least the maiming of the unnamed monk that led to the excommunication of Sigurðr and Hallr. Sturla portrays the killing or maiming a cleric as particularly heinous because of their clerical status; it becomes an atrocity rather than a mere addition to the (admittedly frequent) violence of the *Sturlunga* corpus.[104] Margaret Cormack has argued that these killings are often explicitly hagiographic, for instance when someone is killed while praying or with their arms stretched out in the form of a cross.[105]

101 It is relevant to emphasize here that Sturla himself wrote about the visit of the Cardinal and Papal Legate William of Sabina (also known as William of Modena), who came to Norway to crown King Hákon Hákonarson in 1247. See Sturla Þórðarson, *Hákonar saga Hákonarsonar*, in *Hákonar saga Hákonarsonar Bǫglunga saga, Magnúss saga lagabœtis*, ed. Þorleifur Hauksson et al., Íslenzk fornrit 31–32, 2 vols. (Reykjavík: Hið íslenzka fornritafélag, 2013), 2.136.

102 Notably Skæringr, whose guilt is not disputed.

103 Lára Magnúsardóttir, *Bannfæring og kirkjuvald*, 80; and Walgenbach, "The Canon *Si quis suadente*."

104 Guðrún Ása Grímsdóttir. "Um afskipti erkibiskupa," 28–62.

105 Margaret Cormack, "Saints and Sinners: Reflections on death in some Icelandic sagas," *Gripla* 8 (1994): 187–218.

These killings do not, however, consistently lead to excommunications in Sturla's account, and there is no particular focus on the idea that those maiming or killing clerics were automatically excommunicated, although the idea is present in the case of Hallr and Sigurðr.[106] In another incident a man under attack asks that the priest next to him be spared, presumably on the grounds that a cleric deserved to be spared because of his office.[107] Sturla often emphasizes when a person is a cleric, sometimes specifying, as he did before the Battle of Víðines, the different types of clerics who were involved or killed in the fighting.[108]

The ban on clerics *participating* in violence is not consistently observed in *Íslendinga saga*, but it is sometimes gestured at.[109] There is also at least one case in which a priest seems to have been deposed for being involved in the killing of a priest. There is also a rather odd example of a cleric involved in the thick of a conflict without using any weapons. The scene occurs during the fighting at Flugumýri (*Flugumýrarbardagi*) in 1253 as narrated by Sturla. One member of the defending forces is a priest, Jón Halldórsson, who has no weapons to fight with but joins in the fray by throwing cloths over the swords and axes of the attacking men in an effort to blunt their blows.[110]

In addition to these incidents, which suggest an understanding of canon law concepts defining the special role and limits on the clergy, Sturla's narrative also suggests respect for supernatural phenomena pointing to the power of God and God's potential intervention in earthly conflicts. We can see this in the narration of the events surrounding Kolbeinn's death, both before and after it occurs. Before Kolbeinn is killed, when the bells are ringing in the church for evensong, the night before the fighting, Sturla reports that "it is said that

106 Who maimed an unnamed monk. Sturla Þórðarson, *Íslendinga saga*, ed. Kålund, 1.277, trans. McGrew, 20: 134. Maiming is characteristic of the violence depicted in *Sturlunga saga*, see, Lois Bragg, "Disfigurement, Disability, and Dis-integration in *Sturlunga saga*," *alvíssmál* 4 (1994): 15–32.

107 Sturla Þórðarson, *Íslendinga saga*, ed. Kålund, 1.401, trans. McGrew, 71: 225.

108 Sturla Þórðarson, *Íslendinga saga*, ed. Kålund, 1.282, trans. McGrew, 21: 138: "Með honum voro III abotar oc II mvncar, nær XL presta oc mart klerca."

109 A certain Knútr, although a priest, is said to always carry weapons, "because he was a mettlesome man and held no priestly office." Sturla Þórðarson, *Íslendinga saga*, ed. Kålund, 1.414, trans. McGrew, 76: 236: "þviat hann var v-dæll ok embottis-lavss."

110 Sturla Þórðarson, *Íslendinga saga*, ed. Kålund, 1.576, trans. McGrew, 158: 380. Where it is said that one of the men who came to Iceland with Þórðr kakali in 1242 was "Snorri Þoraalfs son [...] hann var prestr at vigslu ok var þa leik-maðr, þviat hann hafði verit at vigi Knutz prestz i Olafs-firði." Also discussed by Orri Vésteinsson, *The Christianization of Iceland*, 221–222. On Jón Halldórsson see, Sturla Þórðarson, *Íslendinga saga*, ed. Kålund, 2.197, trans. McGrew, 172: 396.

Kolbeinn and his men did not hear" them, a passage implying that Kolbeinn was acting in a way cut off or closed off from God.[111]

A similar focus is also found in the narration of the judicial ordeal that Arnórr Tumason is said to have compelled four followers of Guðmundr to undergo after Kolbeinn's death (which they do successfully, proving their innocence). Priests were banned from supervising ordeals at the church council Lateran IV in 1215.[112] This did not mean, of course, that ordeals instantly disappeared in practice. Sturla himself had a vested interest in believing in ordeals and their validity, even if they were no longer approved and overseen by clerics at the time *Íslendinga saga* was written, in the 1270s or 1280s.[113] An ordeal features prominently in *Hákonar saga Hákonarsonar*, which Sturla also wrote. In this saga, Hákon's mother proved his paternity, and therefore his right to kingship, by successfully undergoing an ordeal by hot iron (in 1218).[114]

Although Sturla depicts both excommunication and outlawry as largely political punishments deployed by rival sides of a conflict, the consequences of both had other ramifications in his account. As emphasized in chapter 3 and also seen in here in *Íslendinga saga,* burial in consecrated ground was a

111 Sturla Þórðarson, *Íslendinga saga*, ed. Kålund, 1.281, trans. McGrew, 21: 138. "oc er sva sagt, at þeir Kolbeinn heyrðv eigi klvckna lioþ." A very similar passage occurs in the narration of the conflict in *Guðmundar saga A*, ed. Stefán Karlsson, 131: 156: "ok er sua s(agt). at K(olbeinn) hafe eigi heyrt klucna hlioþit." *Guðmundar saga B* contains a similar passage, but it adds a comment by Kolbeinn, suggesting that Guðmundr must have been very angry to refuse to ring the church bells on such a holy day, *Guðmundar saga B*, ed. Stefán Karlsson, 89: 112. "Redr er G(vdvmdr) magr min nv er hann lætr eigi hringia at stadnvm slika hatið sem nv er idag." [Guðmundr my brother-in-law is angry now since he does not have the bells rung here on such a holy day as today.]

112 Charles M. Radding, "Ordeals," *Dictionary of the Middle Ages* (New York: Charles Scribner's Sons, 1987), 9.259–260.

113 It seems unlikely that the provision of 1215 would have taken effect immediately, especially in nothern Europe. Given the context of this specific ordeal to prove royal heritage, it is not surprising that ordeals in the thirteenth-century Norwegian codes are both so prominent and so focused on paternity. Ældre Frostathings-lov, 2.1, ed. R. Keyser and P.A. Munch, *Norges gamle love*, 1.130–131, trans. Larson, *Earliest Norwegian Laws*, 225; *Ældre Frostathings-lov*, 45., ed. R. Keyser and P.A. Munch, *Norges gamle love*, 1.145–146, trans. Larson, *Earliest Norwegian Laws*, 244. William Ian Miller notes, but does not discuss the prominence of ordeals in Norwegian lawcodes, "Ordeal in Iceland," *Scandinavian Studies* 60 (1988): 192.

114 Sturla Þórðarson, *Hákonar saga Hákonarsonar*, ed. Þorleifur Hauksson et al., 1.45–47: 218–220. On ordeal in Icelandic sources see, Miller, "Ordeal in Iceland," 189–218. On medieval ordeals generally see, Robert Bartlett, *Trial by Fire and Water: the medieval judicial ordeal* (New York: Clarendon Press of Oxford University Press, 1986); and Peter Brown, "Society and the Supernatural: A Medieval Change," *Daedalus, Journal of the American Academy of Arts and Sciences* 104 (1975): 133–151.

contested and emotionally charged issue both for outlawed men and for those who were excommunicated. It even reached the point that bodies were exhumed and reburied depending on who was in control of a particular area. Fear of damnation and the potential disgrace of unconsecrated burial are surely reasons for Kolbeinn's death bed reconciliation: he may have defied Guðmundr, but even so Sturla depicts him as wanting to reconcile and receive absolution before death.

As argued in chapter 3, when burial is under discussion it is often hard to see a meaningful distinction between the consequences of outlawry and excommunication. A clear example of this can be found in the aftermath of Arnórr Tumason's attack on Hólar in 1209. After this confrontation, Arnórr has men who died under the bishop's excommunication buried in the churchyard. He and his men "said it was just what the bishop would have done, because he had let outlawed men go to church."[115] This is a clear reference to a tradition that outlawed men were not permitted entry into churches or consecrated burial, an idea that Guðmundr's protection of outlaws put into dispute but never quite erased.

Another noticeable feature of Sturla's narration is his use of written documents. In *Íslendinga saga,* clerics in particular communicate with letters (secular chieftains seem to be able to read letters but are not portrayed writing them or giving written responses). Sturla makes relatively frequent reference to letters and other written documents in his saga, sometimes reproducing text said to be taken directly from such letters,[116] for example when he reproduces the text of a letter said to have been sent from the Archbishop of Niðaróss to the northern chieftains in 1211.[117] The reference to these types of documents in *Íslendinga saga* suggest that Sturla understood many key assertions of canon law and the claims that the Church was making for jurisdiction. Even if we attribute some of this knowledge to Sturla's sources and models rather than to him directly, he still understood them and used them to tell his version of events. It is unlikely that they are all or consistently later interpolations because much of the logic of the storytelling relies on an understanding of the special roles and privileges increasingly being assigned to the clergy and the claims of canon law.

115 Sturla Þórðarson, *Íslendinga saga*, ed. Kålund, 1.288, trans. McGrew, 24: 144. "oc collvðvz þat allt licia eptir biskupi, er hann let seca menn i kirkio ganga."

116 It is often imposible to verify if these letters existed independently, if they are fabrications, or were modified by Sturla.

117 Sturla Þórðarson, *Íslendinga saga*, ed Kålund, 1.291–293, trans. McGrew, 26: 147–148.

## 4 Thomas Becket

Sturla also drew on stories from outside Iceland for inspiration. I argue, as others have, that Sturla's story of Guðmundr and Kolbeinn in *Íslendinga saga* was shaped by the stories that circulated and were translated about the conflict between Thomas Becket and King Henry II of England. Becket was killed in Canterbury Cathedral in 1170 and narratives of his struggles against the king, death, and subsequent miracles quickly spread. The story of Thomas was popular in Iceland, where at least two sagas based on the story survive in Old Norse-Icelandic.[118] In this book I focus on *Thómas saga* in the manuscript GKS 1008 fol. (Thómasskina), usually dated to ca. 1400. This is the oldest complete version of the Thomas story to survive in Old Norse-Icelandic.[119]

The parallels between the two stories are all the more compelling because Sturla makes a deliberate effort to identify the conflict with Kolbeinn as a key conflict for Guðmundr and his saintly identity—that is: the one which isolates the key issues of clerical privilege versus secular law. Once both Kolbeinn and his brother are dead, although conflict (and miracles) continued, the bishop seems to have stopped excommunicating people or at least this is no longer of interest to the story teller, although, as discussed above, this could also be related to Guðmundr's diminished power and failing health.

The parallels between Guðmundr and Thomas Becket, while present in *Íslendinga saga*, are made more blatant in later texts like *Guðmundar saga A*, in which Kolbeinn explicitly compares Guðmundr to Thomas Becket in a verse.[120]

---

118 KLNM 18.244–245, s.v. "Thomas Becket," by Hans Bekker-Nielsen; KLNM 18.249, s.v. "Thomas Becket (Norge)," by Lilli Gjerløw; KLNM 18.249–251, s.v. "Thómas saga erkibiskups," by Hans Bekker-Nielsen; and Eiríkur Magnússon, introduction to *Thómas saga Erikbyskups*, vi–clxxv. Scandinavians were making pilgrimages to Caterbury as early as the 1180s. See, Haki Antonsson, "The Lives of Thomas Becket and Early Scandinavian Literature," *Studi e materiali di storia delle religioni (SMSR)* 81 (2015): 392–413; Several versions of *Thómas saga* survive in Old Norse-Icelandic, either in whole or in part. One version is in a manuscript of ca. 1300 and a later version is preserved in a manuscript from ca. 1400. Alfred Jakobsen, "Thómas saga erkibiskups," *Medieval Scandinavia: An Encyclopedia*, ed. by Phillip Pulsiano et al. (New York and London: Garland, 1993), 643–644. There is debate about how Norwegian these versions of *Thómas saga* are, but this issue matters little in the case of Sturla, who also spent time in Norway.

119 On an early version of *Thómas saga* see Peter Foote, "On the fragmentary text concerning St Thomas Becket in Stock. Perg. Fol. Nr. 2," *Saga-Book* 15 (1961): 403.

120 Eiríkur Magnússon, introduction to, *Thómas saga*, 2.xix; and Haki Antonsson, "Lives of Thomas Becket," 396. Eiríkur notes that later *Guðmundar sögur* are more explicit than earlier ones in their identification of Guðmundr with Thomas Beckett. Eiríkur Magnússon, introduction to, *Thómas saga*, 2.xxvii. (Although ideas about the relative age

This version of *Guðmundar saga* also contains the "vision of Rannveig," in which a woman called Rannveig predicts that Guðmundr will have no less a place in heaven than Archbishop Thomas.[121]

Both bishops were put in office in the, it turns out mistaken, presumption that they would be easily led to favor the cause of their secular counterparts.[122] According to the saga, King Henry chose Thomas in part because he trusted him to look after his young son should he die, but "along with these things floated other matters in the heart of the king, but nowise of any great brightness, in that he thought Thomas would be yielding to his will in the keeping of the laws and the kingly customs in the realm."[123] Kolbeinn was rumored to have similar hopes in mind. Sturla reports that "many men commented that Kolbein had wanted Guðmund chosen bishop because he thought he himself would thus control both laymen and clergy in the north."[124]

Another clear parallel concerns the genesis of the actual conflict between each pair, which in both cases centers on jurisdiction. Specifically, both narratives address the judgement of wayward clerics and the question of which courts or under which authority such men should be judged, in other words the above mentioned *privilegium fori*.[125] Guðmundr protected the clerical status and privileges of cleric who fathered a child and others who were outlawed by chieftains. Thomas asserted his right of jurisdiction over a priest who

---

of the various sagas of Guðmundr have shifted since Eiríkur was writing in the 1890s, on this point the analysis still holds.)

The earliest manuscripts that contain this particular verse are AM 396 4to and AM 657 c 4to, both fourteenth-century manuscripts that preserve the verse as part of their versions of *Guðmundar saga biskups*, Finnur, *Norsk-Islandske Skjaldedigtning: A*, 39.

121 Eiríkur Magnússon, introduction to, *Thómas saga*, 2.xxi. For the text see, *Guðmundar saga A*, ed. Stefán Karlsson, 60: 98. "Þat á G(uðmundr) prestr A(ra) s(on). þui at sua hallda benir hans upp lande þesso. sem uarar benir hallda upp Nor(ege) ok Orkneyium. ok man hann uerða mestr upp halldz maðr landi þesso. ok sitea eige i legra sete. enn Thomas erchibyskup a Englandi."

122 Bishops were elected, but it seems clear in both cases that Kolbeinn and King Henry had a great deal of influence over the choices made.

123 *Thómas saga*, ed. and trans. Eiríkur Magnússon, 1.14: 70–71. "Þat flaut með annat, sem eigi var bjart í konungsins hjarta, at hann hugði Thómam eftirlátan sinni vild um lagahald ok konungligar siðvenjur í ríkinn."

124 Sturla Þórðarson, *Íslendinga saga*, ed. Kålund, 1.251, trans. McGrew, 12: 128. "Ok mæltv þat margir, at Kolbeinn vildi þvi Gvðmund til byskups kiosa, at hann þottiz þa raða bæði leicmönnum oc kenni-monnum fyrir norþan land."

125 Eiríkur Magnússon makes this observation, introduction to, *Thómas saga*, 2.xxiv–xxv. He argues that "Not only was [Guðmundr] the first Icelandic bishop who insisted on these clerical immunities, but he carried his theory into practice with a onesidedness as utterly regardless of circumstances as his violence was reckless of consequences."

committed manslaughter.[126] He also asserted that as a cleric he was released from all obligations he had held before taking up the office of archbishop.[127] Guðmundr and Thomas also shared the pain of exile and being driven from their sees. Both men spent significant time in exile or quasi exile—Guðmundr in Norway, various islands off of the north coast of Iceland, and with friendly farmers—and Thomas in France.

The trading of excommunication and outlawry between followers is another compelling similarity between the two stories. In *Thómas saga*, the archbishop does not hesitate to excommunicate either the king or his followers, and the king responds in kind. It is reported that the king banished all those who happened to be related to Thomas in any way from England in 1165: "with unheard of cruelty the king bringeth to bear, that every person, consecrated or not consecrated, man and woman, young and old, rich and poor, on being found to be in any way related to the holy Thomas, is now driven into exile."[128]

In a further similarity between the stories, Kolbeinn's unexpected, almost accidental death is similar to the fate suffered by William Rufus, one of King Henry's predecessors, whom *Thómas saga* portrays in a particularly unfavorable light. His evil character is further emphasized by his death, killed accidentally while hunting by one of his own followers. The saga says that "the arm of the King of heaven fell upon him," when one of his men accidentally shoots him.[129] Kolbeinn's end is similarly unheroic, chaotic even. It comes from a blow to the head from a rock, with no clear idea about where or from whom the rock came. The two unattributed deaths: of William Rufus and of Kolbeinn, point both to unidentifiable social enemies (killers who cannot be identified) and to the hand of God.[130]

---

126 *Thómas saga*, ed. and trans. Eiríkur Magnússon, 1.24: 142–145. The sanction that Thomas suggests for the priest is deposition and lifelong penance. This is echoed in the way in which Bishop Thomas is said to have relagated lay people to a separate table at his court. *Thómas saga*, ed. and trans. Eiríkur Magnússon, 1.22: 106–107. "Ok því skipar erkibyskupinn riddurum ok öðru hoffólki sérligt borð, at þeir megi hafa með lágri hófsemð sína skemtan."

127 *Thómas saga*, ed. and trans. Eiríkur Magnússon, 1.34: 212–213.

128 *Thómas saga*, ed. and trans. Eiríkur Magnússon, 1.54: 348–349. The saga uses the term *útlægðir* to refer to this exile.

129 *Thómas saga*, ed. and trans. Eiríkur Magnússon, 1.1:6–7. "fellr honum handleggr himnakonungsins."

130 Many medieval laws found it hard to define and accept truly accidental harms. In *Grágás* we can see this particularly in the provision declaring that there shall be "no accidents." *Grágás Konungsbók*, Vígslóði 92, ed. Finsen, 1a.92, trans. Denis et al. 1.155. "Þat er mælt. at engi scolo verða vaða verc." Another example can be found in the laws of Henry I of England, which held almost all those who accidentally caused a death, including young children, accountable and in need in the king's pardon, Hurnard, *The King's Pardon*, 26–30.

A subsequent version of the death of Kolbeinn, in *Guðmundar saga B*, written 40–50 years after *Íslendinga saga* (c. 1320),[131] supports this reading of Kolbeinn's death. Rather than just implying that Kolbeinn's killing was divinely ordered or part of a divine order, the later author reworks the story of Kolbeinn's fatal confrontation in a way that leaves little room for ambiguity. Immediately after Kolbeinn falls to the ground the narrator intones that, "it was not certain, who had thrown the stone that killed Kolbeinn, and no one knows still to this day, but it is the report of those men who were there that that stone flew out of the air from above."[132] As I have stated above, the, likely earlier, version of this passage from *Íslendinga saga* insinuates that God signaled his involvement in Kolbeinn's end when the ordeals were successfully passed, a conclusion this writer clearly heard or drew for themselves. The description of Kolbeinn's death in *Guðmundar saga B* is more explicit, but both versions gesture at divine intervention in order to frame Kolbeinn's death in a way that is narratively satisfying. If it does little to console Arnórr, divine wrath to a degree obviates the need to inquire further into Kolbeinn's death.

This reading of Kolbeinn's death accords well with bishop Guðmundr's reputation as a holy man. There are other instances, too, in which he is portrayed as either asking for or receiving the benefit of God's avenging arm.[133] What is most notable about this particular case is that as far as the immediate political situation in the north is concerned, Kolbeinn's death solves nothing. In other words, although God's hand is sketched in retrospectively, his appearance as an

131 Stefán Karlsson, "Guðmundar sögur biskups," *Medieval Scandinavia, An Encyclopedia*, 245–246.

132 Stefán Karlsson ed. *Guðmundar sögur biskups II. Guðmundar saga B*. Editiones Arnamagnæanæ Series B vol. 7 (Copenhagen: Museum Tusculanum Press, 2018), 115: "Ecki vard vist hverr steini þeim hafdi kastað er Kolb(eini) vard at bana ok eingi madr veitt þat enn idag; Enn þat er fra sogn þeira manna er þar voro at or lopti ofan sa þann stein flivga."

133 After the battle on Grímsey, Bishop Guðmundr is said to ask God to avenge him, Sturla Þórðarson, *Íslendinga saga*, ed. Kålund, 1.358–359, trans. McGrew, 44: 188: "Gvðmunðr biskup bað gvð hefna sin, 'þiat ek ma eigi, vesalingr minn;'" When Guðmundr is still a priest, God is said to have taken vengeance on his enemies while at the same time ensuring that Guðmundr himself did not participate directly in any violence, *Sturlunga saga*, ed. Kålund, 1.144–145, trans. McGrew, *The Saga of Guðmundr Arason the Priest*, *Sturlunga saga vol. II Shorter sagas of the Icelanders* (New York: The American Scandinavian Foundation, 1974), 8–9: 110–111; and in another incident, after a priest refuses the bishop and his men hospitality, it is said that his farm burned down to ashes the next summer after the bishop predicted a worse misfortune for him than the responsibility of hosting a bishop and two men, Sturla Þórðarson, *Íslendinga saga*, ed. Kålund, 1.334–35, trans. McGrew, 37: 167.

avenger was never really instrumental in the specific confrontation between Kolbeinn and Guðmundr.[134]

Was Guðmundr positioning himself as Becket to Kolbeinn's Henry? It is difficult to be certain one way or another;[135] the sources are too limited to provide a clear view of how Guðmundr saw himself, but it is clear that he had a strong interpretation of the *privilegium fori*. Although it is probably impossible for us to entirely tease apart how much Guðmundr was modelling himself on Thomas Becket as opposed to how those writing about Guðmundr used Thomas as a model, it remains clear that their stories and the issues over jurisdiction that they document remain connected.

There are rival traditions about Kolbeinn Tumason, traditions that emphasize not his conflict with Guðmundr but rather his own devotion. Perhaps the best known is the attribution of the hymn "Heyr himna smiður" to Kolbeinn, with some traditions suggesting that he composed it on his death bed.[136] It is difficult to pinpoint when this attribution arose, but regardless, there was a rival tradition of Kolbeinn as a deeply spiritual person. These traditions about Kolbeinn also emphasize that whatever he may have stood for, he was not a defiant pagan chieftain.

## 5 Conclusions

This conclusion begins with the caveat that the story of the conflict between Kolbeinn and Guðmundr, as a part of *Íslendinga saga*, is only one narrative and moreover a narrative associated with a man who was positioned within the conflict that he narrates. It is also one of the few narratives from medieval Iceland that positions excommunication and outlawry so squarely against each other, no doubt inspired at least in part by the example from the stories that circulated about Thomas Becket.

---

134 The version of Kolbeinn's death in *Guðmundar saga B*, in which God's intervention is so clearly marked, gives little attention to the political dynamics of the situation (that is, what would have been useful to Guðmundr from a practical perspective is pushed into the background). The hagiographer does not care, and appears to think that his readers will not care either, whether God's aid to the bishop is actually sensible or helpful. What is important for him is to give Guðmundr as imposing an air of divine favor as possible.

135 Eiríkur Magnússon calls Guðmundr Thomas's "avowed disciple and imitator." *Thómas saga Erkibyskups*, 2.xxv.

136 Finnur Jónsson (ed.), *Den Norsk-Islandske Skjaldedigtning: A*, 2.39–40. In its prose context in *Guðmundar saga B* see, *Guðmundar sögur biskups II*, ed. Stefán Karlsson, 112.

Sturla knew a great deal about both outlawry and excommunication and how they were used in Iceland and in conflicts in Iceland. We need not believe everything that he writes as an exact truth, but he provides a thirteenth-century Icelandic perspective on these topics. What emerges from a close examination of his narrative as it relates to excommunication and outlawry is that he wrote about them in a way that shows little difference between the two in terms of implementation or consequences. Kolbeinn used outlawry for the same purposes and in the same way that Guðmundr used excommunication: to assert jurisdiction and punish disobedience.

Sturla's sympathies tend, to a point, to favor the saintly bishop, the claims of the Norwegian archbishop, and question the motives of Kolbeinn and later his brother, Arnórr. His family had long had connections with Bishop Guðmundr and with people who fought for Guðmundr (including Aron Hjǫrleifsson, who will be discussed at length in the next chapter). Sturla was also under the patronage of the Norwegian King Magnús Hákonarson, and it was in his interest to be careful in his narrations of events in both Iceland and Norway. Indeed, there is much discussion of how carefully Sturla had to tread in his depictions of the conflicts and events of his times.[137] Although it is difficult to precisely determine how wealthy a man he was, as an illegitimate son, howbeit of a powerful family, his resources were circumscribed and it is reasonable to expect that he was cautious.

Sturla's understanding of excommunication in canon law focuses on excommunication as potentially contagious, as forbidding consecrated burial, and as a legitimate political tool; he does not appear interested in the development of minor excommunication or the use of excommunication in lawsuits. Sturla also presents outlawry as a punishment that prevented Christian burial and entry into churches (as major excommunication also did), and as a political punishment meted down by a powerful chieftain, not an egalitarian way to police equals or keep society safe. Sturla presents a view of the two sanctions that leaves little distinction between them except that a bishop excommunicates, while a chieftain outlaws.

Sturla's knowledge of vernacular law and lawsuits is frequently mentioned, indeed, Guðrún Ása Grímsdóttir has argued that one of the reasons *Íslendinga saga* was written was to preserve information about how legal cases were conducted before the Norwegian king sent new laws in the 1270s.[138] I would like to argue here that the evidence points to Sturla's knowledge of canon law, at least

137 A point emphasized by Guðrún Ása Grímsdóttir, "Sturla Þórðarson," 33–35.

138 Guðrún Ása Grímsdóttir, "Sturla Þórðarson," 33–35.

in its vernacular forms, being equally deep—without implying that he should be recognized as a canon lawyer.

In the next and final chapter, I focus on Aron Hjǫrleifsson, an outlaw who was also a great friend of Bishop Guðmundr, according to all of the preserved sources about him. The material about Aron is in general not as subtle or sophisticated as the work most closely associated with Sturla Þórðarson, but the tales about him are an underutilized source that illustrates the connections between outlawry and excommunication that I have been arguing for in this book—Aron was an outlaw who expunged his sentence through the Christian ritual of pilgrimage and the patronage of a king.

CHAPTER 5

# Stories of Aron Hjǫrleifsson, Outlaw and Pilgrim

Aron Hjǫrleifsson was an outlaw-hero of the thirteenth century. Narratives of Aron's life illuminate the relationship between conceptions of outlawry, repentance, and royal power in the thirteenth and fourteenth centuries in Iceland. Aron fought as a supporter of Bishop Guðmundr Arason in the conflicts of the early 1220s.[1] A number of different sources, including an eponymous saga probably written in the first half of the fourteenth century document his life.[2]

---

1 The scholarship on *Arons saga* is not extensive see, Guðrún Nordal, "Grímseyjarför," *Viskustykki: Undin Soffíu Guðnýju Guðmundsdóttur fimmtugri 4. apríl 2014*, ed. by Rósa Þorsteinsdóttir and Gunnvör Sigríður Karlsdóttir (Reykjavík: Menningar- og minningarsjóður Mette Magnussen, 2014), 25–27; Guðrún Nordal, *Ethics and action*, 145–146, 150–151; Úlfar Bragason, "*Arons saga*: Minningar, mýtur og sagnaminni," *Ritið: Tímarit Hugvísindastofnunar* (2013): 125–145; Rolf Heller, "Aron Hjörleifssohn und Gisli Surssohn," *Arkiv för nordisk filologi* 81 (1966): 57–63; Stefán Karlsson, "En konjektur til Arons saga," *Bibliotheca Arnamagnæana 31, Opuscula 5* (1975), 412–414; Robert J. Glendinning, "*Arons saga* and *Íslendinga saga*: A problem in parallel transmission," *Scandinavian Studies* 41 (1969): 41–51; Gudrun Lange, "Didatische und typologische Aspekte der Arons saga," *Arbeiten zur Skandinavistik* (1996): 178–193; and Alice Naylor, "Aron Hjörleifsson and the figure of the outlaw in the Icelandic saga," (Master's thesis, University of Iceland, 2009).

Citations for *Arons saga* in this book are taken from Guðbrandur Vigfússon's 1858 edition of the text, which is based on the fragment AM 551 d beta 4to when available and the paper manuscipts AM 212 fol. and what he calls Additam. 27 (folio), See, Guðbrandur Vigfússon, *Biskupa sögur* 1 (Copenhagen: Hið íslenska bókmenntafélag, 1858), 41. The saga itself is printed on pages 619–638 of *Biskupa sögur* 1.

What is printed as chapters 3–10 of *Arons saga* in the 1946 edition of *Sturlunga saga*, is missing from both the fragment AM 551 d 4to. and all of the surviving early modern copies of the saga. Guðbrandur refers readers to chapters 74–90 of the *Guðmundar saga A* preserved in AM 399 4to (Resensbók), which is where the editors of the 1946 reading edition also take their text for this section. I reference these chapters from Stefán Karlsson's edition of *Guðmundar saga* A. *Guðmundar sögur Biskups I: Ævi Guðmundar Biskups, Guðmundar saga A*, Editiones Arnamagnaeanae, Series B, vol. 6. (Copenhagen: The Arnamagnæan Commission, 1983). *Arons saga* is not a part of the *Sturlunga saga* compilation, although it focuses on the same time period and uses some of the same sources.

John Porter has translated *Arons saga* into English, using his own (unpublished) edition as the base text: *The Saga of Aron Hjörleifsson* (London: Pirate Press and Writers Forum, 1975). References to this translation refer to chapter numbers rather than page numbers as there are no page numbers in Porter's translation.

2 Suggested dates for the composition of the saga have ranged between 1270 and the 1330s or 1340s. The earliest manuscript fragment of the saga, AM 551 d beta 4to, is from ca. 1400. I find it most likely that the saga was produced in connection with the effort to canonize Bishop Guðmundr Arason in the early fourteenth century. On the dating of the text see, Úlfar

 | DOI:10.1163/9789004461468_007

*Íslendinga saga,* the A and B texts of *Guðmundar saga biskups*, and stanzas of poetry preserved in these texts, sometimes thought to be remnants of a longer poem (called "Aron's drápa"), also document aspects of Aron's life.[3]

Although stories about Aron were in circulation at the same time that the more famous outlaw sagas were being written, Aron is not as often included in discussions of Icelandic outlaws.[4] Moreover, the manuscripts of *Arons saga* present a variety of challenges. Modern reading editions of the text of *Arons saga* are a pastiche, drawn in part from the earliest manuscript fragment AM 551 d beta 4to of ca. 1400 (which begins during what is now generally labeled chapter 12), and the early modern copies that seem to have been made from AM 551 d beta 4to when it was more complete. These copies are, however, themselves incomplete texts, and modern editors have emended their versions from a manuscript of *Guðmundar saga* that is itself a compilation of several sagas.[5]

---

Bragason, "*Arons saga*," 27–28. Hanna Óladóttir has made an edition of this manuscript in a University of Iceland BA thesis: Hanna Óladóttir, "Arons saga Hjörleifssonar eftir AM 551 d 4to: mállýsing og stafréttur texti," (B.A. ritgerð, Háskóli Íslands, Reykajvík, 1992).

3 Aron also makes a passing appearance in *Þorgils saga skarða* (in 1245). In this saga Aron appears as an established man in Norway, not overwhelmingly rich, but close enough to the king to recommend Þorgils to him and wealthy enough to accommodate some Icelanders in his household. His outlawry by Sturla is presented matter of factly as an identifying marker and perhaps as an explanation for his presence in Norway. *Þorgils saga skarða, Sturlunga saga* ed. Kålund, 2.141–142. "Árón Hjörleifsson var þá með konungi. Hann hafði reynt af Böðvari vináttu mikla, þá er hann var skógarmaðr Sturlu Sighvatssonar. Árón var hirðmaðr Hákonar konungs ok var kærr konungi, var hann ok góðr drengr. Árón gekk at Þorgilsi ok fagnar honum vel, 'ok skal þér heimilt alt þat gott, er ek hefi til at veita þér, hvárt sem þat er fé eða fullting.' [...] Árón hafði fjárkost eigi mikinn, en sparði engan hlut við vini sína."

4 Some reasons for this are the complicated manuscript preservation of the saga, and as Úlfar Bragason has argued, the pro-Norwegian attitude evident in Aron's relationship with King Hákon. Úlfar Bragason, "*Arons saga*: Minningar, mýtur og sagnaminni," 144.

Aron is giving a flattering portrayal in *Arons saga* and is shown in a less favorable light in *Íslendinga saga*, where Sturla Sighvatsson is given a more flattering portrayal. Guðrún Nordal suggests that "Sturla er hetjan í Íslendingasögu, en skúrkurinn í sögunni af Aroni," Guðrún Nordal, "Grímseyjarför," 27. [Sturla is the hero in *Íslendinga saga* but the villian in Aron's story.]

*Arons saga* and the other documentation of his life is contemporary with the production of other outlaw sagas. Aron is better attested as a historical person than, for example, Gísli Súrsson, but stories about them both were being circulated and written down at approximately the same time. Indeed, Rolf Heller has suggested that Aron's outlawry and exploits, most of which take place in Iceland's Westfjords, might have inspired the writing down of *Gísla saga*, which is set in the same landscape. Heller, "Aron Hjörleifssohn und Gisli Surssohn," 57–63.

5 The editors of the 1946 edition of *Sturlunga saga*, where *Arons saga* is also printed, emphasize that a version of *Arons saga* seems to have been used as a source in the *Resensbók* version of *Guðmundar saga*. See, introduction to, *Sturlunga saga*, ed. by Jón Jóhannesson et al., 2.xlix:

In this chapter I argue that these various sources depict Aron's outlawry as a sentence that had spiritual, as well as political, consequences from which it was possible—through pilgrimage and royal favor—to be absolved. More broadly, I address the ideas about outlawry, salvation, and law present in the different accounts of Aron's life and outlawry.[6] These stories suggest that, at least in the late thirteenth and early fourteenth centuries, the idea of a redeemed outlaw was a meaningful one. The materials attesting to Aron's life also emphasize that the distinction between excommunication and outlawry could be blurry. If we consider the stories about Aron Hjǫrleifsson in a legal context, they more closely reflect ideas about the possibility of royal mercy for outlaws found in *Járnsíða* and *Jónsbók*, codes promulgated after the historical Aron had died but not before the major sources about him were composed, than they do earlier legal sources such as *Grágás*.

After a brief account of the events of Aron's life in surviving accounts, I address the reasons that Aron was made an outlaw as well as the enmity between Aron and Sturla Sighvatsson (and the Sturlungs generally). I then analyze the ways that Bishop Guðmundr Arason is presented as Aron's spiritual, and physical, protector. In the latter half of this chapter I explore the ways in which outlawry is depicted as a "hell" that Aron is eventually able to escape from or erase the consequences of in two ways—through pilgrimage to the Holy Land and through the patronage of King Hákon Hákonarson.

---

"Nú vill svo vel til, að 3.–10. kap. sögunnar og nokkur atriði úr næstu kapítulum á eftir hafa verið tekin upp í Guðmundar sögu góða hina eldri í Resensbók, og má fylla tveggja blaða eyðuna eftir henni, en leiðrétta textann annars staðar. Þó er texti 3.–10. kap. ekki óbrjálaður í Resensbók. í honum eru innskot úr *Íslendinga sögu*, og verða þau ekki öll numin brott, án þess að skallar verði eftir," and Guðrún Nordal "Grímseyjarför," 25: "Handrit sögunnar eru brotakennd og sú tilfinning verður æ sterkari að Arons saga hafi kannski aldrei verið til í þeirri mynd sem við finnum í nútímaútgáfum." [Manuscripts of the saga are fragmentary and one has a stronger and stronger sense that, perhaps, *Arons saga* never existed in the form in which we find it in modern editions.] On Resensbók see, Stefán Karlsson, "Guðmundar sögur biskups," *Medieval Scandinavia: An Encyclopedia*, 246.

The early modern manuscripts of *Arons saga* themselves point to these gaps explicitly. In AM 212 fol. on fol. 126v (also labled p. 16), it reads: "hir vanttar stor mikit j þattin." [Here very much is missing in the *þáttur*.] In AM 402 4to. both fol. 4 and 11 are left blank at the same places in the text. In AM 426 fol. there has been an effort made, after then intial copying was completed, to "fill in the blanks." 192v in this manuscript was initially a blank page but a different hand has subsequently added text.

6 As Sverrir Tómasson has observed, *Arons saga* is more hagiographical in tone than many of the bishops' sagas, Sverrir Tómasson, "Old Icelandic Prose," 93. The view of *Arons saga* as a hagiography or hagiographical, however, needs to be considered in light of how many of the most hagiographic elements in the saga actually occur in manuscript lacunae supplied from *Guðmundar saga A* rather than in the earliest manuscripts of the saga itself.

## 1 Aron's Life in Brief

Aron Hjǫrleifsson was born ca. 1200 to a family on Snæfellsnes. Through his mother, he was related to the family of Hrafn Sveinbjarnarson, and both his parents are described as "well born."[7] As a boy Aron was a visitor in the household of Þorlákr Ketilsson in Hítardalir, and he was later fostered in the household of Eyjólfr Kársson at Flatey in Breiðafjǫrðr.[8] Aron fought with Eyjólfr in the following of Bishop Guðmundr Arason. He was involved in the killing of Tumi Sighvatsson (February 1222), who had occupied the bishop's see at Hólar in the autumn of 1221. Aron also fought at the battle on Grímsey that occurred between men supporting Guðmundr and chieftains led by Sighvatr Sturluson and his son Sturla Sighvatsson in the spring of that same year. Aron escaped, albeit wounded, from this battle. Sturla Sighvatsson outlawed Aron a few months later (still in 1222), probably in connection with the killing of Tumi Sighvatsson, Sturla's brother.[9] After surviving for several years in Iceland as an outlaw, periodically hunted by Sturla and his agents but helped by others, Aron escaped to Norway.[10] He went initially to Jarl Skúli, proceeded to go on pilgrimage to Jerusalem, and finally became a member of Hákon Hákonarson's court. According to his saga, he returned at least once to Iceland. He died of sickness in Norway in 1255.

## 2 Aron and His Enemies

Aron, particularly in *Aron's saga*, is presented as an enemy of Sturla Sighvatsson and his allies.[11] The sources account for their enmity as part personal dislike and part political rivalry. (The political rivalry, at least, is attested in all the sources). From childhood, Aron is depicted as having a difficult time getting along with Sturla Sighvatsson, and their relationship did not improve after

7 *Arons saga*, ed. Guðbrandur Vigfússon, 619, trans. Porter, 1: "Bæði vóru þau vel ættuð."

8 *Arons saga*, ed. Guðbrandur Vigfússon, 620, trans. Porter, 2.

9 The precise reason for the sentence is not explicit in any of the surviving sources. Aron was not present at this þing but rather heard about it while still travelling covertly from Svínafell in the east. According to *Arons saga*, ed. Guðbrandur Vigfússon, 621, trans. Porter, 11. "Litlu síðarr kvómu menn af þíngi ok fréttust þau tíðindi, at Aron var sekr gjörr ok xv biskupsmenn aðrir."

10 Frederic Amory emphasizes that Aron's strong social position made it easier for him to seek and receive assistance as an outlaw, "The Medieval Icelandic Outlaw," 198–199.

11 The rivalry is discussed in more detail in *Arons saga* than in *Íslendinga saga*, or *Guðmundar saga A*, where Aron plays a smaller role in the wider narrative.

Aron participated in the killing of Sturla's brother Tumi at Hólar. Aron is also, however, closely identified with Bishop Guðmundr, who was one of the major political rivals of Sturla (and many other chieftains with interests in the north of Iceland) in the first half of the thirteenth century, as has been illustrated in chapter 4. It can be difficult to separate the personal enmity between Sturla and Aron from the fact that they were from families and in alliances that were on opposite sides of the ongoing power struggles in the north.

Years before Sturla outlawed Aron, the two men lived in the same household at Þorlákr Ketilsson's farm in Hítardalr.[12] They were "called the same age" and were more or less foster brothers.[13] In *Arons saga* they are said to have had some difficulty tolerating each other even as children, and their time as foster brothers was short lived: "things went very well with them at that time though their games were rather vigorously fought. But when the two companions began to fall out more, then Helgi, Aron's uncle, invited him to stay with him."[14] It remains unexplained why their games descended into quarrels or fights, but a pattern of antagonism is nevertheless established early in the story. Aron moved on to stay with Helgi, who eventually left Aron with Eyjólfr Kársson when he himself went abroad.[15]

The attack on Sturla's brother Tumi at Hólar and the battle at Grímsey solidified the enmity between Sturla and Aron. Tumi attacked and occupied the episcopal see at Hólar in the fall of 1221.[16] This was both an insult and a material blow to the ambitions of Bishop Guðmundr, who fled to the island of Málmey in Skagafjǫrðr after the attack, along with his supporters, including Eyjólfr Kársson and Aron.[17] The bishop and his forces were soon running out of provisions and were being prevented from landing to seek them on the mainland.[18] Eyjólfr, Aron, and others decided that it would be best to try and retake

12 *Arons saga*, ed. Guðbrandur Vigfússon, 620, trans. Porter, 2.

13 *Arons saga*, ed. Guðbrandur Vigfússon, 620, trans. Porter, 2: "Þeir váru kallaðir jafnaldrar Aron og Sturla, því vóru þeir svo sem fóstbræðr." It is slightly ambiguous if this "svá sem" should be translated as Aron and Sturla being "like" (i.e. like but not quite) foster brothers or if it should be understood that they were together as foster brothers.

14 *Arons saga*, ed. Guðbrandur Vigfússon, 620, trans. Porter, 2: "Var ok þann tíma harla vel með þeim ok þó nökkut kappdrægt í leikum. En þá er meir tók at greinast með þeim kumpánum, þá bauð Helgi, föðurbróðir Arons, honum til sín."

15 *Arons saga*, ed. Guðbrandur Vigfússon, 620, trans. Porter, 2.

16 *Guðmundar saga A*, ed. Stefán Karlsson, 177: 191–192.

17 It is also emphasized as an insult to the saints, whose property Tumi is said to take over as if it was his inheritence. *Guðmundar saga A*, ed. Stefán Karlsson, 178: 192. "lagdi undir sik heilagra manna eign so sem hann uæri erfingi ordin." Cf., Sturla Þórðarson, *Íslendinga saga*, ed. Kålund, 1.352: "Tvmi sez nv a staðinn at Holvm með sveit sina, sva sem þat væri hans föðvr-leifð."

18 *Guðmundar saga A*, ed. Stefán Karlsson, 179: 192–193.

Hólar.[19] On a stormy night they did so, dragging Tumi and his men from the see and killing Tumi.[20]

Aron's role in Tumi's death is a little murky.[21] The sources name Einarr skemmingr as the actual killer,[22] but Aron was present and may or may not have wounded Tumi before he was killed.[23] He also took Tumi's weapons and armor. A few months later, during the counter attack on Grímsey mounted by Sturla Sighvatsson, Aron waved these trophies in Sturla's face.[24] This gesture might be compared to the use of bloody clothing as an incitement to revenge, it is certainly a taunt or dare for Sturla to pursue Aron.[25] Yet despite this incitement, Sturla did not kill Aron during the battle on Grímsey, even after Sighvatr suggested that the boat that Aron was escaping in be rowed after and Aron killed.[26]

Aron is characterized as Sturla's personal outlaw for the rest of the saga. Sturla outlawed Aron and pursued him relentlessly for as long as Aron

---

19 *Guðmundar saga A,* ed. Stefán Karlsson, 177–80: 192–194.

20 *Guðmundar saga A,* ed. Stefán Karlsson, 181–182: 194–197. See also, Sturla Þórðarson, *Íslendinga saga*, ed. Kålund, 1.352–353.

21 Not least because at this point in the narrative all of the manuscripts of the saga that survive are defective. Tumi is wounded when at group of five men attack him. Men assign the wound to Aron, but it is said that he neither affirmed or denied this. *Guðmundar saga A,* ed. Stefán Karlsson, 181: 195: "þa fieck T(umi) sar mikit. og uar þat kent A(roni). enn hann giordi þar at. huorcki bar þat af sier ne a sig."

22 Surviving accounts do not pinpoint Aron but rather Einarr skemmingr as the man who actually killed Tumi Sighvatsson, after he and his men have been forced out of an outbuilding by fire. *Guðmundar saga A*, ed. Stefán Karlsson, 182: 196. "Einar skemmingr kuad hann [Tumi] ecki hafa suo skipt godordum fyrir nordann land. at hann skylldi lifa leingr. og hann uo at honum. þuiat eigi urdu adrir til." See also, Sturla Þórðarson, *Íslendinga saga,* ed. Kålund, 1.353: "Einnar skemmingr qvað hann ekki sva skipt hafa goðorðvunvm firir norðan heiði, at hann skylldi lifa. Ok hann va at honum þviat eigi vrðv adrir til."

23 This made him a fair target in Icelandic legal conceptions of who could be held responsible for a killing.

24 *Guðmundar saga A,* ed. Stefán Karlsson, 198: 207. "A(ron) suar(ar) og hristi saxit Tuma n(aut) brugdit j hendi sier. Hier mättu sia. ragur fiandin m[ækinn] T(uma) naut. brodur þijns."

25 As in *Brennu Njáls saga*, ed. Einar Ól. Sveinsson, Íslenzk fornrit 12 (Reykjavík: Hið íslenzka fornritafélag, 1954), 116: 291, trans. Robert Cook, *Njal's saga* (London: Penguin, 2001), 116: 194–195.

26 *Guðmundar saga A*, ed. Stefán Karlsson, 205: 215, trans. Porter, 8: "Sturla s(egir). Vér þottumz sua við hann skileaz. at ek hugða þat litin drengskap vera. at sekia hann með mannfiølða iþetta sinn. En ef honum verðr lengra lifs auðit enn mic uarir. þa kann vera at þa uerðe en skamt meðar funda." This is a place where the fact that we have only literary presentations of Aron and not a list of facts bears remembering. It is quite possible that Aron simply escaped before any boat was detected.

remained in Iceland. The wording in *Arons saga* emphasizes this connection. It is said that "this same summer (1224) Sturla came to the west fiords and seeks claims against those men who have helped *his* outlaw (*skógarmanni hans*)."[27] Rǫgnvaldr, in the Westfjords hunting for Aron on Sturla's behalf, asked "whether he recognized Sturla's outlaw (*skógarmann Sturlu*) correctly."[28] Years later (1233), Sturla himself came to the Norwegian court when King Hákon was in Bergen. He and Aron had a memorable, if brief, meeting according to *Arons saga*. Aron looked at Sturla and asked him: "How well do you like your outlaw (*skógarmann þinn*), Sturla, since you stare at him so long, or how do I seem to you to have changed since we parted last?"[29] This terminology emphasizes the personal rivalry between the two men and also that a sentence of outlawry did not fall automatically, but needed to be brought by one individual against another. The phrase *skógarmann þinn*, when thrown back at Sturla in Norway (just after Aron has been to the baths no less), also emphasizes how humiliating it was for Sturla to not be able to enforce his own sentence. The saga suggests that the men would not both have survived the encounter had few people been present.[30]

The compiler of *Arons saga* makes every effort to stress how much Sturla hated Aron. In the saga Sturla calls Aron "the devil" before the Grímsey battle,[31] and after Aron is outlawed, it is said that "Sturla wanted to have Aron seized, and intended him more pain in dying than just a blow or two."[32] Sturla's hatred and pursuit of Aron contributes to Lange's reading of the saga as one in which Sturla is not merely a political enemy of Aron, but, in a typological perspective, an agent of the Anti-Christ.[33]

Not only did Sturla pursue Aron to the full extent possible, he also pursued those who helped Aron. As Guðrún Nordal writes, "Sturla Sighvatsson is adamant in accusing people who help his outlawed foster-brother, Aron

27 *Arons saga*, ed. Guðbrandur Vigfússon, 627, trans. Porter, 13: "Þetta sama sumar kom Sturla í Vestfjörðu ok leitar eptir við þá menn, er borgit höfðu *skógarmanni hans*." (emphasis mine).

28 *Arons saga*, ed. Guðbrandur Vigfússon, 624, trans. Porter, 12: "Hvárt hann kenndi rétt skógarmann Sturlu."

29 *Arons saga*, ed. Guðbrandur Vigfússon, 633, trans. Porter, 17: "Hversu lízt [þér] nú á skógarmann þinn, Sturla, er þú horfir á hann svá lengi, eða hversu þykkir þér ek skipazt hafa, síðan vit skiludm næst."

30 *Arons saga*, ed. Guðbrandur Vigfússon, 633, trans. Porter, 17.

31 *Guðmundar saga A*, ed. Stefán Karlsson, 198: 207. "dio[f]ullinn".

32 *Arons saga*, ed Guðbrandur Vigfússon, 629, trans. Porter, 14: "Sturla vildi láta handtaka Aron ok ætlaði honum meiri pínu til dauða en eitt högg eða t[v]au."

33 Lange, "Didatische und typologische Aspekte der Arons saga," 186–187.

Hjǫrleifsson, whom he has convicted."[34] This pursuit continued not simply in the immediate aftermath of the Grímsey battle, but onward for over a decade: "Thirteen years later Sturla is still claiming money from people for helping Aron. Haraldr Sæmundarson, Sturla's brother-in-law, has to pay two farms in compensation. The price seems to have gone up during the period."[35] Childhood difficulties blossomed into full-blown, persistent conflict in adulthood, but Sturla's reasons and the pursuit of Aron were not simply a personal matter.[36]

Aron is also constructed as the enemy of the Sturlungs, particularly in *Guðmundar saga A*. Just before the battle at Grímsey, Bishop Guðmundr himself prophesied that Aron would be pursued by and face harsh treatment from the Sturlungs.[37] Þórarinn Jónsson's willingness to help Aron is explained by his lack of great friendship with the Sturlungs (in contrast to his brother Ormr Jónsson Svínfellingr who wanted to have Aron held captive and handed over to them).[38] Failure to capture or kill Aron was a threat to both Sturla's honor and to the power and prestige of his family. An outlaw walking free was a political liability— a walking reminder of Sturla's failure to execute his own sentence.

Here it is important to interject that while many in the Sturlung family were enemies of Aron and the bishop, this was not universally the case, at least according to some sources. In *Íslendinga saga* Sturla Þórðarson hints that his father Þórðr Sturluson, who was a supporter of Bishop Guðmundr, also helped to protect Aron. Þórðr escorted Bishop Guðmundr back to Skagafjǫrðr about a year after the battle at Helgastaðir, after Guðmundr had spent the winter at Oddi in the south, and Þórðr is then mentioned as being present at Eyri, home of the sons of Hrafn Sveinbjarnarson, who were Aron's allies during this period

34 Guðrún Nordal, *Ethics and action*, 150.

35 Guðrún Nordal, *Ethics and action*, 151.

36 On the limitations of reading the primary motivation for vengeance seeking as an emotional reaction see, Stephen D. White, "The Feelings in the Feud: The Emotional Turn in the Study of Medieval Vengeance," *Disputing Strategies in Medieval Scandinavia*, ed. by Kim Esmark, Lars Hermanson, Hans Jacob Orning and Helle Vogt (Leiden and Boston: Brill, 2013), 281–311.

37 *Guðmundar saga A*, ed. Stefán Karlsson, 196: 206. "Suo s(eigir) mier hugur um ad þu komir hart nidr af Sturl(un)gum. en þo væntir mik at uid siaunst enn sijþar."

38 *Guðmundar saga A*, ed. Stefán Karlsson, 210–215: 219–225. After he escaped from Grímsey, Aron first travelled to the Eastfjords and eventually to Svínafell in the south east, where he was nearly imprisoned by Ormr Jónsson, who thought that it would be a gesture of friendship with Sturla Sighvatsson to deliver Aron to him. With the help of Ormr's brother Þórarinn Jónsson, Aron escapes to seek help in the Westfjords. *Guðmundar saga A*, ed. Stefán Karlsson, 212–215: 220–224. Þórarinn was, according to *Guðmundar saga A*: "ecke iafn mikill vin Sturlunga. sem Ormr." [not as great a friend of the Sturlungs as Ormr].

although they could not always protect him.[39] *Íslendinga saga* is not explicit on the point but makes room for the idea that Þórðr helped to protect Aron in Iceland.[40]

In the aftermath of the attack on Hólar and counter attack on Grímsey, fifteen other men are sentenced to outlawry by Sturla Sighvatsson, but Aron alone is mentioned by name, given a harsher sentence (he is made *óheilagr ok óferjandi ok óráðandi öllum bjargráðum*, i.e. a full outlaw with no mitigation), and persistently tracked by Sturla.[41] This focus can probably be traced to Aron's social prominence – a petty farmer might not be much of a coup to outlaw. And Aron was a prominent figure, connected to historically powerful families,[42] although families not as prominent, nor as talented at literary composition, as the Sturlungs. Another reason for the emphasis on their enmity might be explained as a narrative tactic: it worked to create a compelling picture of Sturla and Aron as archenemies, while underlining that Aron was aligned with the bishop against him.

*Arons saga* also capitalizes on is the political headwinds faced by the Sturlungs in the wake of the battle of Ǫrlygsstaðir in 1238, when Sturla and many of his important allies and relatives were killed.[43] Aron is in Norway at the time of the battle and loses nothing in it. The help Aron subsequently gives Sturla's brother, Þórðr kakali, who was in Norway at the time of the battle, given the history of enmity, might appear an even greater act of charity when it is offered at the end of the saga —although later events suggest that Þórðr was himself a competent leader and politician in his own right.[44]

---

39 Sturla Þórðarson, *Íslendinga saga*, ed. Kålund, 350, 364, trans. McGrew, 181, 193. Aron is mentioned as being at the same farm only a short time later: Sturla Þórðarson, *Íslendinga saga*, ed. Kålund, 1.365, trans. McGrew, 48: 194.

40 A support that makes more sense if we accept interpretations of *Íslendinga saga* as the work of a man reflecting on violent events within his family and their consequences. Helgi Þorláksson, "The Bias and Alleged Impartiality of Sturla," 207–211.

41 *Arons saga*, ed. Guðbrandur Vigfússon, 621, trans. Porter, 11.

42 Aron was related to the Sveinbjarnarsons who helped him early in his outlawry but were not powerful enough to resist pressure from Sturla (they fought on Sturla's side in the battle of Ǫrlygsstaðir and were executed after it). Sveinbjǫrn Hrafsson went to Norway with Guðmundr Arason. Hrafn's daughter Herdís was married to Aron's foster father Eyjólfr Kársson.

43 *Arons saga*, relates the following account, spoken by Hallvarðr to Icelanders in Norway, including Þórðr kakali, ed. Guðbrandur Vigfússon, 635, trans. Porter, 20: "Eigi skortir tíðindi frá frændum yðrum af Íslandi, bardagar stórir ok höfðingjalát ok mannafall mikit. [...] Sighvatr ok Sturla ok allir synir hans." ['There is no lack of news about your kinsmen from Iceland, great battles and death of chieftains, and a heavy loss of men [...] Sighvat and Sturla and all his sons.']

44 *Arons saga*, ed. Guðbrandur Vigfússon, 634–637, trans. Porter, 21.

## 3 Guðmundr Arason and Aron

Aron had keen enemies in Sturla Sighvatsson and his allies, but, he also had a firm friend and patron in Bishop Guðmundr Arason.[45] This is especially true in *Arons saga,* but their friendship is attested in all of the surviving sagas that chronicle Aron's life. The compiler of *Arons saga* is determined to highlight the connections between Guðmundr and Aron. It is one of the major narrative tools of the saga and one of the threads that ties Aron's adventures together, keeping them from becoming a haphazard collection of individual fights and escapes, which is how they tend to appear in *Íslendinga saga,* which shows a more dispassionate attitude towards Aron and his fate, although drawing on much the same raw material.

Bishop Guðmundr blessed Aron before the fighting at Grímsey and Aron's dramatic escape from the island. The specific moment on Grimsey is mentioned in several sources. In *Guðmundar saga A,* after their enemies were sighted off the island, Aron met the bishop in his preparations for battle. The bishop offered to hear Aron's confession. Aron refused, saying that he did not have time. The bishop blessed him instead, saying, moreover: "I have a presentiment, my son, that you will be harshly treated by the Sturlungs, but even so I expect that we shall meet again later."[46] He also reminded Aron to be good to the poor. This statement proved true, as the narrator is not slow to point out, saying, "and that is thought to have been very prophetic."[47] Aron did, in fact, meet Bishop Guðmundr again, three years later in Trondheim, Norway, where they greeted each other joyfully.[48]

Between this meeting in Norway and their parting just before the battle on Grímsey, Guðmundr and Aron never saw each other in person. Nevertheless, surviving narratives do not suggest that the bishop abandoned Aron to his fate.

45 Lange remarks that in *Arons saga* "Guðmundr ist Vertreter Gottes und der Kirche, und Aron ist sein Ritter," [Guðmundr is an agent of God and the Church, and Aron is his knight.] "Didatische und typologische Aspekte der Arons saga," 180.

46 *Guðmundar saga A,* ed. Stefán Karlsson, 196: 206, trans. Porter, 7. "Er nu byskup enn fyrir honum. ok lætur uel yfir þessum til tekium. ok uil ek nu son minn at þu gangir til skriptar uid mig. Ecki er nu tom til þess herra. s(eigir) A(ron). þuiat eigi mun þikia of þyckskipat til uarnarennar. ok er jafnann munur undir mans lide. Uel er slickt mællt. s(eigir) byskup. en þo skylldir þu sem trumestur uera. s(on) minn. ok uertu sem best uid fatæka menn. Nu blezar byskup hann og mæl(lti). Suo s(sigir) mier hugur um ad þu komir hart nidr af Sturl(un)gum. en þo væntir mik at uid siaunst enn sijþar." Not that there seems to be any particular evidence of Aron being generous with poor men.

47 *Guðmundar saga A,* ed. Stefán Karlsson, 196: 206, trans. Porter, 7. "ok þikir þat ordin en mesta späsaga."

48 *Arons saga,* ed. Guðbrandur Vigfússon, 630, trans. Porter, 15.

In *Arons saga* and *Íslendinga saga* (to a lesser extent) the bishop is credited with Aron's continuing survival in Iceland. All the sources agree that Guðmundr protected Aron, howbeit from a distance. When Aron arrived on the mainland from Grímsey, he was severely wounded. According to *Guðmundar saga* A, he treated his wounds with nothing except water that had been blessed by Bishop Guðmundr. Nevertheless, his wounds healed exceptionally well.[49] Guðmundr's protection continued after Aron had been outlawed. According to both *Arons saga* and *Íslendinga saga*, in the summer of 1223, the year after he was outlawed, Aron was sitting in the boathouse of the farm at Geirþjófsfjǫrðr in the Westfjords, when two strangers appeared.[50] Aron told them of a dream that he had had, a dream in which Bishop Guðmundr laid a cloak over him. Aron then learned from them that Sturla was in the area, searching for him and secured their help. As Robert Glendinning has observed, this dream has clear hagiographic features and is connected with a miracle story in which Guðmundr saved a girl from freezing to death on a journey by covering her with his cloak during a blizzard,[51] it also supposedly convinced the two men to fight with Aron.[52]

In 1224 a confrontation is reported to have occurred between Sturla and his men and Aron and those sheltering him at the farm at Lokinhamrar (also in the Westfjords).[53] After he broke away from Sturla and his men, Aron escaped, fleeing across a dangerous heath. The weather was foul and made it difficult to see. Yet Aron was able to cross the heath into safety despite a leg wound. The narrator attributes this success not to Aron's grit but rather to the ongoing protection of Guðmundr and God's mercy.[54]

49 In *Guðmundar saga A* the use of water blessed by Guðmundr to treat Aron's wounds is discussed at considerable length, with a description of the wounds and their healing. *Guðmundar saga A*, ed. Stefán Karlsson, 209: 218.

50 The area of Geirþjófsfjǫrðr is strongly associated with the outlaw Gísli Súrsson. *Gísla saga* says that he spent at least three winters there, sometimes living in hiding with his wife. *Gísla saga*, in *Vestfirðinga sögur, Gísla saga Súrssonar, Fóstbræðra saga, Þáttr Þormóðar, Hávarðar saga Ísfirðings, Auðunar þáttr vestfirzka, Þorvarðar þáttr krákunefs*, ed. by Björn K. Þórólfsson and Guðni Jónsson. Íslenzk fornrit 6 (Reykjavík: Hið íslenzka fornritafélag, 1943), esp. 21: 68–69.

51 *Guðmundar saga A*, ed. Stefán Karlsson, 43–44: 79–81. Robert J. Glendinning, "'Arons saga' and 'Íslendinga saga': A Problem in Parallel Transmission," *Scandinavian Studies* 41 (1969): 49.

52 Glendinning, "'Arons saga' and 'Íslendinga saga.'"

53 *Arons saga*, ed. Guðbrandur Vigfússon, 626–630, trans. Porter, 13–14.

54 *Arons saga*, ed. Guðbrandur Vigfússon, 629, trans. Porter, 14: After this escape, when he is being treated for his wounds by his mother, Aron lays down on the ground, crosses himself, and says two prayers, which he says Bishop Guðmundr taught him to do. *Arons saga*, ed. Guðbrandur Vigfússon, 630, trans. Porter, 14.

In all the sources about Aron but especially in *Arons saga*, this special relationship with Bishop Guðmundr serves to glorify Aron, and gives some of his more violent actions while outlawed at least a vague patina of divine approval. The times when Guðmundr supposedly helps Aron from afar also testify to his spiritual power, even at a distance. Many of these incidents, including Bishop Guðmundr predicting that Aron would survive the Grímsey fighting and Aron's escapes in the Westfjords are recorded not just in *Arons saga* but also in *Íslendinga saga* and *Guðmundar saga A*, emphasizing that these associations with the bishop were firmly in place by the time that *Arons saga* was written and are not the result of a single writer playing up connections between the two men.

The compiler of *Arons saga* was writing at a time when there was an active campaign to canonize Bishop Guðmundr (an effort that was ultimately unsuccessful). The narrative strives to depict Guðmundr as saintly and to make Aron a dutiful recipient of Guðmundr's holy benevolence; we can almost read it as an extended miracle story to be added to Guðmundr's canonization dossier.[55] The saga emphasizes both the loyalty and ultimate triumph of Aron and the protection that Guðmundr offered, however indirectly, to those who supported him in his own lifetime.

Up until now, this chapter has been focusing on the reasons for Aron's outlawry, the political rivalries that help explain the sanction, and some of the ways that his survival was accounted for in surviving sources. The remainder of this chapter examines the portrayal of Aron's outlawry as a religious experience and on the reintegration of Aron into Christian society. I will focus on the text of *Arons saga*, but all the major sources that attest to Aron's existence document his connections with Bishop Guðmundr and his pilgrimage to Jerusalem (discussed below).[56] I will also evaluate the ending of Aron's outlawry in light of the legal developments in Icelandic law, particularly as we can trace them in *Jónsbók*, which was well-established as a source of law by the fourteenth century when much of the documentation about Aron's life was produced.

---

55 The fact that Guðmundr was never formal canonized by the pope is in many ways not important either for the cult of Guðmundr or his portrayal in sagas, which consider him a saint. The process for canonizing a saint became much more complicated and formal in the thirteenth century, Haki Antonsson, "False Claims to Papal Canonisations of Saints: Scandinavia and Elsewhere," *Medieval Scandinavia* 19 (2009): esp. 186–199.

56 *Þorgils saga skarða* also attests to Aron's connections with King Hákon Hákonarson. *Þorgils saga skarða*, *Sturlunga saga*, ed. Kålund, 2.141–144.

## 4 How to Redeem an Outlaw

One of the persistent themes in material about Aron, particularly but not exclusively his saga, is the need to remember Aron as not a good outlaw but a former outlaw. There is an effort to prove that Aron was able to shed, if not exactly the sentence itself, then all of its potential consequences, including damnation, legal handicaps, restrictions on movement, and the denial of Christian burial. There is limited precedent for this effort in other outlaw sagas or in the *Grágás* manuscripts, where the suggestions involve either killing one or more other outlaws, or surviving twenty years in outlawry. The material about Aron takes a different tact. It portrays Christian pilgrimage and royal acceptance as the way back from outlawry, ideas shaped, I argue, in part by religious ideas and imagery and in part by the legal changes brought to Iceland via Norway, in large part through *Jónsbók*.

*Arons saga* is full of religious images and ideas, particularly the power of Bishop Guðmundr to protect Aron from harm. This is most often thought about in terms of the physical protection that a remote but present Guðmundr could offer to Aron—helpful lights, sympathetic ears, and holy water. But Aron was also an outlaw and therefore an imperiled soul. If Sturla had succeeded in capturing and executing him, he would almost certainly have died unshriven and buried in unconsecrated ground, his fate after death followed by a question mark in many minds. Moreover, as an outlaw, Aron would have been forbidden entrance to churches and hence the salvific properties of communion. *Guðmundar saga A*, for instance, mentions specifically that Aron was *í kirkjuskoti* "in the vestibule" or outer entryway of the church at Oddi before leaving Iceland, rather than inside the church, which is a careful distinction to portray Aron as someone who respected the restrictions the law placed on outlaws and their entrance into churches.[57]

## 5 Outlawry as Hell

The possibility of this fate for Aron is probably part of the reason that his outlawry was spoken of as *helja* "hell" in *Arons saga*. In the narration of Aron's escape to Trondheim in 1225, Haraldr Sæmundarson and two of his brothers helped to smuggle Aron out of Iceland on a ship. (According to *Arons saga*,

57 *Guðmundar saga A*, ed. Stefán Karlsson, 222: 232. Also discussed in chapter three, pages 85–87. Here we can see that a – probably clerical – author carefully keeps the outlawed Aron from physically being in the church itself.

they do this in no small part because of their love for Bishop Guðmundr).[58] It is explained that "They got Aron on a ship, with a good band of traveling companions. This ship sailed to Norway, and the voyage went well. They landed at Trondheim, the place that Aron would have most preferred. Bishop Gudmund was staying there, and so was Hjorleifr Aron's father. They welcomed him joyfully, and thought they had got him back from hell."[59] This passage treats Aron's outlawry as a terrible misfortune, a characterization that deemphasizes the role of Aron's actions. It also emphasizes not Aron's luck in escaping but rather the danger and risk that he was under as an outlaw. Some of this risk was spiritual—dying as an outlaw was potentially dying with a soul in some limbo. The "hell" of Aron's outlawry might also be compared with the torments faced by other famous outlaws like Gísli and Grettir, fighting monsters, bad dreams, and the dark.

The wording of the passage is, however, strikingly similar to a passage in *Guðmundar saga A* with reference to Bishop Guðmundr. After Guðmundr survived a journey through a blizzard, in which many of his companions perished it is said in the district that "they had got him back home from hell."[60] The phrase is almost identical to that used of Aron. Perhaps this is a deliberate echo, perhaps a conventional phrase. Regardless, Aron's time as an outlaw, like Guðmundr's being trapped in a blizzard, was likened to hell.

## 6 Outlawry as a Political Consequence

Aron's outlawry is also depicted as a consequence of the political unrest and conflict in Sturlung Age Iceland. In *Guðmundar saga A*, Aron's outlawry is put in a context of unrest and harsh consequences for many men. The saga reads: "At that time there was a great deal of conflict in the north of the country between Bishop Guðmundr and Sighvatr Sturluson. Sighvatr was supported by his son Sturla and his brother Tumi and many other chieftains [...] many

58 *Arons saga*, ed. Guðbrandur Vigfússon, 630, trans. Porter, 15.

59 *Arons saga*, ed. Guðbrandur Vigfússon, 630, trans. Porter, 15: "Um vorit eptir fór Aron suðr um land, ok sækir heim virðuligan mann, Harald Sæmundarson, ok bræðr hans, Vilhjálm ok Filippum; tóku þeir vel við honum, naut hann þar, sem víða annarsstaðar vináttu Guðmundar biskups, því at þeir höfðu hann lengi elskat; kvómu þeir Aroni í skip ok gott föruneyti; fór þat skip til Noregs ok varð vel reiðfara; tóku Þrándheim, þar sem Aron myndi helzt kjósa; þar var firir Guðmundr biskup ok Hjörleifr, faðir hans. Tóku þeir við honum með fagnaði ok þóttust hann or helju heimtan hafa."

60 *Guðmundar saga A*, ed. Stefán Karlsson, 44: 81: "[...] fannz þat a þui huerso mikit Svarfdelar unno G(uðmunde) preste. at þeir þottuz hann hafa or heliu heimtan."

lost property and peace, and got in their place outlawry, and some lost their lives because of the arrogance of Sighvatr and his sons, because they were very aggressive against Bishop Guðmundr with much injustice and violence."[61] This opening passage also places responsibility for Aron's outlawry largely out of Aron's hands. Speaking in general terms, it implies that those who lost their lives or suffered outlawry during this period were victims of the ambitions of Sighvatr, Sturla, Tumi and other chieftains. By this logic Aron's outlawry is narrated more as a natural disaster than as a consequence of Aron's actions.

This pattern, whatever the laws might say, fits well with other Icelandic outlaw narratives. Flawed and violent as a character like Grettir may be, his outlawry is still seen as a misfortune rather than a self-evident consequence.[62] *Íslendinga saga* is less keen to present Aron's misfortunes in quite this way (or devote much attention to Aron in general), but it does not offer a radically different portrayal of events. In *Íslendinga saga*, for instance, Tumi, for whose death Aron is outlawed, is not given a particularly flattering portrayal: he is described as being at the head of a rowdy band of followers and his reasons for occupying Hólar are characterized as personal ambition, not part of a family strategy.[63] Bishop Guðmundr is also portrayed with sympathy, and Sturla Sighvatsson himself is said to have gone on pilgrimage for his role in the attack on Guðmundr at Grímsey.[64]

Once Aron had been welcomed back into the world by Guðmundr and his father in Norway, his reintegration into society was still incomplete. I argue that the remainder of *Arons saga*, and to a lesser extent the information about Aron in other surviving sources, seeks to show how Aron came back from "hell" and probable damnation, from hunted non-personhood back into political and social legitimacy. Aron, freed from the immediate dangers of outlawry in the Westfjords, still needed to atone, not just (or even primarily perhaps) for violent acts, but also for the effective excommunication he had been under as

---

61 *Guðmundar saga A*, ed. Stefán Karlsson, 175: 190: "J þenna tijma horfðizt til mikils ofridar. fyrir nordann land. mill(um) þeirra G(uðmundar) byskups ok Sigh(uats) Sturl(u)s(onar). Þar til styrckti Sturla fodur s(inn) og þeir Tume bræður. og margir aðrir hofdingjar. ok leiddi af þessare til tekiu. mikenn ofagnat. morgum monnum fyrir nordann land. þuiat þeir ueitto mikinn agang G(udmundi) byskupi med myklum ojafnade. og ofridi."

62 Ahola catagorizes all of the major outlaw sagas as "tragic biographies," "Outlawry in the Family Sagas," 105–137.

63 Sturla Þórðarson, *Íslendinga saga*, ed. Kålund, 1.349–353, trans. McGrew 180, 182.

64 In his case, to Rome, Guðrún Nordal, "Grímseyarför," 25. On pilgrimages in the Sturlung Age see also, Guðrún Ása Grímsdóttir. "Um afskipti erkibiskupa," 28–62, and Ásdís Egilsdóttir, "Hrafn Sveinbjarnarson, Pilgrim and Martyr," *Sagas, Saints and Settlements*, ed. by Gareth Williams and Paul Bibire (Leiden and Boston: Brill, 2004), 29–39.

an outlaw without access to communion or Christian burial. Aron's rehabilitation takes two main paths: Aron went on pilgrimage and was accepted as a member of King Hákon Hákonarson's court.

## 7 Aron the Pilgrim

Aron was given a certain religious patina by his association with Bishop Guðmundr, but he also sought his own independent religious credentials. According to *Arons saga*, Aron vowed to go on a pilgrimage, a promise that he kept, even though he had to do so without the permission of his first patron in Norway, Jarl Skúli.[65] Despite not having the jarl's permission, Aron and a group of companions travelled to the Holy Land from Norway. It was reportedly a dangerous and difficult journey and only some of the group of men who set out survived to return, Aron among them.[66]

In travelling to the Holy Land, Aron was in prestigious company. In addition to penitent Icelanders in the contemporary sagas, the kings' sagas discuss two Norwegian Kings, Haraldr harðráði (ca. 1015–1066) and Sigurðr Magnússon (ca. 1090–1130), and their travels to the Holy Land in the eleventh and twelfth centuries.[67] King Sigurðr even had the by-name *Jórsalafari*, "Jerusalem-farer" although Ármann Jakobsson has argued that this name was more popular with nineteenth- and twentieth-century historians than in medieval sources.[68] Both kings might primarily be thought of as crusaders rather than pilgrims although, as Gary Doxey emphasizes, the two were not necessarily mutually exclusive enterprises.[69]

---

65 *Arons saga*, ed. Guðbrandur Vigfússon, 631, trans. Porter, 15. The political conflict between Hákon Hákonarson and Jarl Skúli cannot be treated in depth here, but there is little doubt that it contributed to the depiction of Aron's arrival and treatment in Norway and probably to Aron's decision to leave the country.

66 *Arons saga*, ed. Guðbrandur Vigfússon, 631, trans. Porter, 15.

67 King Sigurðr is particularly discussed in Morkinskinna. Haraldur harðráði spent more time in Byzantium and Kieven Rus' than in the Holy Land, but, at least according to *Heimskringla*, he is also said to have participated in attacks on Muslim controlled Sicily and travelled to Jerusalem, bathing there in the Jordan river, Snorri Sturluson, *Heimskringla*, ed. by Bjarni Aðalbjarnarson, Íslenzk fornrit 26–28, 3 vols. (Reykjavík: Hið íslenzka fornritafélag, 1979), 3.68–90.

68 Ármann Jakobsson, "Image is Everything: The Morkinskinna Account of King Sigurðr of Norway's Journey to the Holy Land," *Parergon* 30 (2013): 121–122.

69 Gary B. Doxey, "Norwegian Crusaders and the Balearic Islands," *Scandinavian Studies* 68 (1996): 156–160.

In Morkinskinna it is reported that Sigurðr decided to go on the journey to obtain "God's mercy and good fame," *Morkinskinna*, ed. by Ármann Jakobsson and Þórður Ingi

Why did Aron go on pilgrimage? The reasons given within his saga are limited. Aron claimed to have made a vow and been determined to carry it out, even if it meant displeasing Jarl Skúli, who was protecting him. Part of what the pilgrimage did was provide a way for Aron to realign his allegiances away from Skúli and toward King Hákon, who is portrayed in *Arons saga* as happy to accept him. Not all the sources mention his connection to Jarl Skúli: in *Guðmundar saga A* it is only mentioned that Aron became a *hirðmaðr* "retainer" of King Hákon after his pilgrimage.[70] But Aron's status as an outlaw in need of atonement features across the sources, and it seems likely that his vow was specifically a penitential vow that would have been considered sinful to break without good cause.[71]

*Guðmundar saga* A, Arons saga, and *Íslendinga saga* all mention Aron's pilgrimage. All of these sources cite a poem attributed to Óláfr Þórðarson hvítaskáld (ca. 1210–1259), Sturla Þórðarson's brother.[72] The stanza, which is thought to be a fragment of a now-incomplete *drápa* about Aron, highlights his journey to the Holy Land and cleansing in the River Jordan. It reads:

> The spear-hurler, he who won honour
> and fame, fared to Jerusalem.
> praise the man's great courage.
> With great spirit the wise warrior

---

Guðjónsson, Íslenzk fornrit 23–24 (Reykjavík: Hið íslenzka fornritafélag, 2011), 2.24: 71: "Guðs miskunn ok góðan orðstír." Ármann Jakobsson observes that Sigurðr's travels seem to be more about earthly glory and prestige than about heavenly rewards, "Image is Everything," 130–131.

70 *Guðmundar saga A*, ed. Stefán Karlsson, 232: "Haralldr kom honum utan. ok for hann þa til Haconar konungs ok gerðiz hirðmaðr hans. þa er hann kom utan fra Iorsølum."

71 The earliest *Grágás* manuscripts do not discuss pilgrimage. The topic is, however, discussed in chapter 19 of Kristinréttr Árna Þorlákssonar. There pilgrimage is discussed under the topic of *heit* "vows," which are defined as promises that one enters into voluntarily for the good of one's soul but that then become binding obligations – although exceptions can be made, in consultation with one's bishop, if health or other circumstances change. Árni Þorláksson, "Kristinréttr Árna," chap. 19, ed. Magnús Lyngdal Magnússon, 165–166. The text in Kristinréttr Árna is itself taken directly from Erkebiskop Jons kristenrett, *Norges gamle love*, 2.365–366.

72 Óláfr was a son of Þórðr Sturluson, a cheiftain on Snæfellsnes who had children by several women. He and the historian Sturla Þórðarson were full brothers. Óláfr spent significant time in the Royal courts in Scandinavia and a number of poems and fragments of poems are attributed to him. Lauren Goetting, "Óláfr hvítaskáld Þórðarson (Ólhv)" [Skaldic Poetry Database] http://www.abdn.ac.uk/skaldic/db.php?id=157&if=default&table=skalds (accessed 22.1.2016)

Fully cleared his outlaw's name out
by the glorious Jordan.[73]

This poem, which we have no reason to suppose was not written sometime before Óláfr died in 1259, is explicit that Aron cleansed himself of outlawry (in this poem using the unmistakable term *skógarmaðr*)—blurring any distinction between secular and ecclesiastical crimes/sins that could be expiated. Of all the sources *Arons saga* speaks the most about the pilgrimage. *Guðmundar saga A* and *Íslendinga saga* merely mention it and cite the poem: in them it does not feed into the wider narrative. To me this suggests that this poem was seen as one of the key sources about Aron and should be taken seriously, although it is short and open, of course, to different interpretations.

This stanza on pilgrimage underlines just how closely outlawry and excommunication could be enmeshed during this period. Even having escaped the immediate hardships of being hunted as an outlaw in Iceland, Aron was still compelled, whether by his own conscience or by pressures from others, to further expiate his outlawry. Even if we want to consider his decision to go on pilgrimage more calculated, an impulse to seek mercy and good fame similar to King Sigurðr's, it was still an important enough feature of the knowledge circulating about Aron that it appears not only in his saga or in *Guðmundar saga* but also in *Íslendinga saga*, which in general is less invested in Aron and the state of his soul. In other words, all the main sources about Aron agree that he went on pilgrimage and implicitly accept the poem's logic that going on a pilgrimage was a valid way to free oneself from the limitations and legal and social restrictions associated with outlawry.

Pilgrimage was one of the ways that a medieval person could show their desire to atone for sins or crimes.[74] One of the reasons that it served this

73 *Guðmundar saga A*, ed. Stefán Karlsson, 222: 232, trans. Porter, 15:
For með fremð ok tire,
flein ryrir, gat stýra.
mest lofa ek micla reyste
mannz Iorsale at kanna.
nafn rak út við itran
Iordan með þrek storan
skilldar freyr enn skyre
skogar mannz at nogu.

74 Pilgrimage is a complex phenomenon that cannot be fully addressed here and was not only undertaken to clease sins. Norman Housley, "Pilgrimage, Western Europe," *Dictionary of the Middle Ages* (New York, 1987), 9.654–661. For pilgrimage as a way to seek healing from disease see, Finucane, Ronald C. Finucane, *Miracles and Pilgrims: Popular Beliefs in Medieval England* (New York: Palgrave Macmillan, 1995). There is at least one Old Norse-Icelandic text detailing a pilgrimage itinerary that includes both Rome and Jerusalem,

purpose, in addition to being a journey to seek holy places and relics, is that pilgrimage journeys entailed significant physical risk;[75] indeed, several of Aron's companions died on the journey.[76] What is most striking about Aron's pilgrimage, which is not narrated in any detail, is his reason for his undertaking it. It seems that Aron's outlawry itself was the major reason that a cleansing pilgrimage, for good measure all the way to the Holy Land, was deemed a necessary or at least a wise decision. Aron undertook a long, difficult pilgrimage to free himself from the constraints of outlawry, almost as if outlawry were itself interchangeable with a grievous sin.

There are other examples in which outlawry is subsequently remedied, at least in part, by a pilgrimage. In *Íslendinga saga*, Kálfr Guttormsson kills Hallr Kleppjárnsson during an ongoing disagreement that takes place in the district of Eyjafjǫrðr in north Iceland. The case is prosecuted and Kálfr's punishment is to pay two-hundred hundreds, be exiled to Norway for three years and (presumably permanent) exile from Eyjafjǫrðr, roughly approximating the *fjǫrbaugsgarðr* type of outlawry (and one of many examples of "district outlawry" that appears in sagas but not in *Grágás* manuscripts). In addition to paying the fine and leaving the country, Kálfr is said to have gone on pilgrimage "south" presumably to Rome or the Holy Land, "where he got absolution for all his actions."[77]

It is hard to know how frequently pilgrimages were undertaken by Icelanders (either from Norway or directly from Iceland) and we cannot be certain that all those said to have gone on pilgrimage actually undertook such journeys, but sources outside of the sagas suggest that, the idea of pilgrimage was at least entertained as a possibility for some sinners. For example, AM 671 4to fol. 1 and AM 625 4to. fol. 162, both contain a similar formula for promising to travel to Rome in search of atonement. The formula in question here reads: "I swear to you and I promise to go out this summer and go south to Rome if God gives me life and health [to do so] and atone for my sins unless you, Lord Bishop, give another counsel."[78] It is worth noting in the context of my larger argument that

see Tommaso Marani, "Contextualising *Leiðarvísir*: Sant' Agnese, the Catacombs, the Pantheon and the Tiber," *Saga Book* 33 (2009): 44–66.

75 George D. Greenia, "Bartered Bodies: Medieval Pilgrims and the Tissue of Faith," *International Journal of Religious Tourism and Pilgrimage* 7 (2019): 38–51. DOI: https://doi.org/10.21427/HRMH-KX63.

76 *Arons saga*, ed. Guðbrandur Vigfússon, 631, trans. Porter, 15.

77 Sturla Þórðarson, *Íslendinga saga*, ed Kålund, 297, trans. McGrew, 29: 152: "Kalfr skylði vera vtan III vetr oc herad-sekr or Eyiafirði. Þetta fe gallt Kallfr alt sem giortt var, oc for vtan oc gekk svðr oc tok lavsn allra sinna mala, hellt oc alla sætt vel."

78 *Diplomatarium Islandicum*, 2.46. "handsala ek þer ok heit ek at fara vtan at sumre ok ganga sudr til roms ef gud gefr mer lif ok heilsu ok beta fyrir syndum minum. nema þit herra biskup seaet annat rad fyrir."

the word used here *beta* a variant spelling for *bœta*, "atone" is the same word that is used for "to compensate" for any number of offenses, further suggesting how intertwined the vocabulary and concepts of outlawry and excommunication could be.[79]

Aron's pilgrimage was a signal to mark that he did not die an outlaw (or an excommunicant) and the verse that attests to it appears in all of the major sources about him. By the logic of this verse, Aron went on pilgrimage to cleanse himself from the taint of being an outlaw as much as from the killings he had committed or any other flaw. To the producers and consumers of material about Aron, it seems that outlawry could be atoned for. At the close of *Arons saga* it is said that Aron is likely in heaven "both through the intercession of his friend, the good Bishop Gudmund Arason, and especially throught [sic] the grace of our most gentle Redeemer, whose pilgrim he may justly be called, because he visited his most holy grave, and many other holy places," underlining the importance of Aron's pilgrimage both with regard to Aron's soul and his reputation.[80]

Aron is also redeemed in another way: in the late 1230s and 1240s after the conflicts of his youth have receded, Aron finds himself in a position to help the brother of his former arch-enemy Sturla. Þórðr kakali is in Norway when he learns of the deaths of Sturla and Sighvatr, and the descent of his own fortunes after the Battle of Ǫrlyggastaðir. With the king reluctant to help, it is Aron who steps in to aid Þórðr.[81] In so doing, he seals the end of the conflict between himself and the Sturlungs. A more cynical interpretation might emphasize that Aron emerges victorious (and alive) while his former enemies are killed in battle. Aron and Þórðr even travelled back to Iceland together, Aron as a free man. In *Arons saga* this return is a more or less unmitigated triumph for Aron, who is portrayed as reconciled with all his (living) former enemies. In

79 "bot." A Lexicon of Medieval Nordic Law. http://www.dhi.ac.uk/lmnl/nordicheadword/displayPa. A similar confluence occurs in Old English, in which compensation and penance are both rendered by the same word, *bōt*. Marafioti, "Secular and Ecclesiastical Justice," 781; Angus Cameron, Ashley Crandell Amos, Antonette diPaolo Healey, et al., eds., Dictionary of Old English: A to H Online (Toronto, 2016), http://doe.utoronto.ca, s.v. "bōt," sections b–c. (last accessed 30 March 2020).

80 *Arons saga*, ed. Guðbrandur Vigfússon, 638, trans. Porter, 22: "bæði firir meðalgöngu vinar síns, hins góða Guðmundar biskups Arasonar, ok einkanliga firir mjúkustu vors lausnara miskun, hvers pílagrímr hann má réttliga kallast, firir þat er hann heimsótti hans helgustu gröf, ok marga aðra heilaga staði."

81 *Arons saga*, ed. Guðbrandur Vigfússon, 634–638, trans. Porter, 19–22.

1254 after a few conversations and agreements it is said that "Aron was at peace with all men in Iceland."[82]

## 8 Outlaws and the Kings of Norway

As mentioned above, Aron became a member of the Norwegian court after he escaped from Iceland. Aron was first sheltered by Jarl Skúli, but Skúli was displeased when Aron left to go on pilgrimage against his wishes.[83] King Hákon Hákonarson (ruled 1217–1263), however, was willing to accept Aron into his court. Indeed, it seems reasonable to suppose that Aron's defiance of Jarl Skúli was a good way to ingratiate himself with King Hákon. According to *Arons saga* the king granted Aron ongoing revenue and married him off to a noble Norwegian widow.[84]

Perhaps Aron's shift in affiliation from Skúli to Hákon made it easier to imagine or reimagine Aron as a political exile rather than a criminal or perhaps supporting Aron was in and of itself a show of aggression to Sturla and his allies. Snorri Sturluson, for instance, supported Jarl Skúli against Hákon and in a way we can imagine that conflicts in Iceland and in Norway were being played out on different stages (in Iceland and in Norway), or on different scales, but were still part of or at least later constructed to be part of the same conflicts. Thus, associating Aron with King Hákon not only conferred on him royal mercy, it also called into question the legitimacy of the sanction he was under in Iceland since it had been put on him by allies of Hákon's rival. But regardless of Aron's particular circumstances, there is a strong thread through many Icelandic narratives of outlaws that has them shining at their best when in the company of Norwegian kings.

The prominence of a Norwegian king in the narration of Aron's life highlights a feature that is actually rather common to outlaws in Icelandic sources: they can be protected, and perhaps even rehabilitated, by association with a king.[85] Other scholars have noted the special relationship between outlaws and kings. Anthony Faulkes, for example, writes that "none of the Icelandic outlaws shows much devotion to either Christ or the Virgin Mary, but Grettir, though he will

82 *Arons saga,* ed. Guðbrandur Vigfússon, 638, trans. Porter, 22: "var Aron sáttr við alla menn á Íslandi."

83 *Arons saga,* ed. Guðbrandur Vigfússon, 630–632, trans. Porter, 15. Skúli was executed by King Hákon in 1240 after declaring himself king.

84 *Arons saga,* ed. Guðbrandur Vigfússon, 632, trans. Porter, 16.

85 This relationship does not hold true for all outlaws.

not accept his sentence of outlawry, is devoted to King (later Saint) Óláfr of Norway, just as Robin Hood rejects the authority of the sheriff of Nottingham but submits to the King of England."[86] Faulkes overstates the a-religious nature of outlaws' devotion,[87] but the observation of a special connection between a king, particularly a holy or successful king, and an outlaw who serves him, whatever his crimes in other areas, is accurate. It was also an image that seems more likely to be of benefit to kings than to many people outlawed in their own conflicts.

The idea of a king as a tamer of outlaws is taken to an extreme in *Fóstbræðra saga,* a saga set in the late tenth and early eleventh centuries about a pair of men who swore allegiance to one another and were both eventually outlawed.[88] In this saga of two Icelandic foster brothers St. Olaf (King Óláfr Haraldsson of Norway) serves as a patron and protector of these otherwise unruly, even ungovernable, men.[89] St. Olaf's ability to turn their violence to social constructive use is mentioned explicitly in Flateyjarbók, where the scribe-compiler Jón Þórðarson integrated *Fóstbræðra saga* into the saga of St. Olaf, explaining that:

> The Lord God, Jesus Christ, saw the need of all us Northmen to choose for us such an intercessor as thus with great goodness strove with our need, as this shining beam and light-shedding lantern, the holy King Óláfr Haraldsson, who not only loved his subjects in Norway, but also equally those who lived in Iceland, those who sought his favour and esteem, decorating each one with worldly honours as he thought appropriate, some with gifts and money, some with titles. Experience also showed that those who loved God the most received the greatest affection and love from King Óláfr. King Óláfr loved his retainers dearly, and he took it very ill if they were treated maliciously, especially those whom he thought the most highly of. Because of this, it seems proper to set down here a

86 Faulkes, "Outlaws in Medieval England and Iceland," 145.

87 It is true that outlaws in the surviving sources show limited devotion to the Church, but that does not necessarily mean that they did not care about their souls. Þormóðr Bersason, one of the outlawed foster brothers of *Fóstbræðra saga*, for example, is said to be afraid of nothing except God, *Fóstbræðra saga*, 13: 191 (*Flateyjarbók* version). "því at Grettir er myrkhræddr, en Þormóðr guðhræddr." [because Grettir is afraid of the dark but Þormóðr afraid of God.]

88 There is little evidence for their existence outside of the saga itself.

89 There is considerable disagreement about when *Fóstbræðra saga* was first put to parchment. Dates as early as 1200 have been suggested although the earliest surviving manuscript witness for the saga is AM 544 4to (Hauksbók), which is from the first half of the fourteenth century.

> certain þáttr about two of his retainers, Þorgeirr Hávarsson and Þormóðr Bersason, who were with him for a long time and in many perils, although they are not always mentioned in *Óláfs saga* itself. From this one must notice the grace and good luck of King Óláfr, that he showed that restraint to such terribly unruly men as those foster-brothers were, who loved the king above all other men. Also, all their deeds, which they performed in honour of the king and which showed their excellent defense, valour and courage, afterwards brought them fame and renown before they ended their life and suffering of this wretched world.[90]

According to this passage, which is an unapologetic panegyric to St. Olaf, one of the things that made St. Olaf so special was his ability to direct the powers of unruly men for good.[91] Under a good king, even the chaotic violence of an outlaw can be channeled appropriately, seems to be the argument presented in this passage, and the explanation for including *Fóstbrœðra saga* in the larger narrative of St. Olaf's life.

Þormóðr, one of the outlawed foster brothers, is further glorified by dying alongside St. Olaf at the Battle of Stiklastaðir (1030). It seems reasonable to conclude that this secured him, for narrators and audiences, a

---

90 *Flateyjarbók: En Samling af norske Konge-Sagaer*, ed. by Guðbrandur Vigfússon and C.R. Unger (Christiania: Malling, 1862), 2.91–92, trans. by Elizabeth Ashman Rowe, *The Development of Flateyjarbók: Iceland and the Norwegian dynastic crisis of 1389* (Odense: University Press of Southern Denmark, 2005), 57: "Gvd drottinn Jesus Christus sa til þess þǫrf vora alla Nordmanna at uelia oss slikan formælanda sem suo kostgæfde med mikille godfyse uora naudzsyn sem þessi skinande gæisli ok lysanda liosker hin heilagi Olafr konungr Haralldzson huerr at æigi at æins elskade sinn undir gefinn lyd j Noregi helldr ok iafnnuel þa sem a Jslande bygdu þa sem sottu hans tign ok virding prydannde huernn eftir þui med veralldar virdingu sem hann fann tilfelldan suma med fegiofum en suma med nafnnbotum. gafuzst ok þær raunir a at þeir fengu mesta ast ok elsku af Olafi konungi sem gud elskudu framazst. Olafr konungr unni mikit hirdmonnum sinum ok þotti ser j þui miog misbodit ef þeim uar med ǫfund misþyrmt ok þeim ollum framazst er honum þotti mestr madr j. þikir af þui tilheyriligt at setia her nockurnn þatt af hird monnum hans tvæimir þorgæiri Hafarssyne ok þormode Bessasyne er leinge voru med honum j moꝛgum mannraunum þo at þeirra se æigi iafnnan vid getith jsealfri Olafs sogu. ma af sliku merkia gætzku ok giftu Olafs konungs at hann uæitti þat athalld suo myklum uæirdarmonnum sem þeir voru fostbrædr at þeir elskodu konunginn yfir alla menn fram. urdu þeim ok sidan sin verk ǫll at frægd ok frama þau sem þeir unnu j heidr vid konunginn ok syndu af ser agæta uǫrnn dad ok dræingskap adr þeir endadu sitt lif ok erfuide þessarar ueslu veralldar."

91 On St. Olaf's role as a mediator in *Fóstbrœðra saga* see, Giselle Gos, "Women as a Source of heilræði, 'sound counsel': Social Mediation and Community Integration in *Fóstbrœðra saga*," *The Journal of English and Germanic Philology* 108 (2009): 297–298.

place in heaven.[92] Just before the narration of the battle, the saga reports that Þormóðr followed St. Olaf back to Norway after his exile because he preferred to die with him rather than to live on after the king was dead, emphasizing his place as a devoted servant of the king, following him into quasi martyrdom.[93]

Aron died of sickness in Norway, not in a battle. King Hákon visited him before he died as "an intimate friend or kinsman" and attended the funeral,[94] once more conferring a sense that Aron was fully reintegrated into society after his outlawry. The idea that a special relationship with the king could ease the stigma (and the dangers) of being an outlaw fits well with ideas put forward in continental Scandinavian lawcodes (also found in Anglo-Saxon legal sources), and discussed previously in chapter 2, that reserving the pardoning of outlaws to kings tied the right to outlaw and release from outlawry to a newer conception of royal authority, one that presented an expanded view of a king's jurisdiction and power, giving him a role as font of mercy.[95] This view was, of course, of particular new relevance to fourteenth-century Icelanders, who were formally under the Norwegian crown.

## 9 Kings and Icelanders

One of the distinctive features in Icelandic narratives of outlaws being helped by kings is that the laws that they were sentenced under were not, generally speaking, royal laws—at least during the time that the events being narrated were taking place. They were not within the king's peace per se, but this did not prevent them from being protected and helped by Norwegian kings. Aron was not outlawed by a king, but it was in part through the power and protection of the king that Aron was able, once again, to become a part of Christian society.

Aron is not the only outlaw to find a special hope and protection through the personal intervention of a king. Stories of outlaws redeemed by kings like Hákon Hákonarson or St. Olaf could have served ambitious Icelanders of the

92 Gos, "Women as a source of *heilræði*," 284.

93 *Fóstbræðra saga*, 24: 260. "Hann fór ok aptr með honum til Nóregs, því at honum þótti betra at deyja með honum en lifa eptir hann."

94 *Arons saga*, ed. Guðbrandur Vigfússon, 638, trans. Porter, 22. "Sem til síns hugarmanns eðr frænda."

95 See Åqvist, *Frieden und Eidschwur*, and Hurnard, *The King's Pardon*.

fourteenth century—whether they were promoting Guðmundr as a saint or Aron as a hero.[96] Here it might be apt to mention that one such fourteenth-century Icelander was almost certainly Haukr Erlendsson, lawman and the main scribe of Hauksbók, a manuscript whose stories of kings and outlaws, including a version of *Fóstbrœðra saga*, are oriented towards the Norwegian royal court.[97] As mentioned above, they may also have been useful ways of discrediting royal rivals and the allies of those rivals, especially once the battles were over and the winners easier to back securely.

The legal changes brought to Iceland with *Jónsbók* might also help to explain the depiction of outlawry and its remediation in stories about Aron. Although *Grágás* (in Konungsbók) provides only one remedy to negate the sentence of full outlawry, killing another outlaw, *Jónsbók* suggests other paths. Most notably, those who felt that their offenses were justifiable or could be explained by mitigating circumstances could, according to section 18 of the chapter on personal rights, throw themselves at the mercy of the Norwegian King as a potential way to end or mitigate the outlawry sentence with a royal pardon. After a person who committed an *wtlegðar werk* was helped abroad or himself escaped abroad, if he managed to do so before any sentence had been passed on him, he is instructed to go to the king and: "When he comes before the king, he shall be the recipient of whatever mercy the king decides to show him regarding his return to Iceland."[98] *Arons saga* and other outlaw narratives (dated from their earliest surviving manuscripts) were written in the fourteenth century, a time when *Jónsbók* and not *Grágás* was the generally accepted legal code. It seems not too far a stretch of the imagination to suppose that the newer way of thinking about outlawry, tying it to the mercy of the king, was influential and understandable to writers and readers in the fourteenth century in Iceland.

96 For further discussion of how medieval Icelanders viewed Norwegian kings see, Ármann Jakobsson, "Hákon Hákonarson: Friðarkonungur eða fúlmenni?" *Saga* 23 (1995): 166–185; and Theodore M. Andersson, "The King of Iceland," *Speculum* 74 (1999): 923–934.

97 Emily Lethbridge, "Hauksbók," *66 Handrit úr fórum Árna Magnússonar*, ed. by Svanhildur Óskarsdóttir, Matthew Driscoll and Sigurður Svavarsson (Reykjavík and Copenhagen: Stofnun Árna Magnússonar and Den Arnamagnæanske Samling, 2013), 90.

98 *Jónsbók*, 4.18, ed. Ólafur Halldórsson, 57; trans. Shulman, *Jónsbók*, 65: "[…] hverja miskunn sem konungr vill þá á gera um landsvist hans, er hann kemr á konungs vald." Note that Iceland is not specifically named in the text, which rather refers to the offender's *landsvist* or right to domicile in the country, which could refer to Norway or Norwegian domains.

## 10 Conclusions

*Arons saga* addresses the possibility that one might cease to be an outlaw. It is not simply a killing that Aron needed to expiate, he did not even kill Tumi Sighvatsson himself after all. Rather, I would argue, what he is expunging is the stain of outlawry itself. Outlawry, much like excommunication, became a barrier to participation in Christian society. In the sources attesting to Aron's life, full outlawry is treated as something that can be reversed, but the means to achieve this are to be found not in formal legal processes but in the rituals of the Church and through the intervention of a benevolent king and a bishop-saint. Aron did not seek out the probably somewhat fantastical solutions to overcoming outlawry suggested in *Grettis saga* (survive for twenty years as an outlaw) or in the Konungsbók manuscript of *Grágás* (kill another outlaw).[99]

Aron is presented as an outlaw who was a casualty of civil conflict, protected by a bishop and a king and, under these new protections and in the afterglow of a pilgrimage, freed from the sentence of outlawry. Another way of reading the moral of Aron's story, or at least his saga, is to see him as a victim of political structures and conflicts of the Sturlung Age. It took the strong hand of a king to save Aron from a grim fate of perpetual outlawry and likely death without last rights or proper burial (i.e. of likely damnation). As Úlfar Bragason has emphasized, part of this might be explained by the political concerns of fourteenth-century Icelanders, who were legal and politically connected to the Norwegian crown in ways they had not been before the 1260s. The king's mercy took on a new prominence as a part of this shift and is emphasized not just in *Arons saga* but also in other stories of outlaws, particularly in narratives that can be associated with the Norwegian court, such as the Hauksbók version of *Fóstbrœðra saga*.[100]

*Arons saga* and Aron's life as depicted in other sources present a situation in which outlawry could be remedied, at least in part, with a show of Christian remorse. The conflation between outlawry and excommunication in this reasoning extends to the point that Christian remedies are applied to secular punishments without comment. All three of the main sources about Aron reproduce the poem about his pilgrimage without any concern about the logic of expiating a sentence of outlawry with a bath in the Jordan.

*Arons saga* and the other surviving sources about Aron make a connection between outlawry and religious concepts of repentance. They also illustrate

99 *Grágás Konungsbók*, Vígslóði 110, ed. Finsen, 1a.187, trans. Denis et al., 1.170–171.
100 Lethbridge, "Hauksbók," 90.

that, at least for fourteenth-century saga compilers and composers, the association between outlawry and damnation was reasonably strong. In these same stories, the remedies provided to protect from the worst consequences of outlawry are few: heroic death in battle for a holy king is one option, pilgrimage another. A newer vision of outlawry is also clearly visible, one that promoted the Norwegian King as the ultimate arbiter of the fate of his subjects, especially for those who committed actions that, absent the king's mercy, could lead to outlawry.

# Conclusion

The central argument of this book is that the sanction of outlawry, as it is presented in thirteenth- and fourteenth-century Icelandic sources, derived many of its features from excommunication. I base this argument on a careful consideration of the nature and dating of the surviving legal evidence, the technical similarities between excommunication and outlawry in surviving sources, and the degree to which outlawry and excommunication were used to punish the same breaches. I also illustrate how the close connections between outlawry and excommunication unfold in several narrative sources.

This argument is by nature not possible to prove in a strict sense. The evidence is too limited, and the compilers of lawbooks were not particularly focused on revealing their methods of composition or the logic behind their choices. This argument is also limited in the sense that it is focused on outlawry in a narrow band of written sources produced and used by an elite, literate minority of people.

Seeing outlawry as derived from excommunication is, nevertheless, the best way to account for the number of similarities between excommunication and outlawry in medieval sources from northern Europe, especially Icelandic sources. In these sources outlawry and excommunication share many detailed features such as being contagious and forbidding those under them from consecrated burial. In narrative sources, both are used in similar ways over the course of political conflicts.

These are not chance resemblances but rather result from a constant dialogue between the two sentences in medieval Iceland. Whatever outlawry may have looked like in the tenth century or earlier (and it almost certainly existed in some form at that time), by the thirteenth it had long been used and developed in a Christian context and in a world in which learned literacy was most often connected, at least indirectly, to the Church.

Focusing on the dates at which surviving manuscripts were produced as is done in this book, rather than on the times that they purport to speak about, shifts most of the evidence about Icelandic outlawry to the late-thirteenth century and later. It leaves us with very few sources about outlawry in Iceland that predate the thirteenth century.[1]

1 In this book I have not engaged with the evidence of Eddic poetry, which I argue has limited value for legal historical study in this particular case.

 | DOI:10.1163/9789004461468_008

The issue is not whether the *Grágás* manuscripts or other manuscripts preserve any older material. They do. I want to emphasize, however, that the material they contain is presented as a whole and as a whole produced in the late thirteenth century. It is not that everything in late-thirteenth-century sources is brand new. Individual words, law terms, and phrases might well be considerably older, but the form in which they are in the manuscripts is what we have and what we can interpret.

Icelandic narrative sources used the dramatic potential of excommunication, which often had connotations of damnation, to full effect. Excommunication was a sanction that never quite shed its associations with penitence and public shame and forgiveness, a feature that also sometimes appears more prominently in narrative than in legal sources, as, for example, in the stories about Aron Hjǫrleifsson, who was an outlaw but also a pilgrim.

The complexities and competing ideas about topics such as excommunication and burial and their potential effects on the afterlife are also, I have shown, topics about which medieval sources contain many competing statements and mutually exclusive ideas. Nevertheless, I suggest that for the group of northern sources that have been the focus of this study, consecrated burial had a fairly consistent meaning and was seen as a punishment with real consequences in both legal and narrative sources. Excommunication can likewise be viewed through a variety of lenses, and it seems certain that people had different beliefs about how significant it was, the potential harm it could do, and the reach of its effects. But even when we consider these complexities, excommunication and outlawry in the legal world of Iceland in the thirteenth and fourteenth centuries remained sanctions in dialogue, sometimes to the point of almost merging.

My arguments are made from a limited pool of sources, produced by elite writers mostly for elite, educated audiences. It is difficult to assess how much of the information and attitudes that they contain affected less privileged people. It is also, arguably, more of a literary phenomenon than a legal one. The stories and the legal sources that discuss outlawry are looking back to earlier times and earlier conflicts; they rarely address contemporary events.

Further work remains to be done on the relationship between canon law and the vernacular law codes of Iceland and northern Europe. The codes of northern Europe, particularly those in vernacular languages, have been studied as separate national entities, but rarely has the group of laws been considered as a whole, much less within the wider framework medieval European law.

From the perspective of saga studies, there is much to be gained by fitting the contemporary sagas into the context of a wider Christian Europe, particularly in the English-speaking world, where the contemporary sagas have not been as extensively studied as the sagas of Icelanders. I have demonstrated with my readings of sagas about Bishop Guðmundr and Aron Hjǫrleifsson that canon law, its ideas and texts, can enrich our readings of the sagas, providing both a fuller context and a greater understanding of their engagement with circulating theological and legal ideas. Icelandic medieval writing, whether it belongs to legal, ecclesiastical, or literary-historical genres, is infused with Christian thought. Religion in sagas like *Íslendinga saga* is not an anomaly or intrusion to be ignored as irrelevant to the mechanics of feuding, but rather to be seen as part of the fabric of saga writing and the structuring of saga conflicts.

There is a fair amount of scholarly discussion of outlaws as not quite human.[2] This study suggests that one of the reasons for this is that outlaws were not quite Christian, not because they were pagan, but rather because outlawry was a sanction that by association (though not one that every medieval theologian would have endorsed) drove the person under it out of Christian society, its rituals and promised protections. Outlawry was secular excommunication.

2 See, for example, Gerstein, "Germanic Warg: The Outlaw as Werewolf," 131–156; Breen, "Outlaws, Assassins, and Avengers Who Cry 'Wolf!' " 31–43; Riisøy, "Outlawry: From Western Norway to England," 107–109; Ahola, "Outlawry in the Family Sagas," 87, 309–310; Harlan-Haughey, *Ecology of the English Outlaw*, 1–18; and Hastrup, *Culture and History*, 142–145.

# Bibliography

## Manuscripts

*Stofnun Árna Magússonar í íslenskum fræðum, Reykjavík.*
GKS 1157 fol. (Konungsbók).
AM 122a fol. (Króksfjarðarbók).
AM 122b fol. (Reykjarfjarðarbók).
AM 212 fol.
AM 334 fol. (Staðarhólsbók).
AM 347 fol. (Belgdalsbók).
AM 350 fol. (Skarðsbók).
AM 351 fol. (Skálholtsbók eldri).
AM 426 fol.
AM 173 c 4to.
AM 186 4to (Hvanneyrarbók).
AM 396 4to.
AM 399 4to (Resensbók).
AM 402 4to.
AM 551 d beta 4to.
AM 544 4to (Hauksbók).
AM 556 a 4to.
AM 657 c 4to.
AM 49 8vo.
*Den Arnamagnæanske Samling, København.*
AM 180 b fol.
AM 671 4to.
*Kungliga biblioteket, Stockholm.*
Stock. Perg nr. 5 fol.
*Det Kongelige Bibliotek, København.*
GKS 1008 fol. (Thómasskina).
*Uppsala Universitetsbibliotek, Uppsala.*
C 564.

## *Primary Sources*

*Acta conciliorum et epistolae, decretales ac constitutiones Summorum Pontificum.* Ed. by Jean Hardouin, Gabriel Cossart, and Philippe Labbe. 11 vols. Paris, 1714–1715.

Ari Þorgilsson. *Íslendingabók, Landnámabók.* Ed. by Jakob Benediktsson. Íslenzk fornrit 1. Reykjavík: Hið íslenzka fornritafélag, 1968.

Ari Þorgilsson. *Íslendingabók, Kristni saga: The Book of the Icelanders, The Story of the Conversion.* Trans. by Siân Grønlie. London: Viking Society for Northern Research, 2006.

*Árna Saga Biskups.* Ed. by Þorleifur Hauksson. Reykjavík: Stofnun Árna Magnússonar á Íslandi, 1972.

"Arons saga Hjörleifssonar eftir AM 551 d 4to: mállýsing og stafréttur texti." Ed. by Hanna Óladóttir. B.A. ritgerð. Háskóli Íslands, Reykajvík, 1992.

*Biskupa sögur* 1. Ed. by Guðbrandur Vigfusson. Copenhagen: Hið íslenska bókmenntafélag, 1858.

*Biskupa Sögur I: Kristni Saga, Kristni Þættir, Jóns saga ins helga.* Ed. by Sigurgeir Steingrímsson, Ólafur Halldórsson and Peter Foote. 2 vols. Íslenzk Fornrit 15. Reykjavík: Hið íslenzka fornritafélag, 2003.

*Biskupa sögur II: Hungarvaka, Þorláks sögur helga, Jarteinabœkur Þorláks helga, Páls saga biskups, Ísleifs þáttur biskups.* Ed. by Ásdís Egilsdóttir. Íslenzk fornrit 16. Reykjavík: Hið íslenzka fornritafélag, 2002.

*Biskupa sögur III: Árna saga biskups, Lárentíus saga biskups.* Ed. by Guðrún Ása Grímsdóttir. Íslenzk fornrit 17. Reykjavík: Hið íslenzka fornritafélag, 1998.

*Brennu Njáls saga.* Ed. by Einar Ól. Sveinsson. Íslenzk fornrit 12. Reykjavík: Hið íslenzka fornritafélag, 1954.

Burchard, Bishop of Worms. *Decretorum libri XX: ex consiliis et orthodoxorum patrum decretis, tum etiam diversarum nationum synodis seu loci communes congesti.* Ed. by Gérard Fransen and Theo Kölzer (reprint of the 1548 Cologne edition, [repr: Aalen: Scientia Verlag],1548 [1992]).

*Canones et Decreta sacrosancti oecumenici Concilii Tridentini.* Lipsiae: Ex officina Bernhardi Tauchnitz, 1863.

*Capitularia Regum Francorum* 2, Ed. by Alfredus Boretius and Victor Krause. Monumenta Germaniae Historica. Hannover: Hahn, 1897.

*Corpus Juris Canonicii,* vol. 1 *Decretum Gratianii, emendatum et notationibus illustratum, Una cum glossis.* Rome, 1582. http://digital.library.ucla.edu/canonlaw/index.html last accessed 27 April 2020.

*Corpus iuris canonici.* Ed. by Emil Friedberg. 2 vols. Leipzig: Ex Officina Bernhardi Tauchnitz, 1879–1882.

*Councils and Synods, with other documents relating to the English Church A.D. 871–1204.* Ed. by Dorothy Whitelock, M. Brett, and C.N.L. Brooke. 2 vols. Oxford: Clarendon Press, 1981.

*Decretum Gratiani,* first recension. Ed. by Anders Winroth. available at Gratian.org.

*The Earliest Norwegian Laws, Being the Gulathing Law and the Frostathing Law.* Trans. by Laurence M. Larson. New York: Columbia University Press, 1935.

*Den elder Gulatingslova*. Ed. by Bjørn Eithun, Magnus Rindal, and Tor Ulset. Norrøne tekster 6. Oslo: Riksarkivet, 1994.

*Flateyjarbók: En Samling af norske Konge-Sagaer*. Ed. by Guðbrandur Vigfússon and C.R. Unger. Christiania: Malling, 1862.

*The General Councils of Latin Christendom: From Constantinople IV to Pavia-Siena (869–1424)*. Ed. by García y García, Antonio, Peter Gemeinhardt, Georg Gresser, Thomas Izbicki, Atria Larson, Alberto Melloni, Jürgen Miethke, Kenneth Pennington, Burkhard Roberg, and Riccardo Saccenti. Corpus Christianorum, Conciliorum Oecumenicorum Generaliumque Decreta 2.1. Turnhout: Brepols, 2013.

*Die Gezetze der Angelsachsen*. Ed. by Felix Liebermann. 3 vols. Halle: Max Niemeyer, 1903.

Gottofredo da Trani (Goffredus Tranensis). *Summa super titulis Decretalium*. Lyon, 1519. Reprint Aalen: Scientia, 1968. Available at: http://works.bepress.com/david_freidenreich/17.

*Grágás efter det Arnamagnæanske Haandskrift Nr. 354 fol., Staðarhólsbók*. Ed. by Vilhjálmur Finsen. Copenhagen: Kommissionen for det Arnamagnæanske Legat; Gyldendal, 1879.

*Grágás: Islændernes Lovbog i Fristatens Tid, udgivet efter det kongelige Bibliotheks Haandskrift*. Ed. by Vilhjálmur Finsen. Copenhagen: Fornritafjelag Norðurlanda í Kaupmannahöfn, 1852.

*Grágás: Lagasafn íslenska þjóðveldsins*. Ed. by Gunnar Karlsson, Kristján Sveinsson and Mörður Árnason. Reykjavík: Mál og menning, 1992.

*Grágás: Stykker, som findes I det Arnamagnæanske Haandskrift Nr. 351 fol. Skálholtsbók og en Række andre Haandskrifter*. Ed. by Vilhjálmur Finsen. Copenhagen: Kommissionen for det Arnamagnæanske Legat; Gyldendal, 1883.

Gregory the Great. *Dialogues*. Ed. by Adalbert de Vogüé and Paul Antin, *Grégoire le Grand: Dialogues, tome III (livre IV)*. Sources chrétiennes 265. Paris: Les Éditions du Cerf, 1980.

*Grettis saga Ásmundarsonar, Bandamanna saga, Odds þáttr Ófeigssonar*. Ed. by Guðni Jónsson. Íslenzk fornrit 7. Reykjavík. Hið íslenzka fornritafélag, 1936.

*Guðmundar sögur biskups I: Ævi Guðmundar Biskups, Guðmundar saga A*. Ed. by Stefán Karlsson. Editiones Arnamagnaeanae, Series B, vol. 6. Copenhagen: C.A. Reitzel, 1983.

*Guðmundar sögur biskups II. Guðmundar saga B*. Ed. by Stefán Karlsson. Editiones Arnamagnæanæ Series B vol. 7. Copenhagen: Museum Tusculanum Press, 2018.

*Hákonar saga Hákonarsonar, Bǫglunga saga, Magnúss saga lagabœtis*. Ed. by Þorleifur Hauksson, Sverrir Jakobsson, and Tor Ulset. Íslenzk fornrit 31–32, 2 vols. Reykjavík: Hið íslenzka fornritafélag, 2013.

*Hauksbók: udgiven efter den arnamagnæanske Håndskrifter no. 371, 544 og 675 4to samt forskellige Papiershåndskrifter*. Ed. by Finnur Jónsson. Copenhagen: Kongelige nordiske oldskrift-selskab, 1892.

*The Icelandic Homily Book, Perg. 15 4° in the Royal Library, Stockholm*. Ed. by Andrea de Leeuw van Weenen. Reykjavík: Stofnun Árna Magnússonar á Íslandi, 1993.

*Islandske originaldiplomer indtil 1450*. Ed. by Stefán Karlsson. Copenhagen: Munksgaard, 1963.

*Íslensk hómilíubók: Fornar stólræður*. Ed. by Sigurbjörn Einarsson, Guðrún Kvaran and Gunnlaugur Ingólfsson. Reykjavík: Hið íslenska bókmenntafélag, 1993.

*Járnsíða og kristinréttur Árna Þorlákssonar*. Ed. by Haraldur Bernharðsson, Magnús Lyngdal Magnússon, and Már Jónsson. Reykjavík: Sögufélag, 2005.

*Jónsbók: Kong Magnus Hakonsson Lovbog for Island vedtaget paa Altinget 1281 og Réttarbætr: De for Island givne retterbøder af 1294, 1305 og 1314*. Ed. by Ólafur Halldórsson. reprint. Odense: Odense Universitetsforlag, 1970.

*Jónsbók: The Laws of Later Iceland*. Ed. and trans. by Jana K. Schulman. Saarbrücken, Germany: AQ-Verlag, 2010.

"Kristinréttur Árna frá 1275: Athugun á efni og varðveizlu í miðaldahandritum." Ed. by Magnús Lyngdal Magnússon. Master's thesis. Háskóli Íslands, 2002.

*Laws of Early Iceland: Grágás, the Codex Regius of Grágás, with Material from other Manuscripts*. Trans. by Andrew Denis, Peter Foote, and Richard Perkins. 2 vols. Winnipeg: University of Manitoba Press, 1980–2000.

*The Laws of the Salian Franks*. Trans. by Katherine Fischer Drew. Philadelphia: University of Pennsylvania Press, 1991.

*Lex Salica*. Monumenta Germaniae Historica, Legum Sectio 1. Ed. by Karl August Eckhardt. Leges Nationum Germanicarum, Vol. 4, Part 2. Hanover: Hahn, 1969.

*Pactus Legis Salicae*. Ed. by Karl August Eckhardt. Monumenta Germaniae Historica, Legum Sectio l, Leges Nationum Germanicarum, Vol. 4, Part 1. Hanover: Hahn, 1962.

*Das Register Gregors VII*. Ed. by E. Caspar. Monumenta Germaniae Historia, Epistolae selectae. 2nd ed. Berlin: Weidmann, 1967.

*Diplomatarium Islandicum: Íslenzkt fornbréfasafn*. Ed. by Þorlákr Jónsson, Ólafur Daviðsson and Jón Þorkelsson 15 vols. Copenhagen and Reykjavík: Hið íslenzka bókmenntafélag, 1857–1972.

*Diplomatarium Norvegicum* 17 B, Tillæg til Syttende samling *Den norske Kirkes Erkebiskoper og Biskoper indtil Reformationen*. Christiania, 1913.

*Morkinskinna*. Ed. by Ármann Jakobsson and Þórður Ingi Guðjónsson. Íslenzk fornrit 23–24. Reykjavík: Hið íslenzka fornritafélag, 2011.

*Njal's saga*. Trans. by Robert Cook. London: Penguin, 2001.

*Norges gamle Love indtil 1387*. Ed. by Rudolph Keyser, P.A. Munch, Gustav Storm, and Ebbe Hertzberg. 5 vols. Christiania: Chr. Gröndahl, 1846–1895.

*Den Norsk-Islandske Skjaldedigtning*, Ed. by Finnur Jónsson. 2 vols. Copenhagen: Gyldendal, Nordisk forlag, 1912–1915.

*Nyere norske Kristenretter (ca. 1260–1273)*. Trans. by Bjørg Dale Spørck. Thorleif Dahls Kulturbibliotek. Oslo: Aschehoug, 2009.

*Patrologia Latina*. Ed. by Jacques-Paul Migne. 221 vols. Paris, 1844–1864.

*The Saga of Aron Hjörleifsson*. Trans. by John Porter. London: Pirate Press and Writers Forum, 1975.

*Skálholtsbók Eldri, Jónsbók etc.* AM *351 fol.* Ed. by Christian Westergård-Nielsen. Copenhagen: Rosenkilde and Bagger, 1971.

*Skarðsárbók. Landnámabók Björns Jónssonar á Skarðsá*. Ed. by Jakob Benediktsson. Reykjavík: Háskóli Íslands, 1958.

Snorri Sturluson. *Heimskringla*. Ed. by Bjarni Aðalbjarnarson. 3 vols. Íslenzk fornrit 26–28. Reykjavík: Hið íslenzka fornritafélag, 1979.

*Sturlunga saga*. Ed. by Jón Jóhannesson, Magnús Finnbogason, and Kristján Eldjárn. 2 vols. Reykjavík: Sturlunguútgáfan, 1946.

*Sturlunga saga efter membranen Króksfjarðarbók udfyldt efter Reykjarfjarðarbók*. Ed. by Kristian Kålund. 2 vols. Copenhagen and Kristiania: Kongelige nordiske oldskrift-selskab, 1906, 1911.

*Sturlunga saga*. Trans. By Julia McGrew and with an introduction by George Thomas. 2 vols. New York: Twayne Publishers and the American Scandinavian Foundation, 1970; 1974.

*Thómas saga Erkibyskups, A Life of Archbishop Thomas Becket, In Icelandic, with English Translation, Notes and Glossary*. Ed. by Eiríkur Magnússon. 2 vols. London: Longmans, 1875–1883.

*Vestfirðinga sögur. Gísla saga Súrssonar, Fóstbræðra saga, Þáttr Þormóðar, Hávarðar saga ísfirðings, Auðunar þáttr Vestfirzka, Þorvarðarþáttr krákunefs*. Ed. by Björn K. Þórólfsson and Guðni Jónsson. Íslenzk fornrit 6. Reykjavík: Hið íslenzka fornritafélag, 1943.

## Secondary Literature

Abrams, Lesley. "The Anglo-Saxons and the Christianization of Scandinavia." *Anglo-Saxon England* 24 (1995): 213–249.

Agnes S. Arnórsdóttir. "Two Models of Marriage? Canon Law and Icelandic Marriage Practice in the Late Middle Ages." *Nordic Perspectives on Medieval Canon Law*. Ed. by Mia Korpiola. Helsinki: Matthias Calonius Society, 1999, 79–92.

Agnes S. Arnórsdóttir. *Property and Virginity: The Christianization of Marriage in Medieval Iceland 1200–1600*. Aarhus: Aarhus University Press, 2010.

Ahola, Joonas. "Outlawry in the Icelandic Family Sagas." Ph.D. Dissertation. University of Helsinki, 2014.

Amory, Frederic. "The Medieval Icelandic Outlaw: Lifestyle, Saga, and Legend." *From Sagas to Society: Comparative Approaches to Early Iceland*. Ed. by Gísli Pálsson. Middlesex U.K.: Hisarlik Press, 1992, 189–203.

Anderson, Joel. "Disseminating and Dispensing Canon Law in Medieval Iceland." *Arkiv för nordisk filologi* 128 (2013): 79–95.

Anderson, Joel. "Bishop Guðmundr's Roman Redemption: Imagining and Suspending Papal Government in Medieval Iceland." *Speculum* 95 (2020): 657–688.

Andersson, Theodore M. "The King of Iceland." *Speculum* 74 (1999): 923–934.

Andersen, Per, Ditlev Tamm and Helle Vogt eds. *How Nordic are the Nordic Medieval Laws?: Proceedings from the first Carlsberg Conference on Medieval Legal History*, 2nd ed. Copenhagen: DJØF Publishing, 2011.

Andersen, Per, Kirsi Salonen, Helle I.M. Sigh, and Helle Vogt (eds.) *How Nordic Are the Nordic Medieval laws? Ten Years After; Proceedings of the Tenth Carlsberg Academy Conference on Medieval Legal History 2013*. Copenhagen: DJØF Publishing, 2014.

Åqvist, Gösta. *Frieden und Eidschwur, Studien zum mittelalterlichen germanischen Recht*. Skrifter utgivna av Institutet för rättskistorisk forskning grundat av Gustav och Carin Olin. Serien 1. Rättshistoriskt Bibliotek 14. Stockholm: A.-B. Nordiska Bokhandeln, 1968.

Ármann Jakobsson. "Hákon Hákonarson: Friðarkonungur eða fúlmenni?" *Saga* 23 (1995): 166–185.

Ármann Jakobsson. "History of the Trolls?: *Bárðar saga* as an Historical Narrative." *Saga-Book* 25 (1998): 53–71.

Ármann Jakobsson. "Image is Everything: The Morkinskinna Account of King Sigurðr of Norway's Journey to the Holy Land." *Parergon* 30 (2013): 121–140.

Ásdís Egilsdóttir. "Hrafn Sveinbjarnarson, Pilgrim and Martyr." *Sagas, Saints and Settlements*. Ed. by Gareth Williams and Paul Bibire. Leiden and Boston: Brill, 2004, 29–39.

Ashman Rowe, Elizabeth. "Literary, Codicological, and Political Perspectives on Hauksbók." *Gripla* 19 (2008): 51–76.

Ashman Rowe, Elizabeth. *The Development of Flateyjarbók: Iceland and the Norwegian dynastic crisis of 1389*. Odense: University Press of Southern Denmark, 2005.

Aston, W.D. "Problems of Roman Criminal Law." *Journal of the Society of Comparative Legislation* 13.2 (1913): 213–231.

Austin, Greta. "Jurisprudence in the Service of Pastoral Care: The 'Decretum' of Burchard of Worms." *Speculum* 79 (2004): 929–959.

Bagge, Sverre. "Kirkens jurisdiksjon i kristenrettssaker før 1277. " *Historisk tidsskrift* 60 (1981): 133–159.

Bagge, Sverre. "Nordic Students at Foreign Universities until 1660." *Scandinavian Journal of History* 9 (1984): 1–29.

Barraclough, Eleanor Rosamund. "Inside Outlawry in *Grettis saga Asmundsonar* and *Gísla saga Súrssonar*: Landscape in the Outlaw Sagas." *Scandinavian Studies* 82 (2010): 365–388.

Bartlett, Robert. *Trial by fire and water: the medieval judicial ordeal*. New York: Clarendon Press of Oxford University Press, 1986.

Björn Þorsteinsson and Guðrún Ása Grímsdóttir. "Norska öldin." *Saga Íslands: Saminað tilhlutan Þjóðhátíðarnefndar 1974*. Ed. by Sigurður Lindal. 5 vols. Reykjavík: Hið íslenzka bókmenntafélag, 1974–1990, 4.61–258.

Beistad, Heidi Anette Øvergård. "Kirkens frihet: Biskop Arne Torlaksson som Islands reformator." Master's thesis. NTNU, Trondheim, 2008.

Boulhosa, Patricia Pires. *Icelanders and the Kings of Norway: Medieval Sagas and Legal Texts*. Leiden and Boston: Brill, 2005.

Boulhosa, Patricia Pires. "Ideals and Aspirations: Democracy and Law-Making in Mediaeval Iceland." *The Secret History of Democracy*. Edited by Benjamin Isakhan and Stephen Stockwell. London: Palgrave Macmillan, 2011, 92–104.

Bragg, Lois. "Disfigurement, Disability, and Dis-integration in Sturlunga saga." *alvíssmál* 4 (1994): 15–32.

Breen, Gerard. " 'The Wolf is at the door' Outlaws, Assassins, and Avengers Who Cry 'Wolf!' " *Arkiv för nordisk filologi* 114 (1999): 31–43.

Breisch, Agneta. *Frid och fredlöshet: sociala band och utanförskap på Island under äldre medeltid*. Studia Historica Upsaliensia 174. Uppsala: Uppsala Universitet, 1994.

Briem, Ólafur. *Útilegumenn og auðar tóttir*. 2nd ed. Reykjavík: Bókaútgáfa menningarsjóðs, 1983.

Brink, Stefan and Lisa Collinson (eds.) *New Approaches to Early Law in Scandinavia*. Turnhout: Brepols, 2014.

Brown, Peter. "Society and the Supernatural: A Medieval Change." *Daedalus, Journal of the American Academy of Arts and Sciences* 104 (1975): 133–151.

Brown, Peter. *The Cult of the Saints: Its Rise and Function in Latin Christianity*. Chicago: University of Chicago Press, 1981.

Brundage, James A. *Medieval Canon Law*. London and New York: Routledge, 1995.

Buc, Philippe. *The Dangers of Ritual: Between Early Medieval Texts and Social Scientific Theory*. Princeton: Princeton University Press, 2009.

Bullough, Donald. "Burial, Community and Belief in the Early Medieval West." *Ideal and Reality in Frankish and Anglo-Saxon Society: Studies Presented to J.M. Wallace-Hadrill*. Ed. by Patrick Wormald. Oxford: Blackwell, 1983, 177–201.

Burden, John. "Reading Burchard's *Corrector*: canon law and penance in the High Middle Ages." *Journal of Medieval History* 46:1 (2020): 77–97. DOI: 10.1080/03044181.2019.1671892.

Byock, Jesse L. *Feud in the Icelandic Saga*. Berkeley and Los Angeles: University of California Press, 1982.

Byock, Jesse L. "The Power and Wealth of the Icelandic Church: Some Talking Points." *The Sixth International Saga Conference, Helsingør, 28.7–28.8 1985: Workshop*

*Papers I–II*. Ed. by Jonna Louis-Jensen, Christopher Sanders and Peter Springborg. Copenhagen: Det arnamagnæanske Institut, 1985, 89–101.

Byock, Jesse L. "The Age of the Sturlungs." *Continuity and Change: Political Institutions and Literary Monuments in the Middle Ages*. Ed. by Elisabeth Vestergaad. Proceedings of the Tenth International Symposium Organized by the Center for the Study of Vernacular Literature in the Middle Ages (Odense: Odense University Press, 1986), 27–42.

Byock, Jesse L. *Medieval Iceland: Society, Sagas, and Power.* Berkeley and Los Angeles, 1988.

Cameron, Angus, Ashley Crandell Amos, Antonette diPaolo Healey, et al., (eds.) Dictionary of Old English: A to H Online (Toronto, 2016), http://doe.utoronto.ca.

Carella, Bryan. "The Earliest Expression for Outlawry in Anglo-Saxon Law." *Traditio* 70 (2015): 111–143.

Cheney, C.R. "King John's Reaction to the Interdict on England." *Transactions of the Royal Historical Society* 31 (1949): 129–150.

Chodorow, Stanley. "Dishonest Litigation in the Church Courts, 1140–98." *Law, Church, and Society: Essays in Honor of Stephan Kuttner*. Ed. by Kenneth Pennington and Robert Somerville. Philadelphia: University of Pennsylvania Press, 1977, 187–206.

Ciklamini, Marlene. "Biographical Reflections in 'Íslendinga saga:' A Mirror of Personal Values." *Scandinavian Studies* 55 (1983): 205–221.

Ciklamini, Marlene. "The Hand of Revision: Abbot Arngrímr's Redaction of *Guðmundar saga Biskups*." *Gripla* 8 (1993): 231–252.

Clark, Peter D. "A Question of Collective Guilt: Popes, Canonists and the Interdict c. 1140–c. 1250." *Zeitschrift der Savigny-Stiftung für Rechtsgeschichte, Kanonistische Abteilung* 116 (1999): 104–146.

Clark, Peter D. *The Interdict in the Thirteenth Century: A Question of Collective Guilt.* Oxford: Oxford University Press, 2007.

Cleasby, Richard, and Gudbrand Vigfusson. *An Icelandic-English Dictionary* 2nd ed. Revised by William A. Craigie. Oxford: Clarendon Press, 1957.

Cole, Richard. "Árna saga biskups / Kafka / Bureaucracy / Desire." *Collegium medievale* 28 (2015): 37–69.

Cormack, Margaret J. The *Saints in Iceland: Their Veneration from the Conversion to 1400. Subsidia Hagiographica* 78. Brussels: Société des Bollandistes, 1994.

Cormack, Margaret J. "Saints and Sinners: Reflections on death in some Icelandic sagas." *Gripla* 8 (1994): 187–218.

DeAngelo, Jeremy. *Outlawry, Liminality, and Sanctity in the Literature of the Early Medieval North Atlantic*. Amsterdam: Amsterdam University Press, 2019.

Doxey, Gary B. "Norwegian Crusaders and the Balearic Islands." *Scandinavian Studies* 68 (1996): 139–160.

Duggan, Anne J. "Clerical Exemption in Canon Law from Gratian to the Decretals." *Medieval Worlds* 6 (2017): 78–100. DOI 10.1553/medievalworlds_no6_2017s78.

Edwards, Genevieve Steele. "Ritual excommunication in medieval France and England, 900–1200." Ph.D. Dissertation. Stanford University, 1997.

Effros, Bonnie. "Beyond cemetery walls: early medieval funerary topography and Christian salvation." *Early Medieval Europe* 6 (1997): 1–23.

Eichmann, Eduard. *Acht und Bann im Reichsrecht des Mittelalters*. Paderborn: Ferdinand Schöningh, 1909.

Einar Ól. Sveinsson. *The Age of the Sturlungs: Icelandic Civilization in the Thirteenth Century*. Trans. by Jóhann S. Hannesson. Islandica vol. 36. Ithaca: Cornell University Press, 1953.

Elliott, J.H. "A Europe of Composite Monarchies." *Past and Present* 137 (1992): 48–71.

Estes, Heide. "Raising Cain in Genesis and Beowulf: Challenges to Generic Boundaries in Anglo-Saxon Biblical Literature." *The Heroic Age* 13 (2010). http://www.heroicage.org/issues/13/estes.php.

Faulkes, Anthony. "Outlaws in Medieval England and Iceland." *Greppaminni, Rit til heiðurs Vésteini Ólasyni sjötugum*. Reykjavík: Hið íslenska bókmenntafélag, 2009, 139–151.

Finucane, Ronald C. *Miracles and Pilgrims: Popular Beliefs in Medieval England*. New York: Palgrave Macmillan, 1995.

Foote, Peter. "On the fragmentary text concerning St Thomas Becket in Stock. Perg. Fol. Nr. 2." *Saga-Book* 15 (1961): 403–450.

Fritzner, Johan. *Ordbog over Det gamle norske Sprog*. 4 volumes. Kristiania: Norske Forlagsforening, 1883–96. [corrected and expanded by Finn Hødnebø. Oslo, Bergen, Tromsø: 1972].

Gerstein, Mary. "Germanic Warg: The Outlaw as Werewolf." *Myth in Indo-European Antiquity*. Ed. by G.J. Larson. Berkeley: University of California Press, 1974, 131–156.

Glendinning, R.J. "Saints, Sinners, and the Age of the Sturlungs: Two Dreams from *Íslendinga saga*." *Scandinavian Studies* 38 (1966): 83–97.

Glendinning, R.J. "*Arons saga* and *Íslendinga saga*: A problem in parallel transmission." *Scandinavian Studies* 41 (1969): 41–51.

Glendinning, R.J. *Träume und Vorbedeutung in der Islendinga Saga Sturla Thordarsons: Eine Form- und Stiluntersuchung*. Bern and Frankfurt: Herbert Lang, 1974.

Goetting, Lauren. "Óláfr hvítaskáld Þórðarson (Ólhv)." http://www.abdn.ac.uk/skaldic/db.php?id=157&if=default&table=skalds last accessed 22 January 2016.

Gos, Giselle. "Women as a Source of heilræði, 'sound counsel': Social Mediation and Community Integration in *Fóstbræðra saga*." *The Journal of English and Germanic Philology* 108 (2009): 281–300.

Greenia, George D. "Bartered Bodies: Medieval Pilgrims and the Tissue of Faith." *International Journal of Religious Tourism and Pilgrimage* 7 (2019): 38–51. DOI: https://doi.org/10.21427/HRMH-KX63.

Griffiths, John. "What is Legal Pluralism?" *Journal of Legal Pluralism and Unofficial Law* 24 (1986): 1–55.

Guðrún Ása Grímsdóttir. "Um afskipti erkibiskupa af íslenzkum málefnum á 12. og 13. öld." *Saga* 20 (1982): 28–62.

Guðrún Ása Grímsdóttir and Jónas Kristjánsson (eds.) *Sturlustefna, ráðstefna haldin á sjö alda ártíð Sturlu Þórðarsonar sagnaritara 1984*. Reykjavík: Stofnun Árna Magnússonar á Íslandi, 1988.

Guðrún Nordal. "*Sturlunga saga* and the context of saga-writing." *Introductory Essays on Egils saga and Njáls saga*. Ed. by John Hines and Desmond Slay. London: The Viking Society for Northern Research, 1992, 1–14.

Guðrún Nordal. *Ethics and action in thirteenth-century Iceland*, Odense: Odense University Press, 1998.

Guðrún Nordal. "Grímseyjarför." *Viskustykki: Undin Soffíu Guðnýju Guðmundsdóttur fimmtugri 4. apríl 2014*. Ed. by Rósa Þorsteinsdóttir and Gunnvör Sigríður Karlsdóttir. Reykjavík: Menningar- og minningarsjóður Mette Magnussen, 2014 25–27.

Guðrún P. Helgadóttir. introduction to *Hrafs saga Sveinbjarnarsonar*. Oxford: Oxford University Press, 1987.

Guðrún Þórhallsdóttir. "Bragur og breytingar: Kolbeinn og himnasmiðurinn." lecture given 4.2.2016 at the University of Iceland.

Guðvarður Már Gunnlaugsson. " 'Grettir vondum vættum, veitti hel og þreytti': Grettir Ásmundarson og vinsældir *Grettis sögu*." *Gripla* 11 (2000): 37–78.

Gunnar F. Guðmundsson. *Kristni á Íslandi 2, Íslenskt samfélag og Rómarkirkja*. Reykjavík: Alþingi, 2000.

Gunnar Karlsson. "Goðar and höfðingjar in Medieval Iceland." *Saga-Book* 19 (1977): 358–370.

Haki Antonsson. "Some Observations on Martyrdom in Post-Conversion Scandinavia." *Saga-Book* vol. 28 (2004): 70–94.

Haki Antonsson. "Two Twelfth-century Martyrs: St Thomas of Canterbury and St Magnús of Orkney." *Sagas, Saints and Settlements*. Ed. by Gareth Williams and Paul Bibire. Leiden and Boston: Brill, 2004, 41–64.

Haki Antonsson. "False Claims to Papal Canonisations of Saints: Scandinavia and Elsewhere." *Medieval Scandinavia* 19 (2009): 171–203.

Haki Antonsson. "The Lives of Thomas Becket and Early Scandinavian Literature." *Studi e materiali di storia delle religioni* (*SMSR*) 81 (2015): 392–413.

Haki Antonsson. "*Árna saga biskups* as Literature and History." *Journal of English and Germanic Philology* 116 (2017): 261–285.

Haki Antonsson. *Damnation and Salvation in Old Norse Literature*. Cambridge: D.S. Brewer, 2018.

Harlan-Haughey, Sarah. *The Ecology of the English Outlaw in Medieval Literature: From Fen to Greenwood*. London and New York: Routledge, 2016.

Hartmann, Wilfried and Kenneth Pennington. *The History of Medieval Canon Law in the Classical Period, 1140–1234. From Gratian to the Decretals of Pope Gregory IX*, (History of Medieval Canon Law III), Washington, D.C.: Catholic University of America Press, 2008.

Hastrup, Kirsten. *Culture and history in medieval Iceland: An Anthropological Analysis of Structure and Change*. Oxford and New York: Oxford University Press, 1985.

Haug, Eldbjørg. "Concordants, Statute and Conflict in *Árna saga biskups*." *Collegium Medievale* 28 (2015): 70–104.

Thomas and Richard Landes (eds.) *The Peace of God: Social Violence and Religious Response in France around the Year 1000*. Ithaca and London: Cornell University Press, 1992.

Helgi Skúli Kjartansson. "Quousque? Um latínuglósur í Grágásarlögum." *Heimtur, Ritgerðir til heiðurs Gunnari Karlssyni sjötugum*. Ed. by Guðmundur Jónsson, Helgi Skúli Kjartansson and Vésteinn Ólason. Reykjavík, 2009, 201–214.

Helgi Þorláksson (ed.) *Church Centres: Church Centres in Iceland from the 11th to the 13th Century and their Parallels in other Countries*. Reykholt: Snorrastofa, 2005.

Heller, Rolf. "Aron Hjörleifssohn und Gisli Surssohn." *Arkiv för nordisk filologi* 81 (1966): 57–63.

Helmholz, Richard H. "Excommunication as a Legal Sanction: The Attitudes of the Medieval Canonists." *Zeitschrift Der Savigny-Stiftung fur Rechtsgeschichte, Kan. Abt.* 68 (1982): 202–218.

Helmholz, Richard H. " 'Si quis suadente' (C.17 q.4 c.29): Theory and practice." *Proceedings of the Seventh International Congress of Medieval Canon Law, Cambridge, 23-27 July 1984*. Ed. by Peter Linehan. Vatican City: Biblioteca Apostolica Vaticana, 1988, 425–438.

Helmholz, Richard H. "Excommunication in Twelfth Century England." *Journal of Law and Religion* 11 (1994–95): 235–253.

Helmholz, Richard H. *The Spirit of Classical Canon Law*. Athens GA: University of Georgia Press, 1996.

Helmholz, Richard H. *The ius commune in England*. Oxford and New York: Oxford University Press, 2001.

Heusler, Andreas. *Das Strafrecht der Isländersagas*. Leipzig: Duncker & Humblot, 1911.

Heusler, Andreas. *Zum Isländischen Fehdewesen in der Sturlungenzeit*. Berlin: Verlag der Königl. Akademie der Wissenschaften, 1912.

Hinschius, Paul. *System des katholischen Kirchenrechts*. 6 vols. Berlin: Guttentag, 1869–1897.

Hjalti Hugason. *Kristni á Íslandi 1, Frumkristni og upphaf kirkju.* Reykjavík: Alþingi, 2000.

Hoff, Hans Henning. *Hafliði Másson und die Einflüsse des römischen Rechts in der Grágás.* Ergänzungsbände zum Reallexikon der Germanischen Altertumskunde, vol. 78. Berlin and Boston: De Gruyter, 2012.

Hoffmann, Hartmut and Rudolf Pokorny. *Das Dekret des Bischofs Burchard von Worms: Textstufen, frühe Verbreitung, Vorlagen.* Hilfsmittel, 12. Munich: Monumenta Germaniae Historica, 1991.

Housley, Norman. "Pilgrimage, Western Europe." *Dictionary of the Middle Ages* (New York: Charles Scribner's Sons, 1987) 9.654–661.

van Houts, Elisabeth. "The Vocabulary of Exile and Outlawry in the North Sea Area around the Frist Millennium." *Exile in the Middle Ages: Selected Proceedings from the International Medieval Congress.* Ed. by L. Napran and E. van Houts, International Medieval Research, 13. Turnhout: Brepols, 2004, 13–28.

Hurnard, Naomi D. *The King's Pardon for Homicide before A.D. 1307.* Oxford: Clarendon Press, 1969.

Hyams, Paul R., *Rancor and Reconciliation in Medieval England.* Ithaca and London: Cornell University Press, 2003.

Jacoby, Michael. *Wargus, vargr 'Verbrecher' 'Wolf' eine sprach- und rechtsgeschichtliche Untersuchung.* Uppsala: Almqvist & Wiksell, 1974.

Jones, Gwyn. "Fjörbaugsgarðr." *Medium Aevum* 9 (1940): 155–163.

Jones, Timothy S. *Outlawry in Medieval Literature.* New York: Palgrave Macmillan, 2010.

Jón Jóhannesson. *A History of the Old Icelandic Commonwealth: Íslendinga saga.* Trans. by Haraldur Bessason. Winnipeg, 1974.

Jón Viðar Sigurðsson. *Chieftains and Power in the Icelandic Commonwealth.* Trans. Jean Lundskær-Nielsen. Odense: Odense University Press, 1999.

Jón Viðar Sigurðsson. "Allir sem sjá líta þó ekki jafnt á: Sagnaritun um íslenskar miðaldir fram um 1300." *Saga* 38 (2000): 33–57.

Jón Viðar Sigurðsson and Sverrir Jakobsson (eds.) *Sturla Þórðarson: Skald, Chieftain and Lawman.* Leiden and Boston: Brill, 2017.

Jordan, William Chester. "A Fresh Look at Medieval Sanctuary." *Law and the Illicit in Medieval Europe.* Ed. by Ruth Mazo Karras, Joel Kaye, and E. Ann Matter. Philadelphia: University of Pennsylvania Press, 2008, 17–32.

Jørgensen, Torstein. "Excommunication – an act of expulsion from heaven and earth." *The Creation of Medieval Northern Europe: Christianisation, Social Transformations, and Historiography, Essays in Honour of Sverre Bagge.* Ed. by Leidulf Melve and Sigbjørn Sønnesyn. Oslo: Dreyer Forlag, 2012, 58–69.

Keen, Maurice. *The Outlaws of Medieval Legend.* 2nd ed. London and Toronto: Routledge, 1977.

King'oo, Clare Costley. *Miserere Mei: The Penitential Psalms in Late Medieval and Early Modern England.* Notre Dame IN: University of Notre Dame Press, 2012.

*Kulturhistoriskt lexikon för nordisk medeltid.* Malmö: Allhem, 1956–1982.

Kålund, Kristian. *Katalog over den Arnamagnœanske Håndskriftsamling.* Copenhagen: Kommissionen for det Arnamagnæanske Legat, 1889–1894.

Landro, Torgeir. "Kristenrett og kyrkjerett: Borgartingskristenretten i eit komparativt perspektiv." Ph.D. Dissertation. University of Bergen, 2010.

Lange, Gudrun. "Didatische und typologische Aspekte der Arons saga." *Arbeiten zur Skandinavistik* (1996): 178–193.

Lára Magnúsardóttir. *Bannfæring og kirkjuvald á Íslandi 1275-1550: Lög og rannsóknarforsendur.* Reykjavík: Háskólaútgáfan, 2007.

Lára Magnúsardóttir. "Icelandic Church Law in the Vernacular 1275–1550." *Bulletin of Medieval Canon Law* 23 (2015): 127–143.

Lethbridge, Emily. "*Gísla saga Súrssonar*: Textual Variation, Editorial Constructions, and Critical Interpretations." *Creating the Medieval Saga: Versions, Variability, and Editorial Interpretations in Old Norse Saga Literature.* Ed. by Judy Quinn and Emily Lethbridge. Odense: University Press of Southern Denmark, 2010.

Lethbridge, Emily. "Dating *Gísla saga*: Methodological Problems and Alternative Approaches." *Dating the Sagas: Reviews and Revisions.* Ed. by Else Mundal. Copenhagen: Museum Tusculanum Press, 2013, 77–113.

Lindow, John. review of Michael Jacoby, *Wargus, vargr 'Verbrecher' 'Wolf' eine sprach- und rechtsgeschichtliche Untersuchung* (Uppsala: Almqvist and Wiksell, 1974). *Speculum* 52 (1977): 382–385.

Little, Lester K. *Benedictine Maledictions: Liturgical Cursing in Romanesque France.* Ithaca and London: Cornell University Press, 1993.

Logan, F. Donald. *Excommunication and the Secular Arm in Medieval England: A Study in Legal Procedure from the Thirteenth to the Sixteenth Century.* Toronto: Pontifical Institute of Medieval Studies, 1968.

Logan, F. Donald. "Excommunication." *Dictionary of the Middle Ages.* Ed. by Joseph R. Strayer. New York: Charles Scribner's Sons, 1984, 4.536–538.

Lúðvík Ingvarsson. *Refsingar á Íslandi á Þjóðveldistímanum.* Reykjavík: Bókaútgáfa Menningarsjóðs, 1970.

Lundgreen, M. "Friedlosigkeit (Acht)." *Reallexikon der Germanischen Altertumskunde.* Band 9. Berlin: Walter De Gruyter, 1995, 613–621.

Magnús Lyngdal Magnússon. "Kátt er þeim af kristinrétti, kærur vilja margar læra: Af kristinrétti Árna, setning hans og valdsviði." *Gripla* 15 (2004): 43–90.

Magnús Stefánsson. *Staðir og staðamál: Studier i islandske egenkirkelige og beneficialrettslige forhold i middelalderen I.* Historisk institutt. Universitetet i Bergen. Skrifter 4. Bergen: Historisk institutt, 2000.

Mansfield, Mary C. *The Humiliation of Sinners: Public Penance in Thirteenth-Century France*. Ithaca: Cornell University Press, 1995.

Marani, Tommaso. "Contextualising *Leiðarvísir*: Sant' Agnese, the Catacombs, the Pantheon and the Tiber." *Saga Book* 33 (2009): 44–66.

Már Jónsson. *Blóðskömm á Íslandi 1270-1870*. Reykjavík: Háskólaútgáfan, 1993.

Marafioti, Nicole. "Unconsecrated Burial and Excommunication in Anglo-Saxon England: A Reassessment." *Traditio* 74 (2019): 55–123.

Marafioti, Nicole. "Secular and Ecclesiastical Justice in Late Anglo-Saxon England." *Speculum* 94 (2019): 774–805.

Matthías Þórðarson. "Tveir Grettisbústaðir." *Árbók hins íslenzka fornleifafélags* 45 (1936): 49–60.

Maurer, Konrad. *Island von seiner ersten Entdeckung bis zum Untergange des Freistaats*. Munich: C. Kaiser, 1874.

McDougall, David. review of Andrea de Leeuw van Weenen, editor. *The Icelandic Homily Book, Perg. 15 4° in the Royal Library, Stockholm* and Sigurbjörn Einarsson et al, editors. *Íslensk hómilíubók: Fornar stólræður. alvíssmál* 5 (1995): 107–111.

McSweeney, Thomas J. "Law and Fiction in Medieval Iceland: The Story in the *Grágás* Manuscripts." American Society for Legal History's pre-conference workshop, 2014.

McTurk, Rory ed. *A Companion to Old Norse-Icelandic Literature and Culture*. Malden, MA, Oxford, and Victoria: Blackwell, 2007.

Merkelbach, Rebecca. "'He Has Long Forfeited All Kinship Ties': Monstrosity, Familial Disruption, and the Cultural Relevance of the Outlaw Sagas." *Gripla* 28 (2017): 103–137.

Miller, William Ian. "Ordeal in Iceland." *Scandinavian Studies* 60 (1988): 189–218.

Miller, William Ian. *Bloodtaking and Peacemaking: Feud, Law, and Society in Saga Iceland.* Chicago: University of Chicago Press, 1990.

Murphy, Margaret. "Ecclesiastical Censures: An Aspect of Their Use in Thirteenth Century Dublin." *Archivium Hibernicum* 44 (1989): 89–97.

Murray, Alexander. *Excommunication and Conscience in the Middle Ages: The John Coffin Memorial Lecture, 13 February 1991*. London: The University of London, 1991.

Naylor, Alice. "Aron Hjörleifsson and the figure of the outlaw in the Icelandic saga." Master's thesis. The University of Iceland, 2009.

Nedkvitne, Arnved. *The Social Consequences of Literacy in Medieval Scandinavia*, Turnhout: Brepols, 2004.

Nedkvitne, Arnved. *Lay Belief in Norse Society 1000–1350*. Copenhagen: Museum Tusculanum Press, 2009.

Nilsson, Bertil. *De sepulturis. Gravrätten i Corpus iuris canonici och i medeltida nordisk lagstiftning*. Stockholm: Almqvist & Wiksell, 1993.

Lexicon of Medieval Nordic Law. https://www.dhi.ac.uk/lmnl/.

*Ordbog over det norrøne prosasprog*. http://onp.ku.dk/.

Orri Vésteinsson. *The Christianization of Iceland. Priests, Power, and Social Change 1000–1300*. Oxford: Oxford University Press, 2000.

Pavlac, Brian A. "Excommunication and Territorial Politics in High Medieval Trier." *Church History* 60 (1991): 20–36.

Pennington, Kenneth. "Moderamen inculpatae tutelae: The Jurisprudence of a Justifiable Defense." *Revista Internazionale di Diritto Comune* 27 (2014): 27–55.

Pharr, Clyde. "A Thirteenth Century Formula of Anathema." *The American Journal of Philology* 66 (1945): 135–150.

Poilvez, Marion. "The Inner Exiles: Outlaws and Scapegoating Process in *Grettis saga Ásmundarsonar* and *Gísla saga Súrssonar*." Master's thesis, University of Iceland, 2011.

Pollock, Frederick and Frederic William Maitland, *The History of English Law before the Time of Edward I*, 2nd ed., 2 vols. Cambridge: Cambridge University Press, 1898.

Porter, John. "Some aspects of Arons saga Hjörleifssonar." *Saga Book* 18 (1973): 136–166.

Pulsiano, Phillip. Kirsten Wolf, Paul Acker, and Donald K. Fry (eds.) *Medieval Scandinavia: An Encyclopedia.* New York and London: Garland, 1993.

Radding, Charles M. "Ordeals." *Dictionary of the Middle Ages*. Ed. by Joseph R. Strayer. New York: Charles Scribner's Sons, 1987, 9.259–60.

Riisøy, Anne Irene. "Outlawry: From Western Norway to England." *New Approaches to Early Law in Scandinavia*. Ed. by Stefan Brink and Lisa Collinson. Turnhout: Brepols, 2014, 101–129.

Rohrbach, Lena (ed.) *The Power of the Book. Medial Approaches to Medieval Nordic Legal Manuscripts*. Berliner Beiträge zur Skandinavistik vol. 19. Berlin: Nordeuropa-Institut der Humboldt-Universität, 2014.

Ross, Richard J. and Philip J. Stern. "Reconstructing Early Modern Notions of Legal Pluralism." *Legal Pluralism and Empires, 1500–1850*. Ed. by Richard J. Ross and Lauren Benton. New York: NYU Press, 2013, 109–141.

Scott, James C. *Weapons of the Weak: everyday forms of peasant resistance*. New Haven: Yale University Press, 1985.

Scott, James C. *Seeing like a state: how certain schemes to improve the human condition have failed*. New Haven: Yale University Press, 1998.

Shoemaker, Karl. *Sanctuary and Crime in the Middle Ages, 400–1500*. Bronx, NY: Fordham University Press, 2011.

Sigurdson, Erika. *The Church in Fourteenth-Century Iceland: The Formation of an Elite Clerical Identity*. Leiden and Boston: Brill, 2016.

Sigurður, Líndal. "Um þekkingu Íslendinga á rómverskum og kanóniskum rétti frá 12. öld til miðrar 16. öld." *Úlfljótur. Afmælisrit 50*. Ed. by Þórólfur Jónsson. Reykjavík, 1997, 241–273.

Simons, Kenneth W. "The Crime/Tort Distinction: Legal Doctrine and Normative Perspectives." *Widener Law Journal* 17 (2008): 719–732.

Siuts, Heinrich. *Bann und Acht und ihre Grundlagen im Totenglauben*. Berlin: Walter de Gruyter, 1959.

Stefán Karlsson. "En konjektur til Arons saga." *Bibliotheca Arnamagnæana 31, Opuscula 5* (1975): 412–414.

Svanhildur Óskarsdóttir, Matthew Driscoll and Sigurður Svavarsson (eds.) *66 Handrit úr forum Árna Magnússonar*. Reykjavík and Copenhagen: Stofnun Árna Magnússonar and Den Arnamagnæanske Samling, 2013.

Sveinbjörn Rafnsson. "Grágás og Digesta Iustiniani." *Sjötíu Ritgerðir Helgaðar Jakobi Benediktssyni 20. júlí 1977*, síðari hluti, Reykjavík: Stofnun Árna Magnússonar á Íslandi, 1977, 720–732.

Sveinbjörn Rafnsson. "Skriftaboð Þorláks Biskups." *Gripla* 5 (1982): 77–114.

Sveinbjörn Rafnsson. "Um grið og griðastaði á Sturlungaöld." *Saga* 54.2 (2016): 90–107.

Sverrir Jakobsson. "Heaven is a Place on Earth: Church and Sacred Space in Iceland." *Scandinavian Studies* 82 (2010): 1–20.

Sverrir Tómasson. "Trúarbókmenntir í lausu máli á síðmiðöld." *Íslensk bókmenntasaga*, Ed. by Guðrún Nordal, Sverrir Tómasson and Vésteinn Ólason. 3 vols. Reykjavík, 1992–. 1.265–418.

Sverrir Tómasson. "The Middle Ages. Old Icelandic Prose." *A History of Icelandic Literature.* Ed. by Daisy Neijmann (Lincoln: University of Nebraska Press, 2006), 64–173.

Tanner, Norman and Sethina Watson. "The Least of the laity: the minimum requirements for a medieval Christian." *Journal of Medieval History* 32 (2006): 395–423.

Taranger, Absalon. *Den Angelsaksiske kirkes indflydelse paa den norske.* Den Norske Historiske Forening, Kristiania: Norsk Historisk Forening, 1890.

Tarsi, Matteo. "On the origin of the oldest borrowed Christian terminology in Icelandic." *Orð og tunga* 18 (2016): 85–101.

Tranter, Stephen Norman. *Sturlunga Saga: The rôle of the Creative Compiler*. Frankfurt am Main: Peter Lang, 1987.

Treharne, E.M. "A unique Old English formula for excommunication from Cambridge, Corpus Christi College 303." *Anglo-Saxon England* 24 (1995): 185–211.

Trenholme, Norman Maclaren. "The Right of Sanctuary in England." *The University of Missouri Studies* 1 (1903): 1–31.

Turville-Petre, G. "Outlawry." *Sjötíu Ritgerðir Helgaðar Jakobi Benediktssyni 20. júlí 1977*, síðari hluti. Reykjavík: Stofnun Árna Magnússonar á Íslandi, 1977, 769–778.

Úlfar Bragason. "The Art of Dying: Three Death Scenes in *Íslendinga saga*." *Scandinavian Studies* 63 (1991): 453–465.

Úlfar Bragason. "In the Scriptorium of Sturlunga's Compiler." *International Scandinavian and Medieval Studies in Memory of Gerd Wolfgang Weber*. Ed. by Michael Dallapiazza, Olaf Hansen, Preben Meulengracht Sørensen, and Yvonne Bonnetain. Trieste: Edizioni Parnaso, 2000, 471–482.

Úlfar Bragason. "*Arons saga*: Minningar, mýtur og sagnaminni." *Ritið: Tímarit Hugvísindastofnunar* (2013): 125–145.

Vadum, Kristoffer. "Bruk av kanonistisk litteratur i Nidarosprovinsen ca. 1250–1340." Ph.D. Dissertation. University of Oslo, 2015.

Vadum, Kristoffer. "Canon Law and Politics in Grímr Hólmsteinsson's *Jóns Saga Baptista II*." Trans. by Alan Crozier. *Intellectual Culture in Medieval Scandinavia, c. 1100–1350*. Ed. by Stefka Georgieva Eriksen. Turnhout: Brepols, 2016, 175–209.

Vogt, Helle. *The Function of Kinship in Medieval Nordic Legislation*. Leiden and Boston: Brill, 2010.

Walgenbach, Elizabeth. "Church Sanctuary in the Contemporary Sagas." *Íslensk klausturmenning á Íslandi á miðöldum*. Ed. by Haraldur Bernharðsson. Reykjavík: Miðaldastofa Háskóla Íslands og Háskólaútgáfan, 2016, 103–117.

Walgenbach, Elizabeth. "The Canon *Si quis suadente* and Excommunication in Medieval Iceland." *Gripla* 30 (2019): 155–185.

Walther, Hans. *Lateinische Sprichwörter und Sentenzen des Mittelalters in alphabetischer Anordnung*. 5 vols. Göttigen: Vandenhoeck und Ruprecht, 1963–1967.

Wei, John C and Anders Winroth (eds.) *Cambridge History of Medieval Canon Law*. Cambridge: Cambridge University Press, forthcoming.

White, Stephen D. "The Feelings in the Feud: The Emotional Turn in the Study of Medieval Vengeance." *Disputing Strategies in Medieval Scandinavia*. Ed. by Kim Esmark, Lars Hermanson, Hans Jacob Orning and Helle Vogt. Leiden and Boston: Brill, 2013, 281–311.

Winroth, Anders. *The Making of Gratian's Decretum*. Cambridge: Cambridge University Press, 2000.

Winroth, Anders. "Neither Slave nor Free: Theology and Law in Gratian's Thoughts on the Definition of Marriage and Unfree Persons." *Medieval Church Law and the Origins of the Western Legal Tradition: A Tribute to Kenneth Pennington*. Ed. by Wolfgang P. Müller and Mary E. Sommor. Washington D.C.: The Catholic University of America Press, 2012, 97–109.

Winroth, Anders. "The Canon Law of Emergency Baptism and of Marriage in Iceland and Europe." *Gripla* 29 (2018): 203–229.

Winroth, Anders. "Goffredus och Västgötalagen." *Kyrkohistorisk årsskrift* 1:119 (2019): 183–188.

Wormald, Patrick. *The Making of English Law: King Alfred to the twelfth century*. vol. 1. Oxford and Malden, Mass.: Blackwell, 1999.

Wormald, Patrick. *Legal culture in the early medieval West: law as text, image and experience*. London and Rio Grande, Ohio: The Hambledon Press, 1999.

Þórður Ingi Guðjónsson. "Editing the Three Versions of *Gísla saga Súrssonar*." *Creating the Medieval Saga: Versions, Variability, and Editorial Interpretations in Old Norse Saga Literature*. Ed. by Judy Quinn and Emily Lethbridge. Odense: University Press of Southern Denmark, 2010, 105–121.

Þorsteinn Bjarnarson. "Fjalla-Eyvindur og niðjar hans." *Blanda* 7 (1940–1943): 91–96.

# Index

Icelandic and Old Norse-Icelandic names as well as medieval names are alphabetized by given name. The alphabetical order is: a á b c d ð e é f g h i í j k l m n o ó p q r s t u ú v w x y ý z þ æ ö/ ǫ å


absolution 13–14, 30–31, 109–110, 118–119, 129, 145
Alþingi 14, 44–47, 68–69, 80–81, 93–94, 96, 97
anathema 9, 10n15, 17–19, 25–26
Ari Þorgilsson (d. 1148) 68–69
Arnórr Tumasson (d. 1221) 102, 109, 110–111, 112–114, 118, 119, 125
*Arons saga Hjǫrleifssonar* 127, 128, 129n6, 136–137, 138, 139–140, 151
  manuscripts of, 128, 128n4, 128n5
Aron Hjǫrleifsson (d. 1255) 4, 86, 98, 101, 125, 126, 127–128, 130
  outlaw sagas and, 128
  pilgrim 142
"Aron's drápa" 127–128, 143–144
Ármann Jakobsson 142
*Árna saga biskups* 5, 32, 33–34
Árni Þorláksson, Bishop of Skálaholt (d. 1298) 29, 31–34, 80–82
Ásbjǫrn, priest 102–103

*bannfæring* see excommunication, translation into Old Norse-Icelandic
baptism 82, 89, 97
Battle at Helgastaðir see *Helgastaðabardagi*
Battle of Víðines see *Víðinesbardagi*
Battle of Ǫrlygsstaðir see Ǫrlygsstaðir, Battle of
Beistad, Heidi Anette Øvergård 66
Belgdalsbók (AM 347 fol.) 70n23
Boulhosa, Patricia Pires 70–71
Brandr Sæmundarson, Bishop of Hólar (d. 1201) 24, 25
breaking the confessional 93, 98
Burchard, Bishop of Worms (d. 1025) 11, 36, 67–68
burial, consecrated 13, 76
  *ad sanctos* 65, 83
  denial of, 8, 13, 14–15, 78–79, 80–84
  development of, 8n10, 13–14n34
  in Anglo-Saxon sources 84
  in *Grágás* 65
  in Iceland 76–77
  in *Íslendinga saga* 109–110, 118–119
  salvation and, 13–14
burial, unconsecrated 5, 13, 84
  and suicide 30, 78–79n54

canon law 1, 3, 4, 6, 67
  Bishop Árni Þorláksson and, 29, 32–34
  development in high and late Middle Ages 16–17
  local usage of (*ius particulare*) 3, 33, 97
  Sturla Þorðarson's understanding of 125
  translation(s) into Old Norse-Icelandic 29–32
  works known to have been in Iceland 28–29, 31–33
Canterbury 21–22, 120
Carella, Bryan 41–42, 89–90
clerical impediment 105
clerical violence 24–25, 117
Cnut/Knútr, King of England, Denmark, and Norway (d. 1035) 41–42, 66, 88, 89–90
compensation 10n16, 39–40, 44, 46, 58–59, 61, 105, 133–134, 145–146, 145–146n79
  to church 78–79
confession 8, 26, 80–81n60, 136
consecrated ground, origins of, 8n10, 13–14n34
consecrated burial see burial, consecrated
conversion to Christianity, Iceland 76–77, 84–85
Cormack, Margaret 116
church buildings
  ban on entry into, 85
  bloodshed and, 22, 108–109
  sanctuaries see, sanctuary
crusader(s) 142

Dalir 108
*Decretum*, of Gratian 15–16, 19, 21, 29, 31–32, 36–37, 81–82

*Decretum*, of Burchard of Worms 11–12, 13, 67–68
Doxey, Gary 142
dreams, prophetic 108

Edwards, Genevieve 37
Eichmann, Eduard 67
Eidsivatings law 90
Einarr Hafliðason (d. 1393) 32
Einarr skemmingr 132
Eiríkr, Archbishop of Niðaróss (d. 1205) 24
excommunication 1, 4, 6
  abuses of 20–21
  consequences of 8
  damnation and, 11–13, 15, 36–37, 83
  enforcement of 22
  early medieval 10
  for disobedience 19
  formulas for 11–13, 33–34
  imposed by bishops (*ferendae sententiae*) 7, 18, 27, 103
  in Icelandic sources 23, 28
  *latae sententiae* see excommunication, *Si quis suadente*
  minor and major 17
  Old English 11
  political conflicts and, 21–23, 99, 125
  rituals 10
  secular sanctions and, 8–10, 88–91
  *Si quis suadente,* 5, 18–19, 24, 29, 31–33, 37, 82–83, 89, 103–104, 116–117
  The Council of Trent and, 20–21
  translation into Old Norse-Icelandic 25–26, 27, 29–30, 32–33, 116
  unjust 15–16, 20–21
  exile 22n68, 50, 94–95, 100–101, 122, 145, 147, 149–150
Eyjafjǫrðr 145
Eyri (farm) 134–135
Eyjólfr Kársson 85–86, 111–112, 130, 131–132

Fagurey, Breiðafjǫrðr 101
Faulkes, Anthony 147–148
Fjalla-Eyvindur (Jónsson), útilegumaður 2n3, 63n112
*fjǫrbaugsgarðr* 38, 93
  as a fine 50
  as temporary banishment from Iceland 50
  as uniquely Icelandic 50
  for breaches of Church law 26–27, 51–52, 94, 98
  in the context of *Grágás* 38
  literal meaning of 49
  minor excommunication and, 53, 72–74
  offenses leading to 51
Flateyjarbók (GSK 1005 fol.) 148–149
*Flugumýrarbardagi* 117
*Fóstbræðra saga* 65, 84–85, 149, 150–151, 152
Frederick II, Holy Roman Emperor (d. 1250) 23
Frostathing law, older 51, 68–69, 78, 84, 88–89, 94–95

Geirþjófsfjǫrðr 137
*Gísla saga Súrsonar* 38n110, 128n4
Gísli Markússon 85–86
Gísli Súrsson 55–56, 85n6, 128n4, 136–137n50, 139–140
Glámr 85
Glendinning, Robert 136–137
Goffredus of Trano (d. 1245) 17–18, 28, 75–76
Gratian 15–16, 52n66, 78–79n54, 81–82
*Grágás* 1, 26, 52, 68, 70–72, 93–94, 129
  Konungsbók manuscript see Konungsbók, *Grágás*
  Staðarhólsbók manuscript see Staðarhólsbók, *Grágás*
Grettir Ásmundarson 55–56, 84–85n76, 139–140, 141, 147–148n87
  buried as Christian 84–85
  not entering a church 86
  St. Olaf and, 147–148
*Grettis saga* 38, 55–56, 84–85, 84–86, 152
Grímsey 114, 130, 131–132, 133–134, 135, 136–137, 138, 141
Grímseyjarför 114, 130, 131–132, 133–134, 135, 136–137, 138, 141
Guðmundr Arason, Bishop of Hólar (d. 1237) 4, 99, 102, 112
  Aron Hjǫrleifsson and, 98, 127–128, 136–140, 142
  final years 114n96
  protector of outlaws 106, 109–110, 119
  sagas of 23–24n72
  Thomas Becket as model 120–121
Guðmundr inn seki 85–86

*Guðmundar saga A* 86, 117–118n111, 120–121, 127–128, 134, 136, 139, 140–141, 143, 144
*Guðmundar saga B* 117–118n111, 123, 127–128
Guðrún Ása Grímsdóttir 125
Guðrún Nordal 133–134
Gulathing law, older 43, 61, 68–69, 72–75, 78, 84
Gulathing law, newer Christian 29, 80–81

Hafliði Másson (d. 1130) 68–69
Hallr Kleppjárnsson 103–105, 117
Haraldr harðráði, Norwegian king (d. 1066) 142
Haraldr Sæmundarson 86, 133–134
Hauksbók (AM 544 4to) 28n95, 75–76n41, 150–151, 152
Hákon Hákonarson, Norwegian king (d. 1263) 90–91, 98, 129, 130, 132–133, 141–142, 143, 147, 150–151
*Hákonar saga Hákonarsonar* 100, 118
*Helgastaðabardagi* (1220) 113, 134–135
Helgi Skúli Kjartansson 71
Henry ii, English king (d. 1189) 21–22, 99, 120, 121, 122, 124
heresy 7, 19, 21, 88
"Heyr himna smiður" 107, 113
Hincmar, Bishop of Rheims (d. 882) 9–10, 15n41
Hítardalr 131
Hjǫrleifr Gilsson 139–140
Holy Land 129, 142, 143–145
Hólar 70n23, 104, 107–108, 111–112, 112n84, 113–114, 131–132, 141
Hrafn Sveinbjarnarson (d. 1213) 130

Icelandic Homily book 26, 76–77
interdict 14, 22
*Íslendinga saga* 65, 99, 100, 102, 108, 115–116, 118–120, 124, 127–128, 134, 136, 138, 141, 144, 155–156
*Íslendingabók* 65

Jarl Skúli Bárðarson (d. 1240) 142, 143, 147
*Járnsíða* 38, 43, 60, 62, 70, 100–101, 115, 129
Jerusalem, see also Holy Land, 130, 138, 142, 143, 144–145n74
John, English king (d. 1216) 23n69
Jones, Gwyn, 50, 53–54, 70–71, 76
Jón Halldórsson, priest 117
Jón rauði, Archbishop of Niðaróss (d. 1282) 22n68
*Jónsbók* 1, 51–52, 59–62, 66, 74, 129, 138–139, 151
judicial ordeal 14–15n39, 110, 118, 123
jurisdiction(s) 5, 8–9n13, 22, 36, 58–59, 61, 77–78, 88–89, 91–92, 93, 94–95, 115–116, 119, 121–122, 124, 125, 150
Jörundr, Archbishop of Niðaróss (d. 1309) 35

Kálfr Guttormsson 145
Kolbeinn Tumason (d. 1208) 4, 124, 125
  Bishop Guðmundr Arason and, 102, 105, 120
  death of, 107, 110, 117–119, 122–124
  excommunication of, 103, 104
Kolbeinn ungi Arnórsson (d. 1245) 114note 95
Konungsbók manuscript of *Grágás* (GKS 1157 fol.) 43–44, 46, 47, 48–49, 51, 52–53, 57, 61, 68–69, 71, 77–79, 80, 94, 151, 152
Kristinréttr Árna Þorlákssonar 29–30, 80–81, 89, 91–92
Kristinna laga þáttr 2–3, 78–79

*Landnámabók* 38
Lange, Gudrun 133
Lateran, Fourth Council (1215) 15–16
Lateran, Second Council (1139) 18
Laurentius Kálfsson, Bishop of Hólar (d. 1331) 32, 33–35, 90–91
Lára Magnúsardóttir 6, 23–24, 26, 66, 96
*Lárentíus saga biskups* 5, 33–34, 90–91
lesser outlawry see *fjǫrbaugsgarðr*
*Liber extra* (*Decretales Gregorii IX*) 5, 13–14n35, 29, 31–32, 36, 93n105, 103n21
Liebermann, Felix 66, 96
Logan, F. Donald 16–17, 19–20
Louis iv, Holy Roman Emperor (d. 1347) 23
Lyon, First Council of (1245) 15

Magnús Hákonarson "lagabætir," Norwegian king (d. 1280) 60n97, 125
maiming of clerics 24, 116, 117
Maitland, Frederic William 66, 96–97
manuscript(s) 3–4
  of Frostathing law, older 43
  of *Grágás* 65, 71–72, 155
  of Gulathing law, older 43

of Kristinréttr Árna Þorlákssonar 91–92
of Merovingian laws 40–41
of outlaw sagas 54, 56, 62
Marafioti, Nicole 84
Málmey 131–132
McSweeney, Thomas 70–71
miracle(s) 112, 114–115, 120, 136–137, 138
Mǫðruvellir 107

Niðaróss 23–24, 28, 111, 119
cathedral canons of, 35, 90–91
Nikolaus Árnason, Bishop of Oslo (d. 1225) 111
Nilsson, Bertil 82–83, 98
*Njáls saga* 38, 76, 115, 132note 25
Norway, Icelandic submission to 1–2, 51–60

Oddi 86, 103, 113, 134–135, 139
Ogmundr sneis 107–108
Old English 11, 41–43, 145–146n79
ordeal see judicial ordeal
Ormr Jónsson 134
outlawry 2, 38
as hell 139–140
Church law and, 30–31, 93
consequences of 45
district 54n75, 145
escaping or annulling 46
full 38, 44, 57, 86–87, 151, 152 see also, *skóggangr*
in early English/Anglo-Saxon law 41–42
in Merovingian law 39–41 see also Salic law
in saga literature 2, 54, 57
landscape and, 56
lesser see *fjǫrbaugsgarðr*
Norwegian legal influence on Iceland and, 60
political 56–57, 99, 125
social status and, 54–55
state power and, 57
outlaw(s)
burial of 79–80, 84–85
forbidden in churches 85
helping or associating with 47–48, 72–74, 103
impunity for killing 45–46, 80, 106
kings and, 60, 147, 152–153
*óferjandi* 43–46, 61, 77, 135

Óláfr Haraldsson, Norwegian king see St. Olaf
Óláfr Þórðarson, hvítaskáld (d. 1259) 101, 143–144

penance 7, 72, 94–95, 103, 145–146n79
papal ban (papal excommunication), see also excommunication, *Si quissuadente* 5, 31–33
papal letters 19–20, 23–24
Páll Jónsson, Bishop of Skálaholt (d. 1211) 103
pilgrimage 21–22, 89, 95, 126, 129, 130, 138, 141, 142, 143–144, 147
as atonement 89, 94–95, 144–146
as atonement for outlawry 129, 139, 141–142, 145, 146, 152–153
Pope Clement III (d. 1191) 24
Pope Gregory VII (d. 1085) 8, 72
Pope Innocent IV (d. 1254) 15, 36
Pope Leo I (d. 461) 8n10, 13–14, 83
Pope Nicholas III (d. 1280) 19–20n60
*privilegium fori* 99, 102–103, 115–116, 120–122, 124 see also, jurisdiction

*Quoniam multos* 8, 72–75

Rauðasandr 85
Raymond of Penyafort (d. 1275) 28, 29n96, 31–32n108, 75–76n41
Regino of Prüm (d. 915) 67–68
Reykholt 110
ritual, for excommunication 10, 33
River Jordan 143–144, 152
Rohrbach, Lena 71
Rome 13, 144–145n74, 145–146
Rǫgnvaldr Kársson 132–133

sacrament(s) 7, 8–9, 17–18, 22
St. Olaf, King Óláfr Haraldsson, St. Olav, Norwegian king (d. 1030) 30–31, 69–70, 84–85, 148–151
Salic law(s) 39–42
sanctuary 8, 40–41, 61–62, 86–87, 108
in the context of *fjǫrbaugsgarðr* 38, 76
*sekr* 38, 57, 60
*Si quis suadente* see excommunication, *Si quis suadente*
Sighvatr Sturluson (d. 1238) 108, 112–114, 130, 132, 140–141, 146–147

Sigurðr Magnússon, Norwegian king (d. 1130) 142, 144
Sigurðr Ormsson 103–105, 117
Siuts, Hinrich 67–68
Skagafjǫrðr 108, 131–132, 134–135
Skarðsbók (AM 350 fol.) 81–82n63
Skálaholt 29, 70n23, 103
*skogar kaup* 65, 94–95
*skógarmaðr/skógarmenn,* 38, 46, 57, 63, 115n100, 132–133, 144 see also, outlawry, full and *skóggangr*
*skóggangr* 38, 57, 82–83, 86–87, 89, 151, 152
Skæringr, cleric 105–106, 109
Snorri Sturluson (d. 1241) 100–101, 108, 109, 110, 147
Staðarhólsbók (AM 334 fol.), manuscript of *Grágás* 38, 44, 45–46, 47, 60, 68–69, 70, 75, 79–80, 93
Stiklastaðir, Battle of 84–85, 149–150
Sturla Þórðarson, historian and lawman (d. 1284) 99–102, 120
  Bishop Guðmundr Arason and, 101, 110–111
  *Íslendinga saga* and, 99–102
  knowledge of canon law 125
  knowledge of secular law 100–101, 115
  ordeal and, 118
  The Norwegian court and, 100–101
Sturla Sighvatsson (d. 1238) 129–130, 132, 133–136, 140–141
*Sturlunga saga* 99, 112
Sturlung family 100–101, 129, 134–135, 136, 146–147
Sveinbjarnarsons (sons of Hrafn Sveinbjarnarson) 134–135, 135n42
Sæmundr Jónsson, of Oddi (d. 1222) 103

Thomas Aquinas (d. 1274) 15
Thomas Becket, Archbishop of Canterbury (d. 1170) 21–22, 101, 120–122, 124
*Thómas saga Erkibyskups* 21–22n65, 99, 122
Thómasskina, GKS 1008 fol. 120
Treharne, Elaine 89–90
Trondheim 136, 139–140
Tumi Sighvatsson (d. 1222) 113–114, 130–132, 140–141, 152

*udaða menn* 5, 30–31, 78
unbaptized, denied consecrated burial 77–78
Úlfar Bragason 152
Úlfljótr 68–69
*útilegumaður/útilegumenn* 2, 63

*Víðinesbardagi* 107, 117
Vodola, Elisabeth 8–9, 10
vow(s) 142, 143, 145–146

*wargus*, as term for outlaw 39–41
  in *Grágás*, Konungsbók 41n14
Westfjords 85, 108, 128n4, 132–133, 136–137, 138, 141
William Rufus, English king (d. 1100) 122
William II see William Rufus
Winroth, Anders x, 97n115
Wormald, Patrick 69–70

Þorgeirr Hávarsson, 84–85, 148–149
Þorlákr Ketilsson (d. 1240) 131
Þorlákr Þórhallsson, saint, Bishop of Skálaholt (d. 1193) 23–24n71, 24, 25
Þormóðr Bersason 84–85, 147–148n87, 148–150
Þórarinn Jónsson 134
Þórðr kakali Sighvatsson (d. 1256) 117n110, 135, 146–147
Þórðr Sturluson (d. 1237) 100–101, 114n96, 134–135, 143–144n72

Ǫrlygsstaðir, Battle of 135, 135n42, 146–147

Åqvist, Gösta 58–59, 66